CERAMICS

CERAMICS

A WORLD GUIDE TO
TRADITIONAL TECHNIQUES

BRYAN SENTANCE

WITH 848 ILLUSTRATIONS, 753 IN COLOUR

Thames & Hudson

ONE

TWO

THREE

FOUR

FIVE

SIX

SEVEN

EIGHT

PAGE 1: *Painted 'Tree of Life', Oaxaca, Mexico.*
PAGE 2: *Tin-glazed plates, Andalucia, Spain.*
PAGE 3: *Display of unglazed pottery from around the world.*
PAGE 5: *Jar decorated with overglaze enamels, Macao, China.*
PAGE 6, ABOVE, RIGHT: *Painted bird from Puebla, Mexico.*
LEFT: *Water jar painted in the Sitkyatki style by a member of the Frogwoman family, Hopi Reservation, Arizona, USA.*
BELOW, RIGHT: *Contemporary Peruvian pot painted in the style of the Nazca culture.*
PAGE 7, ABOVE, LEFT: *Berber earthenware vessel from southern Morocco.*
RIGHT: *Terracotta model of a cook by Kojo Darko, a Ghanaian potter born in England.*
BELOW, LEFT: *Portuguese tin-glazed casserole.*

Designed by David Fordham

First published in the United Kingdom in 2004 by Thames & Hudson Ltd,
181A High Holborn, London WC1V 7QX

www.thamesandhudson.com

British Library Cataloguing-in-Publication Data
A catalogue record for this book is available from the British Library

ISBN 0-500-51177-2

Printed and bound in Singapore

For Polly

AND

Luke James Worship

B. 22.02.04

When I was in my Native place I was
A lump of Clay and digg'ed was out of the Earth
And brought from thence away but now I am a jugg
Becambe by Potters Art and Skill and now your
Servant am becombe and carry Ale I will

Inscription on a North Devon Harvest Jug, 1795

CONTENTS

INTRODUCTION

Few of us are immune to the joy found in squeezing an amorphous lump of clay between the fingers. Just observe the relish with which a child makes mud pies. There are not many crafts that are so 'hands on', the fingers in direct contact with the raw material – feeling it yield to the touch. We are enthralled by the magic of a craft that involves all four of the elements: earth mixed with water cooked in a fire and coloured by the presence or absence of air. It feels as though, while moulding the clay to our will, we could almost breathe life into it.

There are folk tales that tell of how when Jesus was a child he shaped mud into birds and was reproached for labouring on the Sabbath. His smiling response was to open his hands and let the birds fly away. We may not be able to work such miracles, but our interaction can give us the sensation that our creations have a life of their own which is generally lacking from mass-produced articles.

There is no doubt that there is enormous satisfaction to be gained from the craft of making objects from clay, but even those of us who do not have such skill surround ourselves with pots, jars, cups and bowls, jugs, vases, teapots and *objets d'art* made from fired earth. It is a humble, grounding material that keeps us in touch, even unconsciously, with nature. It is the fabric from which our planet is made.

Top; and above: *Pinched pot blackened by oxygen reduction in an open fire; Mende potter adding a rim to a coiled pot in Sierra Leone.*

Below, left: *Clay votive plaque of the Babylonian goddess Ishtar, 2000–1600 BC. Ishtar sometimes took on the role of earth goddess.*

Opposite: *Coiled water pot from KwaZulu Natal, South Africa; oxygen-rich firing.*

MYTHOLOGY

Clay appears frequently in myths and folk tales – in several languages the name for our planet and the material from which our ancestors thought it had been made are the same, for example, earth in English and terra in Latin. In many cultures people have revered Mother Earth – she is our mother because it is from clay, according to the ancients, that we ourselves have been made. In Peru the mother goddess was Pachamama (Mother Earth) and her husband was the creator god Pachacamac (he who animates the Earth). In the Pueblos of New Mexico she is called the Clay Mother. Similar myths exist all over the world – in China the goddess Nü Wa created the first humans from mud and water. The Greeks told how Prometheus, the benevolent titan, fashioned the first people from clay mixed with his own bitter tears, while the Babylonians recalled how the gods had mixed the clay with blood spilt by the decapitation of the great god Merodach. In West Africa the Fon tell of how the creator mixed clay with water to make the first man and woman and set them to live on a world shaped like a giant calabash. He mixed the materials as if he was building a house, a task accomplished by adding straw or dung.

LEFT: THE FIRST MAN AND WOMAN, MADE FROM CLAY BY THE CREATOR; DEPICTED ON A FON WOOD CARVING FROM BENIN.

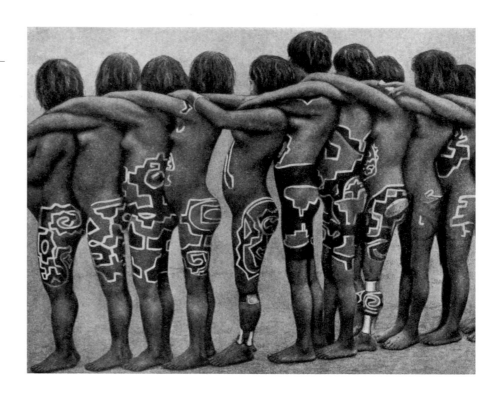

ABOVE: *Amazonian girls painted with pigments derived from clay and natural earth colours for the Snake Dance.*

BELOW, LEFT: *Reproduction of an Egyptian faience* shabti *intended to carry out the physical labour expected of the deceased in the afterlife. The tombs of the wealthy contained many of these figures.*

Myths also explain the colour of our skin, usually biased in favour of the storyteller. In the Sudan a Shilluk story tells how the creator god Juok made all the men on Earth – where he found white clay he made white people, from the mud of the Nile he made brown people and from the black clay of the Sudan he made the handsome black Shilluk. Among the Romanies and some Native American tribes the difference in skin colour is explained as the result of trial and error on the creator's part when he was firing his modelled figures. The story goes that first the fire is too cool, so the figures are too pale and then the fire is too hot and his figures are burnt black. Finally, he gets it right and his men are a beautiful reddish brown.

ABOVE: TANAGRA CLAY STATUETTE OF GAEA, THE EARTH GODDESS, ITALY.

It is not only the gods who have tried to animate a figure made of clay. Since the Middle Kingdom (2055–1650 BC) Egyptians placed figures made from wood, metal, stone, wax or clay in their tombs. These statuettes were called *shabti* (answerers) as they were inscribed with a charm that would animate them so they could take on menial tasks such as ploughing and irrigating that were otherwise expected of the deceased in the afterlife. In China this concept was taken to extremes by the Emperor Qin Shi Huang Di who died in 210 BC. Believing the next life to be much like this one, his tomb in Xi'an was surrounded by a whole army of thousands of life-sized terracotta warriors ready to fight the wars he would have to wage to maintain his status.

In the Jewish communities of Eastern Europe dark tales tell of the making of the golem. Successful attempts are credited to the Prophet Jeremiah and also to Rabbi Judah Loew who lived in Prague in the 16th century. An artificial human made of clay was activated when touched with an incantation written on a strip of parchment. This golem, slave to its master's commands, was possessed with superhuman strength, but when disabled by reversing the charm would crumble into a heap of clay.

ABOVE: *Unfired human figures modelled from different clays by the author. From left to right: red earthenware, white stoneware, grogged black clay which works best at higher temperatures.*

BELOW: *Earthenware beer pot with inscribed patterns from KwaZulu Natal, South Africa.*

SYMBOLISM

IN SPITE of the advanced state of medical science we still employ phrases such as 'our mortal clay', associating our short lifespan with the soil in which our bodies may one day decompose. Clay is a symbol of life and specifically of the body, of resurrection or reincarnation. Mythically, we came from clay and to it we will return.

The psychoanalyst Sigmund Freud recognized the obvious feminine symbolism of hollow forms such as pots and bowls. In Africa, where potters are traditionally women, a pot symbolizes the body of a woman – it is like a bulging womb. Ceramic decoration is often derived from aspects of a woman's daily life, for instance, the pattern of ritual scars on the body of a Congolese woman or the beaded belt that protects Zulu fertility. In Zimbabwe the symbolism is overt, so when a Shona woman places an upturned pot outside her hut, her husband knows that she will not be granting him any sexual favours that night. The female symbolism is also present during a pot's manufacture. Before firing, a pot is like a pre-pubescent girl and so young maids should keep away lest the latent force of their future menstrual flows should cause the pot to crack. During firing the heat of a pot is like a girl's first menstruation and should a man be present the heat will wither his virility. Nor should a man be the first to eat from a new pot.

CRAFT VERSUS INDUSTRY

FOR MILLENNIA potters have sought to push their skills to new heights, mastering chemistry and harnessing mechanics to transcend the limitations of their down-to-earth materials. Ceramic components are now used in Outer Space. In our modern industrial society ceramics can be virtually any shape or colour, without blemish and reproduced identically millions of times. These incredible achievements are undeniably admirable, bringing cheap products within the reach of virtually everyone. Our only limitations are our imaginations and our sense of aesthetics.

To the Japanese the aberrant reaction of an individual pot to the atmosphere of a kiln can make it not only different, but also special and their tea masters say that there is a particular pleasure to be savoured from a hand-made bowl, just as one savours the tea within it. It is the imperfections, the mark of the maker's fingers that give a pot character. It is as though each pot carries within it the living memory of the hand that made it.

LEFT: *Clay cooking pots on a kitchen range built from mud near Lake Titicaca in the High Andes, Peru. A clay structure is efficient and protects the home from the risk of fire. Clay ranges can be seen in many homes and include the mirror-studded versions found in Gujarat, northwest India.*

ABOVE: *Unpredictable natural ash glazing on a thrown stoneware jar; made by Stephen Parry in England and fired in a Japanese-style kiln.*

BELOW: *Demonstration impressed on a clay tablet by the author of how Sumerian cuneiform writing developed from pictograms.*

USES OF RAW CLAY

CLAY HAS been used in an unfired state since ancient times, a fact attested to by the existence of raw clay bison in the caves of Tuc d'Audoubert, France, preserved for an estimated 12,000 years by the stable atmosphere. Few such examples exist as they are so easily abraded and destroyed – either they are washed away or they crumble into dust, but by studying pre-industrial societies and our own society today we can observe considerable evidence of the use of clay. In parts of Africa and India this impermanence is spiritually significant as votive offerings of clay are immersed in rivers and lakes to be returned to nature. Evidence of the world's first writing system, dating from 5,000 years ago in Sumeria, has been found in the form of clay tablets impressed with a code of wedge-shaped marks and dried in the sun. There are many modern uses for clay, ranging from plastics to paper polishing – of all the clay mined at the china clay pits in Cornwall, England, only ten per cent is actually used for pottery.

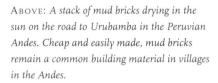

ABOVE: *A stack of mud bricks drying in the sun on the road to Urubamba in the Peruvian Andes. Cheap and easily made, mud bricks remain a common building material in villages in the Andes.*

RIGHT: *The El Glaoui kasbah at Ouarzazate, Morocco, built from mud bricks and plastered with clay. Although vulnerable, houses of mud brick can be easily re-built.*

BELOW, RIGHT: *Mud building at Kano in northern Nigeria. Such buildings are regularly repaired with fresh coatings of clay.*

BUILDINGS

THE MASSIVE ziggurats of Ur in Mesopotamia (modern-day Iraq) were built from mud bricks, as were the homes of Ancient Egyptians, and mud or 'adobe' bricks are still to be seen, constructed in the same tried and tested way, from Karnak in Egypt to Cusco in Peru. Quantities of straw are generally mixed with the clay before it is dried in the sun. Buildings of mud bricks, mortared with clay and plastered with mud and dung may last far longer than one might think, but are vulnerable to heavy rain or flooding. Excavations have shown that the mounds or 'tell' on which many villages in Turkey and Egypt are built are in fact the remains of the mud buildings of previous centuries.

Clay, generally mixed with dung or straw, has been used widely as a form of plaster, coating the surfaces of buildings. Known as daub, this mixture may be smeared over mud brick or pressed on to wattle panels of interwoven sticks.

ABOVE: *Clay bread oven at Sky City, the Acoma Pueblo in New Mexico, USA. Acoma is thought by some to be the oldest inhabited village in the USA.*

PRESERVATION

A s DISCUSSED previously, the first pots may have been a by product of cooking in baskets lined with clay. Clay is a useful medium for waterproofing and is used not only for baskets, but also for the lining of dew ponds which collect water – many of which can still be seen by village greens in the English countryside.

Rubbed on the skin, clay is used by the inhabitants of insect-infested areas to protect themselves from bites and, just so, the wooden furniture and grain stores of the Rabari people in the Rann of Kutch in India is coated with layers of sculpted clay mixed with donkey dung, inset with mirrors, to prevent the depredations of hungry insects.

Clay will also offer some protection from fire and is often used for ovens and hearths. Pioneers such as the Polynesians, whose voyages crossed thousands of miles of ocean, were able to cook without setting their boats alight by lighting fires on clay hearths. (Clay is also a poor conductor of electricity and is now an important material in the manufacture of fuses and high-voltage insulators.)

LEFT: *Australian Aborigine in festive body paint made from earth pigments and natural materials. A coat of clay is also used in many places to protect against insect bites.*

RIGHT: *Mud house on the outskirts of Jaisalmer, Rajasthan, northwest India. In this part of India the decoration of houses with clay and earth pigments has developed into a form of folk art.*

COLOUR

T RAVELLING FROM one region to another one is often struck by the changing colour of the soil, a result of the presence of minerals such as iron in varying proportions. Soil taken from different sites has been used to provide a palette of pigments which, mixed with oil, water and juice or fat, can be used to colour anything from buildings to bodies. Wodaabe men in Niger parade themselves in yellow ochre face paint, while the Maasai of Kenya and Tanzania smear their hair and bodies with red ochre. Earth pigments such as umber and sienna, named after their Italian places of origin, are still a major ingredient in commercially produced oil- and water-based paints used by artists and decorators.

RIGHT: POT WITH IMPRESSIONS OF CORDS, INCIPIENT JOMON CULTURE (10000–7000 BC), JAPAN.

LEFT: *Food laid out in an assortment of locally produced clay bowls, Sillustani, Peru. One bowl to the right of centre contains a surprisingly tasty relish made from clay.*

BELOW: *Coiled earthenware jar with black and white spirals typical of pottery found at Kayenta, Arizona, USA, made between 800 and 1200. Clay forms such as this were often inspired by vessels exploiting the natural shape of locally grown gourds. In other regions containers may originally have been inspired by the form of coconuts, seashells or baskets. Spherical forms predominate as these have the most structural integrity.*

OTHER USES

BIRDS AND animals have no qualms about swallowing small amounts of clays to benefit from the minerals they contain. For generations, kaolin and morphine has been used to treat digestive problems, soothing the pain and lining the stomach and gut. Kaolin is in fact none other than china clay disguised under a more palatable title. Not all people have the same reservations – on the Peruvian Altiplano one may be served potatoes accompanied by a relish of surprisingly tasty local clay.

ORIGINS

WHILE EXPERIMENTING with open-air firings it became very clear to me that, when subjected to intense heat, the heavy clay soil into which I had dug my pit became extremely hard. This is the basis of the 'hearth' theory of the invention of ceramics which suggests that, in much the same way, early people could have observed that a fire in a clay-lined pit would accidentally produce a crude vessel. Other theories have put forward the idea that birds' nests or baskets insulated with clay may have been used as cooking vessels, burning away in the flames to leave a clay form. This possibility is reinforced by the presence of the imprint of basketwork on Neolithic pots in Europe and the Middle East. Evidence of deliberate firings has been interpreted from the existence of small, modelled figurines of baked clay, probably votive offerings – some found in the Czech Republic are almost 30,000 years old.

Nomadic societies rely on basketry, wood and textiles for their utensils rather than on pottery which is easily broken when travelling. Ceramic manufacture is the preserve of

LEFT: *Basket-wrapped gourd bottle made by Akha tribespeople living near Chiang Rai in Thailand.*

RIGHT: *Fante women making pottery in the open air, Ghana. In Africa ceramic forms often resemble the calabash, a large member of the gourd family.*

settled societies with an adequate supply of raw materials and fuel, as well as time to see the process through from preparing the clay to the actual firing. There is no evidence of the manufacture of utilitarian pottery dating from before the communities who lived after the last Ice Age. The establishment of these sedentary societies was made possible either by advances in agriculture or the presence of a rich natural stock of food such as fish. Early pottery manufacture was practised in the valleys of the Nile, the Indus and between the Tigris and Euphrates, but the first known utilitarian ceramics were produced in about 10,700 BC by settlers on the coast of Japan. Archaeologists named the culture that produced this ware Jomon (cord pattern) after the impressions of cordage with which the pots were decorated. Since that time pottery skills have developed around the world on independent timelines and with different criteria – compare, for example, the sophistication of celadon 'greenwares' of the Koryo Dynasty in Korea (AD 918–1392) with the earthy appeal of coiled, burnished black Zulu pots of modern times.

BELOW, LEFT: *Gourds and impressed clay vessels on sale side by side at a market in Cameroon.*

BELOW, RIGHT: *Flask made from a naturally formed gourd, Cameroon.*

The shape of pottery vessels varies considerably from one region to another, but the sphere or cylinder is the most common element as this is much stronger and considerably easier to construct than a shape with corners. The nature of the material dictates the shaping of the pot. Variations in form have often been inspired by natural forms, such as coconut shells, which have themselves been used as receptacles. Studies of the Ancestral Puebloan peoples (formerly known as the Anasazi) have identified a repertoire of pottery forms, from dishes to jugs, based upon different cross-sections of the gourd, one of their main food crops.

The methods used to build pottery have been heavily influenced by other familiar crafts. In KwaZulu Natal, South Africa, for example, women in adjacent homes can be observed making ilala palm baskets and clay pots using very similar coiling techniques. In western India, in Rajasthan and Goa, you can see both clay and brass pots being beaten or hammered into shape. In Britain's industrial Midlands it is possible to watch molten metal and runny clay slip being cast in moulds.

PYROTECHNOLOGY, POTTERS AND SMITHS

A S POTTERS sought to improve the quality of their wares with hotter, better controlled firings, they achieved temperatures at which metals could be smelted. Copper, the first widely used metal, melts at 1083°C (1981°F) which is within the range achieved when firing earthenware. Because of the dependence of both potters and smiths on fuel for their fires they have often sited their workshops close together and have frequently been members of the same families. The awe that primitive peoples had for fire surrounded both crafts with an aura of magic and mystery and allocated their exponents a wary position on the edge of society. This remains particularly clear in the Cameroon where the potter and smith are traditionally wife and husband. The association of pottery with femininity, the womb and life contrasts with metal which symbolizes hard masculinity, penetration and death, and here the female potter serves the community as midwife, while her smith husband serves as undertaker.

BELOW, LEFT: *Statuette of the Hindu gods Shiva and Ganesh, made in Bastar, India, using the lost-wax technique. Molten metal was poured into a clay mould formed around a wax original which melts and runs away. Each piece is unique as the clay mould is broken to release the casting.*

BELOW, RIGHT: *Clay structure erected outside a village smithy in Kirdi, Cameroon, where the workers' relationship with metal and clay is particularly apparent. In some tribal societies the female potter is traditionally married to the male smith.*

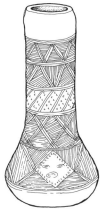

ABOVE: CLAY NOZZLE FOR A SMITH'S BELLOWS, LUVALE, ZAMBIA.

The lost-wax technique of sculpture requires the use of both clay and metal. Fine work produced by the famous bronze casters of Benin (who more accurately worked in brass) or the metalworkers of Bastar in India employ basically the same technique. A rough core is built from clay and then covered in wax which can be built up or cut away into a detailed form. This is coated with layers of clay and allowed to dry out thoroughly before being heated over a fire until all the wax melts and runs out. The empty mould is filled with molten metal and when cool all the clay is broken off and discarded to reveal a metal version of the wax sculpture.

RIGHT: POTTER
AT HIS WHEEL
ON A GREEK
BLACK FIGURE CUP,
ATHENS, 490 BC.

TECHNICAL IMPROVEMENTS

THE MOST far-reaching impact on construction came with the invention of the potter's wheel which was probably developed in Mesopotamia some time around the 4th millennium BC. Interestingly, in Egypt the wheel was used for pottery before transport. Although the wheel remained unknown in the Americas and sub-Saharan Africa until modern times, the speed and efficiency with which pots could be thrown on a wheel was a major factor in the increase in the number of professional workshops all over Asia, Europe and North Africa. There is evidence that prior to 2000 BC workshops in Ur, Mesopotamia, sometimes employed up to ten people on a seasonal basis.

The increase in the efficiency of kilns meant that higher temperatures could be achieved which resulted in harder, less porous vessels. At the forefront of kiln technology were the Chinese who had developed kilns capable of reaching over 1200°C (2192°F) by the time of the Warring States period (403–221 BC) and the quality of Chinese ceramics continued to be such that ceramics are now commonly referred to as china. Also affecting the porosity of pottery was the development of glazes, probably pre 3000 BC as a by product of Egyptian glass-making technology. Spreading rapidly through the Middle East this new process made vessels waterproof and introduced the opportunity of decorating with colours of a wider, brighter spectrum than had previously been possible with slips and earth colours. Among the most impressive examples of this technology is the monumental Ishtar Gate built in Babylon by Nebuchadnezzar II (604–562 BC) from bricks coated in glaze largely tinted with iron and copper.

TOP LEFT: *Indian potter throwing on a wheel. Periodically speed is increased with the aid of a stick inserted into a notch in the circumference of the flywheel.*

ABOVE: *Potter using an electric wheel at a modern pottery in Urubamba, Peru. Electrical equipment and the electricity itself are an extra expense, if available at all, and many potters prefer traditional body-powered machinery which may be constructed by a local craftsman.*

LEFT: *Working on a foot-powered kickwheel in Cameroon.*

ABOVE: *Fragments of Samian ware excavated at Barcombe Roman Villa in Sussex, England. Using moulds and stamps, this Roman pottery, decorated with a fine red slip, was produced in large quantities in industrial workshops to furnish the dining tables of the wealthy.*

PIECING TOGETHER THE PAST

UNLIKE METAL, which will rust, or wood and plant fibres, which will rot, fired clay can survive for vast periods of time. Many examples of pottery were placed in the graves and tombs of ancient notables, either in the form of burial urns or as equipment for the afterlife, and have survived intact to have their stories interpreted by historians. Even the fragments of broken pots, known as sherds, thrown out upon the midden of history survive – they literally allow archaeologists to piece together the past. Their forms and decoration speak volumes about the lifestyle and culture of their former owners. Often pottery sherds are the most common and, therefore, significant artefacts to be found during an excavation. Some sherds were recycled by the ancients, leaving us records of their daily lives. The Egyptians, for instance, used them as a cheap substitute for papyrus, for sending messages, keeping tallies or practising their writing, while the Greeks recorded their votes to banish politicians on ostraka (pieces of broken pottery) which has given us the word ostracize.

BELOW, RIGHT: *Kabyle platter, from Algeria, with Phoenician motifs. The design repertoire of the Phoenicians, a people who originally came from the Middle East, was disseminated through their extensive trading network and colonies, such as Carthage, established around the shores of the Mediterranean, particularly in North Africa, where their legacy is still visible today.*

LEFT: PHOENICIAN INFLUENCED 19TH-CENTURY STORAGE VESSEL FROM THE RIF MOUNTAINS, MOROCCO.

RIGHT: PHILISTINE POTTERY JAR FROM ASKELON, MADE IN THE 12TH OR 11TH CENTURY BC.

By studying the remains of ceramics it is possible to discern stylistic and technological changes which allow us to establish a chronology not only of the pottery, but also of the civilization that produced it. It has allowed us great insight into the rise and fall of the cultures of Paracas and Nazca on the coastal plains of Peru and has revealed the widespread influence of Phoenicians trading in ancient times from the Levant to the Atlantic. Pottery such as terra sigillata, a fine red-slipped tableware, can be easily dated as it was so highly valued that it was stamped before export from Gaul to Roman settlements in Britain. Because of the presence of unused Samian ware, as it was called in Britain, in the remains of a pottery shop in Colchester its destruction has been attributed to insurgents in the rebellion of the Iceni (AD 60) led by Queen Boudicca. This form of dating, known as terminus post quem, is not infallible as it can only provide a date after which an event must have taken place. Terminus ante quem, on the other hand, would provide a date before which an event occurred – for instance, the terra sigillata still packed in a crate found in Pompeii buried by the ashes of Vesuvius in AD 79.

The dating of pottery using scientific technology is a recent development. Radiocarbon dating, in which age can be assessed by measuring the amount of carbon 14 remaining in organic materials, is of no use for mineral substances such as clay, but can be helpful for dating pottery bodies which have been mixed with organic temper such as shell, chaff or bone ash. A more useful technique is thermoluminescence (TL) dating which measures the light emitted when a fragment is heated, so indicating the amount of radiation to which an object has been exposed and therefore the length of time since it was fired.

REPLICATING THE PAST

TODAY, WHEN visiting the sites of what were once great cultural centres one is often surrounded by souvenir shops selling copies of the ceramics of a golden age. Some are no doubt shoddy, but many are works of art in their own right, made by local potters using the old techniques. Buying one puts much needed money into the pockets of genuine craftsmen. Pottery from the past is also a great source of inspiration to today's potters as can be seen among the potters on the Hopi Reservation in the American Southwest.

ABOVE, RIGHT: *'Anasazi bowl' by Otis Wright of Blanding, Utah, USA; painted with minerals and plant extracts. The bowl is a copy of ceramics made in Mesa Verde, Colorado, between 500 and 1400.*

LEFT: *Modern Peruvian reproduction of a stirrup jar made by people of the Nazca culture (AD 300–600). Both original and modern versions are generally made with a mould.*

ABOVE: *A family of potters in Gujarat, India. Born into a caste of pottery makers, children begin at an early age to learn the skills handed down through their family from ancient times. Some tasks are assigned specifically to men, such as throwing at the wheel, while decoration is generally carried out by women. Firing is a communal task.*

MATRILINEAL HERITAGE

SINCE THE days of the first primitive settlements there has generally been a clear division of labour between the sexes. While men have been free to hunt and care for livestock, the child-bearing role of women has linked them more closely to the home and the chores related to its running. In societies where survival rather than financial remuneration is the motivation, pottery, like basketmaking and weaving, is generally part of the domestic work of women meeting the needs of their families by providing vessels for the fetching and storage of water and foodstuffs, and for the cooking of meals. Often this work is seasonal, dependent on periods of fine weather suitable for the drying and firing of pots.

Like cookery, craft skills have been handed down from mother to daughter for many generations – this practice can still be observed in many regions, including Africa and among the peoples in the Pueblos in the American Southwest. Among the most influential Native American potters of modern times was Nampeyo (1860–1942), a Tewa woman living at Hano on the Hopi Reservation in Arizona. During the 1880s Nampeyo was shown fragments of ancient pottery from Sitkyatki, a ruined village below First Mesa, and was inspired to develop a style of pottery decoration employing the colours and designs which is now known as the Sitkyatki style. She taught her techniques to her daughters and they passed them on to theirs so that there are many descendants who sign their work with the Nampeyo family name. Some of the patterns are considered the property of the family, not to be used by outsiders, and serve as a kind of trademark. Unbroken matrilineal descent alone gives the right to use these designs and a man who has been taught by his mother does not have the right to teach his daughter. Many other Puebloan families have a continuing pottery tradition, now yielding a substantial income, among them the Frogwoman clan of Hopi and the descendants of Maria Martinez at San Ildefonso, New Mexico. In South Africa, too, it is not difficult to find Zulu and Venda potters who can trace their skills back beyond their grandmothers.

ABOVE: *Nampeyo, 'the serpent that has no tooth', (1860–1942); a photograph by Edward S. Curtis of one of the most inspirational and influential of all Native American potters.*

ABOVE, LEFT: *Modern painted pot from the Hopi Reservation in Arizona, USA, decorated with designs in the Sitkyatki style made popular by Nampeyo.*

BELOW: *'Blue Dahlia' dish hand painted in underglaze colours by Susie Cooper, who set up her own studio in England in 1929.*

COMMERCIALIZATION

WHEN THE manufacture of pottery becomes a commercial concern, supplying the needs of others, it is common for production to become a family venture and in many traditional societies ceramics are made by a potter's caste. In Indian villages women prepare the clay and paint the finished pots but, although they may make coiled vessels and use the paddle and anvil, it is men who throw on the wheel and oversee production. Until the 20th century the wheel remained virtually the preserve of men all over the world, while painting was often carried out by women. Even on the industrially produced – moulded, cast or thrown – pottery of early 20th-century Britain, factories employed armies of women equipped with brushes and some, for instance, Susie Cooper and Clarice Cliff, achieved international recognition for their work. In the West the growth of the population and the increase in industrialization led to the building of large factories sited near the best sources of clay, preferably near a source of fuel and a river or canal for ease of transportation. Using swiftly evolving scientific and technological developments, and employing large numbers of workers, sophisticated machinery and enormous kilns, these establishments have for several centuries produced mountains of standardized, reasonably priced ceramics which can be adapted to suit contemporary ideas of taste and style.

STUDIO POTTERY

UNFORTUNATELY, IN the eyes of many, the precise repetition of identical objects, however well designed and made, lacks the charm and appeal of individual, hand-crafted objects. During the late 19th century the Arts and Crafts Movement in Britain, figureheaded by visionaries such as William Morris, championed the production of well-designed, hand-made goods including the Islamic-influenced ceramics of William De Morgan and the eccentric creations of the Martin brothers. Bernard Leach (1887–1979) followed the banner and set up a pottery in St Ives, Cornwall, in 1920. Leach had studied pottery in Japan and, combining the restrained aesthetic of Japanese ceramics with English traditions, created a range of tableware and one-off pieces which brought new life to the craft. Although quite eclectic in his approach, working with earthenware and raku, it was probably his use of stoneware glazed with a subtle range of 'natural' colours that was most influential. Working in 'studio potteries', subsequent generations of potters have been liberated from the restrictions of industry and are able to produce forms inspired by the nature of the clay itself, experimenting and learning day by day just as the first potters did.

ABOVE: *Late 19th-century English majolica fireplace tile decorated with thick, brightly coloured lead glazes. The aesthetic pretensions of the late 19th century saw a boom in the industrial production of pottery and tiles.*

BELOW, RIGHT: *Somerset-based studio potter Michael Gaitskell throwing stoneware clay on an electric wheel. Most individual potters in England worked in earthenware until stoneware became popular under the influence of Bernard Leach and his Japanese collaborator Shoji Hamada.*

LEFT: *Memorial mug fired in a reduced atmosphere in a wood-burning kiln by John Leach, Bernard Leach's grandson. John Leach runs his own pottery in Somerset, England.*

BELOW: *Slip-trailed earthenware tile made using local Devon clays by Philip Leach, one of Bernard Leach's grandsons, who runs a pottery with his wife, Frannie, at Hartland in Devon, England.*

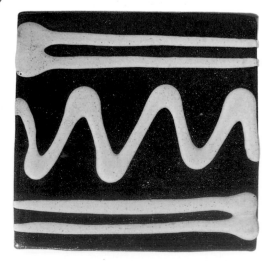

Making pottery with traditional and modern methods and selling it is a way of bringing money into deprived or undeveloped areas, boosting the economy and helping to preserve local culture. International aid agencies and fair-trade businesses have sponsored the establishment of workshops all over the world, while tribal communities such as the Utes in Colorado, USA, have set up their own, harnessing modern technology such as kilns and moulds to produce pottery in both contemporary and traditional Native American forms even though they have no pottery heritage of their own. Since the late 20th century pottery has also been introduced as an artistic medium to Aboriginal craftsmen in Australia. Many of them are now producing high-quality works incorporating traditional painting styles.

ABOUT THIS BOOK

I T IS with a sense of awe that I approached this book, sensing a ghost within the clay, a ghost hard to trace in the machine-formed products of factories. Many books have been published about the great ceramic producers – Limoges, Sèvres, Wedgwood, Meissen and the tableware of the rich and influential – but I want to celebrate the potter with clay under his or her fingernails who makes everyday wares for ordinary folk, a potter who is continuing the ancient tradition of an elemental craft. By looking at the many techniques a potter exploits and illustrating each with examples from disparate regions of the world I hope to give a basis for comparison that will help the reader understand these techniques better, while gaining a greater insight into the cultures in which they have been produced. Beneath the veneers of local culture, people the world over face the same technical problems working with clay and making a living from doing so.

ABOVE, LEFT: *Underglaze painted jar by Irene Entata, an Aborigine artist from the Aranda tribe, who works at Hermannsburg near Alice Springs, Australia. Although ceramics are not a traditional Aboriginal craft, during the 20th century workshops producing wares with great character were set up in many tribal centres.*

ABOVE, RIGHT: *Plate by a Greek potter; decorated with carving and sgraffito.*

CONCLUSION

C LAY CAN tell us a great deal about cultures both living and past. We know, for instance, more about the Incas and the pre-Columbian cultures of Latin America from their pottery than virtually anything else. Pottery is shaped more easily by the hand than any other medium and, therefore, there is less inhibition to the creative flow from the unconscious mind to the fingertips. The shapes built by a craftsman in clay are formed by the joy and pain, the beliefs and fears of everyday life.

THE RAW MATERIAL

FAR LEFT: *Unfired tile panel of white earthenware clay from Devon and red clay from Staffordshire, England.*
LEFT: *Jaipur blueware vase, India.*
ABOVE: *Portuguese moulded, earthenware, tin-glazed dish.*
BELOW, CENTRE, RIGHT: *Micaceous clay bowl made by Jicarilla Apache potter Sheldon Nunez-Velarde, New Mexico, USA.*

BELOW, LEFT: *'Agateware' vase made from two earthenware clays.*
BELOW, RIGHT: *Ghanaian necklace of Venetian glass trade beads.*

THE RAW MATERIAL

Clay is one of the world's most abundant resources. Although commercial production has now brought a certain uniformity to the material available, generations of potters were limited to the clays that they could obtain in the vicinity of their homes or workshops, clays that varied in plasticity, colour and their reaction to heat and while one clay may be ideal for throwing another may be better suited for slip casting. Experimentation with the idiosyncrasies of local materials has led to a rich diversity of regional styles and techniques.

THE ORIGIN OF CLAY

IGNEOUS ROCKS such as granite were created by volcanic activity many millions of years ago. Weathering and erosion caused their gradual decomposition and the release of particles of feldspar, composed of alumina and silica, which formed deposits around their mother rock. When found in their place of origin they are known as primary clays and include china clay (or kaolin) and bentonite. Other clays may be transported considerable distances by water and deposited in layers of sediment – for instance, in the rainforests of Amazonia or on the banks of the Nile in Egypt. These deposits are referred to as secondary clays. They pick up a considerable range of impurities before deposition and so their properties vary far more than those of primary clays.

PLASTICITY

THE MICROSCOPIC particles of which clay is composed are flat and by making them lie in one direction, a task accomplished by wedging, plasticity can be improved. Plasticity can also be increased by the addition of foreign matter and primary clays are therefore less plastic than secondary. Potters often perform this task themselves by adding materials such as sand or by mixing different clays together.

TOP LEFT: *Sherds of pre-Columbian earthenware pottery found near Sillustani on the Peruvian Altiplano.*

ABOVE: *Roman terracotta tile made by the 2nd Augustan Legion between AD 60 and AD 80; excavated in Usk, Wales. Roman legionaries were generally trained in a craft, such as carpentry, pottery or metalworking, so that a legion could be self sufficient when based in hostile territory.*

LEFT: *Heavily tempered earthenware cookery pots, southern Turkey.*

OPPOSITE, CENTRE, LEFT: *Slipware tile by English ceramist Philip Leach; made from two naturally coloured North Devon clays.*

OPPOSITE, BELOW, LEFT: *Sherd of post-Medieval slipware excavated in South Wales.*

COLOUR

CLAY IS available in a range of colours from white to black and the spectrum includes not only reds, but also blues. Even in one area the colour of local clays may vary considerably. Beot in France, for example, developed its own distinctive style of trailed slipware pottery using white and brown clays available locally. Pure china clay is white, but the colour of secondary clays depends on the impurities that have been mixed into them. Principal among these colourants is red iron oxide which, depending on the concentration, can produce reds, yellows and black.

ABOVE, LEFT: *Unfired sgraffito wares of red and white clays dug in North Devon; made by Harry Juniper.*

RIGHT, FROM TOP TO BOTTOM: *Figures pinched from red terracotta clay; from white stoneware clay; and from black clay suitable for firing at high temperatures.*

FIRING

THE PROCESS of firing may cause alterations in colour – for example, some browns become red or orange. Before firing, the white clay from the village of Peters Marland used on Devon slipware is actually grey. The dark colours of secondary clays dug in Malaysian rainforests are the result of organic materials. During firing the organic colours are burnt away leaving the rusty red tints of laterite, a type of iron oxide.

Further to the differences between clays described above is the temperature at which they mature when fired. This is somewhere between the point at which they become hard due to the fusing of the body and the temperature at which they begin to bloat and collapse as they approach a molten state. Earthenware clays mature between 1000 and 1180°C (1832–2156°F) while stoneware clays mature between 1200 and 1300°C (2192–2372°F). Refractory clays will not vitrify at temperatures over 1400°C (2552°F) and can therefore be used in the construction of kilns.

EXCAVATING AND PREPARING CLAY

Working with clay involves a very close relationship with the substance from which our planet is made and in many traditional cultures the term Mother Earth is still imbued with spiritual meaning and a feeling of reverence. All parts of the ceramic process, particularly the digging of clay from the Earth, may be accompanied by meditation, prayer and acts of purification. In Malaysia taboos even demand the banning of menstruating women from the vicinity when clay is being excavated.

Excavation

For thousands of years Egyptian potters have been collecting alluvial silt from the banks of the Nile, but it is more common in other areas to dig clay from a hole or a mine. At the Acoma Pueblo of Sky City in northwest New Mexico, USA, generations of potters have kept the whereabouts of the sources of local white clay to themselves as they consider the sites to be holy places. Collecting the clay is a family affair which begins with the offering of food and corn pollen to the Clay Mother. Family and friends dig clay out of a mine and break it into lumps that can be taken home in a wheelbarrow or a pick-up truck; once they were carried in sacks.

Removing impurities

Excavated clay generally contains impurities such as grit, rock and roots which must be removed as they make the clay less plastic and can cause problems

TOP LEFT: *Wheal Martyn china clay pit near St Austell in Cornwall, England; established by Elias Martyn in the 1820s.*

ABOVE: *Plates from the Comte de Milly's L'Art de la Porcelaine, published in France in the 18th century, showing various stages in the refining and preparation of clay.*

BELOW, LEFT: *Sand and mica drags at Wheal Martyn, Cornwall, England. As clay slurry flows down, coarse and heavy particles sink to the bottom.*

BELOW, RIGHT: *Settling pits at Wheal Martyn, Cornwall, England. As clay particles sink to the bottom, water is gradually strained off.*

LEFT: KNEADING CLAY BY FOOT, AFTER AN EGYPTIAN TOMB PAINTING, 1900 BC.

THE RAW MATERIAL

ONE

when firing. The sequence of the processes varies regionally and may involve both dry and wet methods. Dried clay can be pulverized by beating with a club or in a mortar and then ground on a saddle quern similar to those used for grinding meal for food. During the beating and grinding all visible impurities are picked out by hand. The clay powder may then be winnowed (tossed into the air with a basket, allowing the wind to blow away organic debris), or filtered through sieves.

Soaking is a slow but less physically exhausting method of extracting detritus in which the clay is watered down in a large vat and allowed to settle. Particles of different sizes settle in layers which allows the separation of the slurry into useful and unwanted constituents. Water running down a gradient can also be used as a separator, as in gold prospecting – the heaviest materials are deposited first and the lightest last. In living memory in northern Peru impurities were sometimes filtered out by straining slurry through cloth suspended like a hammock.

TOP, FROM LEFT TO RIGHT, AND TOP TO BOTTOM: *The process of preparing clay in Urubamba, Peru: resoaking lumps of clay in a bathtub; rolling out wedged and kneaded clay; drying out soaked clay to a workable consistency; dried out clay awaiting resoaking. At any stage before the firing process, clay can be recycled by breaking up and soaking.*

RIGHT: *Zulu woman grinding on a saddle quern, a technique used for preparing both food and clay.*

Wedging and kneading

ONCE purified, powdered clay must be soaked, while wet clay must be dried until a suitable consistency is achieved. At this point all uneven lumps have to be broken down and all the air pockets, which could cause explosions during firing, must be expelled. Wedging is a vigorous technique performed on a solid surface. A lump of clay is sliced in two with a wire and then one half is lifted above the head and slammed down on the other. Slicing and slamming are repeated many times, perhaps for fifteen minutes, until the clay is ready. This process can be mechanized using a pug mill. The clay may then be stored in a cool damp place until required.

Kneading should be carried out immediately before the clay is shaped into pottery and is in essence the same as kneading dough when making bread, although in many places the clay may be worked with the feet as much as the hands. As well as guaranteeing an even consistency, kneading improves the plasticity of the clay by causing its flat particles to lie in the same direction.

MIXTURES

RATHER THAN accept the limitations imposed by the characteristics of any one clay body, potters commonly mix two or more together, altering the colour, plasticity and the temperature to which the clay can be effectively fired. Further improvements may also be made with the addition of ingredients as diverse as quartz, shell, animal dung and other non-plastic materials, a process known as tempering.

Tempering

EARLY potters were aware that the addition of non-plastic materials to their clay served two valuable functions. Firstly, during the actual construction of a pot wet clay would hold its shape better and secondly, as it dried out it would shrink less and was less likely to warp or crack. During firing the more open structure of the pot (created because it was able to hold its shape) allowed moisture and air to circulate and escape, making the stress of thermal shock less damaging. Firing at higher temperatures becomes more feasible, so ceramics that are less porous can be produced. Mica was added to clay by

ABOVE, RIGHT: *Funerary figures made from coarsely tempered clay, Chancay culture of northern Peru (1200–1460).*

LEFT: *Stonepaste bowl from Nishapur, Iran, 11th century.*

the Jomon in Japan 12,000 years ago, by the Medes in what is now Iran during the 7th century BC and is still being used today in the construction of Turkish cooking pots. Mineral tempering has included sand, ground rocks such as flint or quartz and grog made from ground up potsherds either saved from broken items or picked up among the debris of earlier civilizations.

Organic tempering

Both animal and vegetable material can be used as temper. In China moulded toys are made from clay mixed with hemp, cotton rags or paper pulp for Spring festivities. For thousands of years in Middle Eastern regions such as Yemen and Palestine chaff, chopped straw, fluff from seed heads, animal hair and even dried dung have been added to clay, particularly for the construction of larger pots to make them lighter and more porous. The fine-walled, but low-fired, pottery of Amazonia is made possible by tempering with the ashes of tree bark or freshwater sponges. The long filaments of organic silica present in this ash act like reinforcing rods, making the structure strong and resilient. Also widely used are ground shell and the ashes of animal bones.

Porcelain and its imitations

The most highly prized recipe for a clay body is, without doubt, that of porcelain and its ingredients were for centuries kept a closely guarded secret by the Chinese. The elements used were white china clay, also called kaolin after the place it was mined, and pulverized china stone, which was composed of quartz, mica and feldspar.

Attempts to imitate its translucent whiteness have inspired many experiments since porcelain wares first travelled the Silk Route to the West. By the 11th century AD Muslim potters in Syria, Egypt and Iran were using a body known as stonepaste or fritware which was made from quartz, glass and clay fired to a low temperature up to 1150°C (2102°F). This was the forerunner of 'soft-paste' bodies used by European potters from the 17th century until the discovery of sources of china clay in Europe. One great money spinner, exported from England all over Europe, was bone china which was made from a body that did not contain ground quartz, but an alkali-rich ash made from burning animal bones.

ABOVE, LEFT; AND OPPOSITE, BELOW, RIGHT: *English bone china saucers with hand-painted decoration; here, the body is made from clay mixed with the ashes of animal bones.*

TOP RIGHT: *Shipibo bowl, from Amazonian Peru, made with organic temper.*

CENTRE, RIGHT: *Vase by Terrance M. Chino, an Acoma potter from New Mexico, USA. The Acoma temper their clay with the ground up sherds of old pottery.*

BOTTOM RIGHT: *Hand-painted Chinese porcelain bowl. Porcelain is tempered with china stone composed of quartz, mica and feldspar.*

CERAMICS WITHOUT CLAY

A NUMBER of ceramic mixtures contain only a very small quantity of clay, but just a few contain no clay at all. As clay provides plasticity, the clay-free mixes are harder to work and are more often formed by press moulding.

BELOW, LEFT; AND BELOW, RIGHT: Glass vase made in Herat, Afghanistan, using technology handed down within one family for hundreds of years; copy of an Egyptian faience hippo with copper blue glaze, after an original dating from the 12th or 13th Dynasty (1985–1750 BC).

Egyptian faience

ALSO referred to as Egyptian paste or fritware, Egyptian faience was erroneously named faience by archaeologists because of its resemblance to European tin-glazed pottery of the same name. It was in use in Pre-Dynastic times (5500–3050 BC) and is actually a mixture of ground minerals that fuse together, like clay or glass, when fired. The body was composed of quartz and sand, in varying proportions, with smaller quantities of lime and natron or plant ash. Less plastic than clay, this material could be modelled, moulded or ground into shape and then decorated with a blue-green copper-based glaze, fired at 800–1000°C (1472–1832°F).

The Egyptian name for this material was *thenet* which means dazzling or shining and refers to the jewel-like quality of the glaze. It was a cheaper substitute for semi-precious stones such as turquoise or lapis lazuli which had to be imported from distant lands at great expense. Several techniques could be employed for the glazing, but all were dependent on the way alkali salts on the surface melt and fuse during firing. These salts naturally formed a crust due to efflorescence from the body during drying, but could also be applied directly to the surface. It is likely that the observation of this process led to the invention of glass.

Blueware

NORTHERN India is home to the production of a distinctive style of pottery inspired by Persian and Chinese porcelain during the time of the Mughals. The white body is decorated in bright colours dominated by blues and has therefore become known as blueware. While the mixture used in Khurja, Uttar Pradesh, contains 50 per cent clay, the mix

in Jaipur, Rajasthan, is totally clay free, consisting mainly of ground quartz with smaller amounts of glass, fuller's earth, borax and gum.

When the paste has been kneaded to a workable, dough-like consistency it can be thrown on a wheel or pressed into a mould. A variety of cups, vases and bowls are produced, many of which are assembled from separate components. Once the pots are dry and ready for decorating, floral patterns are painted in outline using cobalt oxide before they are filled in with a palette of oxides that typically includes two blues, yellow, green and brown. A glaze of borax, glass and lead oxide is applied before a six-hour firing at 800–850°C (1472–1562°F).

The production of Jaipur blueware has become a serious export industry and its manufacture has now spread to other sites, including villages in the vicinity of Lucknow, Uttar Pradesh.

Glass

GLASS is the result of fusing together silica, alkali and lime and was probably discovered before 2000 BC by potters in Mesopotamia or Egypt during their experiments with glazes. As glass is only plastic at a high temperature it must

OPPOSITE, ABOVE, RIGHT: *Modern copies of Ancient Egyptian faience scarab beetles, a symbol of rebirth.*

BELOW: *Blueware vase and bowl from Jaipur, Rajasthan, India; strongly influenced by porcelain prized by the Mughals.*

RIGHT: GLASS LAMP CREATED IN THE 14TH CENTURY FOR A MOSQUE IN CAIRO, EGYPT.

ABOVE, CENTRE: *Venetian glass* millefiore *beads from Ghana.*

ABOVE, RIGHT: *Necklace excavated at Balkh, Afghanistan, which includes natural objects and Roman trade beads.*

be shaped by grinding, moulding, blowing or stretching. The greatest masters of glasswork were the Venetians whose products were exported all over Europe by the 11th century. Venetian beads were used as trade currency as far afield as Africa, Canada and Central Asia.

33

ALTERNATIVE MATERIALS

MIXED WITH some liquid or binding agent, all manner of mineral and organic substances can be modelled or moulded into shape. Powdered marble or semi-precious stones are widely employed to cast cheaper copies of hand-crafted originals; in Kashmir and Russia the making of intricately painted domestic articles from the pulp of paper in the form of papier mâché is a major export industry. Even animal dung has been used, hand crafted into ceremonial – they could neither hold water nor withstand the heat of a fire – bowls by the inhabitants of the Nuba Hills in the Sudan.

ABOVE: SUDANESE RITUAL BOWL MADE OF PAINTED COW DUNG, NUBA HILLS, C. 1910.

Paste and dough

BREAD dough was used over 3,000 years ago for religious offerings by the people of Ancient Egypt and the Minoan civilization in the Mediterranean and has been used in Europe, Latin America and China for modelling festive decorations right up to the present day. Dough must be dried or baked and in 19th-century Germany it was discovered that if salt was also added to the

mix (two parts flour to one part salt) then the dough would last indefinitely and rats and mice would not be tempted to eat it. Bright colours can be produced by dyeing the raw dough or by painting and varnishing the finished article. In Peru a vast number of figures are modelled from a paste made from plaster and mashed potato to inhabit *retablos* depicting religious scenes and tableaux of everyday life.

ABOVE: *Painted salt dough figure of a peasant woman, Central America.*

BELOW, LEFT: *Four salt dough figures, from Otovalo, Ecuador, sold as Christmas decorations.*

Plaster and stucco

PLASTER of Paris, made from calcinated gypsum, is a white powder that becomes a fast-setting paste when mixed with water. When ground marble is added to the mix it is possible to achieve a hard surface, known as stucco, which can be polished to a lustrous sheen. Plaster can be smeared over a surface or, to some extent, carved, but is most often used in its

BELOW, RIGHT: *A wooden retablo made in Lima, Peru, with figures constructed from plaster and mashed potato. Originally housing religious scenes, these boxes now contain lively tableaux of everyday life.*

NEAR RIGHT:
*Model guinea fowl, from
Zimbabwe, of wire and
window putty.*

FAR RIGHT: *Polymer clay
imitation of an African
millefiore glass trade
bead necklace.*

BELOW, LEFT: *Papier mâché
pot, from Kashmir, made using
moulded reconstituted paper.*

BELOW, RIGHT: *Plaster casts in the
Cornice Museum of Ornamental
Plasterwork in Peebles, Scotland.*

liquid form for casting. It has been widely
used in the manufacture of decoration
in the form of relief designs on walls
and ceilings which reached their most
elaborate in the extravagant European
concoctions of the 16th and 17th centuries
and also in the complex geometric
creations found in Islamic mosques and
palaces. Plaster is the ideal material for
the construction of moulds intended
for shaping clay in both its plastic and
liquid forms.

Polymer clay

THE 20th century saw the development
of synthetic materials for use in
many fields and included the invention
of Plasticine, a flexible substance available in a number of colours, ideal as a
modelling material for children. A certain
amount of kneading is necessary to make
it easy to work and it can be reused
again and again as it never sets hard.
An advance was achieved more recently
with the development of synthetic polymer
clay which is now widely available from
craft shops under brand names such as
Cernit, Fimo and Sculpey. Easily worked

and available in a range of exciting
colours, this substance can be fired at a
low temperature, 15 to 20 minutes at 130°C
(266°F). A domestic oven can be used, but
the instructions should be read carefully
as some products may be toxic. Although
more expensive than Plasticine, polymer
clay is ideal for children and has also been
taken up enthusiastically as a medium by
ceramic artists, particularly in the USA,
notably for the manufacture of beads.

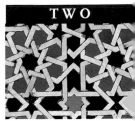
FORMING TECHNIQUES

LEFT: *Mosaic of tiles cut from fired slabs, Marrakesh, Morocco.*
TOP: *Moulded dish by Philip Leach, England.*
ABOVE, LEFT: *Modelled and carved 'Christ', unfired; made by the author.*
ABOVE, RIGHT: *Acoma coiled water jar in the Zuni style, signed M. Antonio, New Mexico, USA.*
NEAR RIGHT: *Javanese 'teapot' with modelled spout and handle.*
FAR RIGHT: *English thrown stoneware bottle by Rupert Andrews.*

FORMING TECHNIQUES

POTTERS AT the opposite ends of the Earth have developed variations on the same few basic methods of forming clay, all dependent on the manipulation of the raw material with the hands, the fingers and occasionally the feet. Even the more recent slip-casting technique requires the construction of a hand-built original matrix. The oldest surviving clay objects appear to have been votive offerings, anthropomorphic and zoomorphic, which were squeezed into shape with the fingers. Archaeological evidence surviving from 12,000 years ago during the Incipient Jomon period in what is now Japan suggests that the first functional wares were made by joining hand-moulded slabs together. This method was soon superseded by smoothing together large coils of clay which were then paddled with the hand or a piece of wood. Coiling remains the most geographically widespread traditional technique to this day, although thrown wares are produced in larger numbers because of the speed with which they can be turned out.

LEFT: *Indian potter shaping a jar with a paddle and anvil.*

RIGHT: *Thrown stoneware vase by Elizabeth Aylmer; influenced by the coiled pottery of Zimbabwe where she lived for many years.*

BELOW: *Coiled jar by Terrance M. Chino, an Acoma potter from New Mexico, USA.*

WEATHER

THE WEATHER has a considerable effect on the traditional potter. For many, particularly women in tribal communities making pots for their own use, pottery is a seasonal activity as it must be fitted in between the tasks of the agricultural year – ploughing, sowing, harvesting and the movement of flocks and herds – as well as the daily tasks of cultivation, food preparation and childcare. The weather also has a direct effect upon the clay itself. In many hot climates finished wares are still placed in the sun to dry and harden, but this is not feasible during the rainy season without special facilities or if there is no dry fuel to spare for firing. Conversely, if the sun is strong pots must be constantly turned or placed in the shade to avoid drying unevenly and subsequently cracking. Full-time potters are able to set up better facilities for work all year round, in a workshop with heating, often the secondary effect of a kiln, and a controlled atmosphere.

LEFT: *Mende potter, from Sierra Leone, forming the lip of a coiled pot by squeezing the edge with her fingers.*

RIGHT: *Mende potter smoothing a leatherhard pot with a scraper, Sierra Leone.*

THE INFLUENCE OF OTHER CRAFTS

POTTERY IS an ancient craft, younger than basketry but of a similar age to metalworking, and over the millennia the techniques of one craft have influenced those of another, although it is not always possible to ascertain which came first. In its plastic state clay can be manipulated and coiled like the fibres used in basketmaking. Rolled into slabs it can be assembled like wood or metal, luting the roughened edges coated with slurry just as a woodworker might use glue or a metalworker would use a flux with welding gear. Both clay and metal can be beaten into shape and, when liquid, poured into a casting mould. Pots can be thrown and turned on a wheel just as wood and metal can be shaved into shape on a lathe.

CENTRE, RIGHT: *Thrown wares on a drying rack in Michael Gaitskell's studio in Somerset, England.*

BELOW, LEFT: *A display of hand-built figures and animals from around the world.*

RIGHT: *Slip-cast pots on a drying rack at the Ute Mountain Pottery, Colorado, USA. Whatever the mode of construction, pottery must be thoroughly dry before firing.*

CHANGING TRADITIONS

CRAFTSPEOPLE AROUND the world use the same skills as their grandparents and their distant ancestors, but global culture has exposed many of us to the styles and techniques of distant lands. Now the coiled pots of southern Africa may be sold alongside moulded raku animals, while the wheel, unknown in pre-Columbian America, is a major feature of many workshops in Peru.

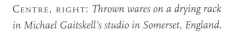

39

TOOLS AND EQUIPMENT

THE RANGE of tasks that can be accomplished by the supreme tool, the human hand, may be extended with a variety of tools. While some may be impromptu and as simple as a handy stick, others may be specially made for the individual potter's needs or bought from a professional manufacturer. Traditionally tools are made from local materials and so, for example, while the modelling tools of a Western European potter are usually made from box wood, in Japan they are probably made from bamboo.

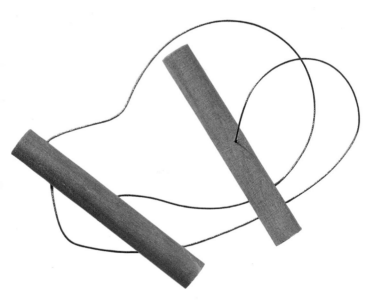

The workshop

IN ideal conditions a potter works in a specially designed studio with equipment conveniently placed ready for use. A potter may need a solid slab for wedging, a work surface and turntables, a wheel, a cool place for storing clay and a kiln, but in many parts of the world working conditions are far more basic – Zuni potters in New Mexico, USA, generally work in their kitchens, while Nigerian or Egyptian potters may sit outdoors paddling their work as they revolve it in a hollow in the ground.

Natural objects

NATURALLY formed objects, sometimes with a little adaptation, can make handy tools. Stones smoothed by a river are excellent for smoothing and burnishing and shells can be good for scraping or smoothing. Seashells found in a Palestinian cave at Lachish were used by a potter 3,000 years ago, probably for this purpose. The shell or rind of the large calabashes grown in West Africa make excellent turntables, one half inverted on the other, convex surfaces together, while

TOP: *English ceramist Stephen Murfitt pinching the rim of a thrown bowl with the aid of a turntable. This process is also known as 'rusticating'.*

ABOVE, LEFT, CENTRE: *Potter's knife.*

ABOVE, LEFT: *'Cheese' wire used for cutting lumps of clay or removing thrown wares from the wheel.*

ABOVE, RIGHT: *English-style kickwheel with a foot treadle that spins a heavy flywheel.*

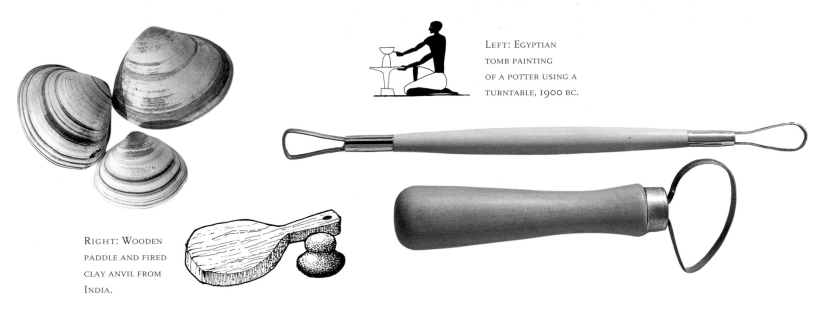

LEFT: EGYPTIAN TOMB PAINTING OF A POTTER USING A TURNTABLE, 1900 BC.

RIGHT: WOODEN PADDLE AND FIRED CLAY ANVIL FROM INDIA.

pieces of the rind can be employed for scraping. In Central America smoothing may be done with a corncob after the corn has been removed. Even contemporary Western potters regularly employ a marine sponge when throwing on the wheel.

Recycling

CRAFTSPEOPLE are great improvisers and discarded objects are often adapted for tools. In Mexico potters frequently smooth the clay with a *cuero* (hide), once made from a scrap of leather, but now more predominantly cut from an old felt hat. In the American Southwest starter moulds, turntables and ribs for scraping are often made from pieces of broken pottery or old tin cans. Bernard Leach used an old umbrella spoke for making holes and many modern Western potters have broken hacksaw blades for scraping.

Tools designed for other purposes

TOOLS for other crafts can often be used in pottery – for instance, the surform blade used by woodworkers for shaping wood. Kitchen utensils, including knives for cutting clay, apple corers for making large holes, pot scrubbers for smoothing or rolling pins for making slabs, are also handy. Even dentists' equipment can be useful, whether tongue depressors for modelling or drills for etching decoration used by Jemez potters on the Rio Grande, New Mexico, USA.

Custom-made tools

BESPOKE tools are made by both individual potters and professional suppliers from materials ranging from wood to rubber and plastic. Clay, too, may be used for kiln furniture and moulds. The *molde* and *volteador* (a turntable system used in Mexico) is built from baked clay.

ABOVE, LEFT: *Seashells have been widely used since ancient times for scraping and smoothing clay, and sometimes for impressing patterns into the surface.*

ABOVE, RIGHT: *Hooped wire tools for trimming, carving and hollowing clay.*

BELOW, LEFT: *An assortment of hardwood modelling tools. Hardwoods (particularly boxwood), bone or bamboo are excellent as tools because they are less likely than softwoods to decay in damp conditions.*

BELOW, CENTRE, RIGHT: *Metal kidney and wooden shaper for smoothing and refining forms.*

BOTTOM RIGHT: *Piece of old surform blade used for shaving away unwanted clay.*

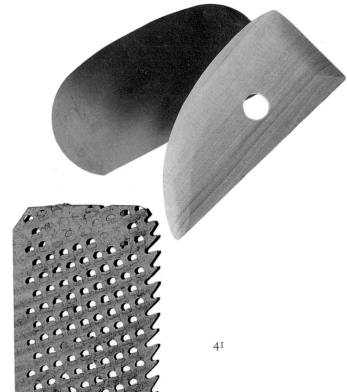

MODELLING

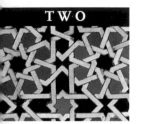

TWO

MODELLING IS the most ancient clay-shaping technique and the oldest surviving ceramic objects are not pots, but votive figures offered to the fire in Eastern Europe 30,000 years ago. It seems a reasonable assumption that unfired figures could have been made much earlier, but failed to survive without hardening in the fire.

BELOW, LEFT: *Terracotta frieze modelled in relief, Kalna, India.*

BELOW, RIGHT: *Modelled terracotta figure from the Nok Culture, Nigeria, c. 1st century AD.*

OPPOSITE, ABOVE, LEFT; AND OPPOSITE, ABOVE, RIGHT: *Modelled fish, Aldeburgh, Suffolk, England; ram's head in Hatherleigh, Devon, made by Steve Hunton to commemorate the British foot and mouth epidemic of 2001.*

Models

EARLY models may have served a religious purpose just as today both crude and sophisticated figurines are fashioned for the use of the devout, but often modelling serves a less righteous function, adding faces or legs to mundane household objects such as jugs and vases. Artists use clay as a medium for sculpture both in its own right and as a preliminary to casting a form in metal. At the end of the day, as they have done for millennia, potters use up their left over scraps by making play things for their offspring. But not all modelling is figurative and – notably in Nepal and Indonesia – handles and spouts may be squeezed and pulled into shape for addition to some functional vessel.

Technique

JUST handling clay subtly alters its form. Slight changes wrought by pressing and squeezing fire the imagination and prompt further manipulation, pushing, prodding and pulling until a recognizable shape appears. There is an ideal consistency, when the clay is not so dry it cracks or so wet it sticks to the hands, and in this state inspired fingers can work their magic upon it.

Additive modelling

IN its plastic state, it is a simple task to add more clay to the original lump as work progresses, pressing and smearing the two surfaces firmly together to achieve a sound join. However, it is often easier to build large or complex forms in separate sections that can be joined together when firm

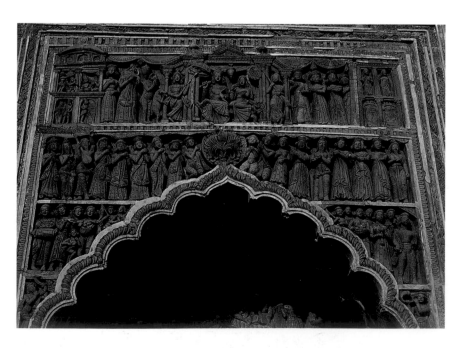

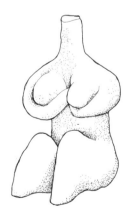

ABOVE: POTTERY FIGURINE MADE IN AROUND 5000 BC, HALAF CULTURE, MESOPOTAMIA.

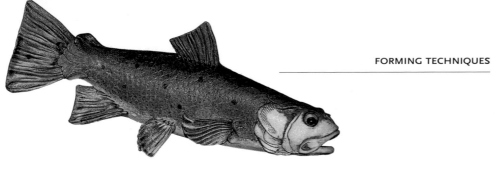

enough to maintain their shape. In this case, it is necessary to employ a process known as luting in which both surfaces must be roughened or scored before 'gluing' together with a thick slip or slurry.

Subtractive modelling

Sᴏᴜʟᴅ a form need refining at the plastic stage pieces can be pinched out with the fingers or cut away with a modelling tool. At the leatherhard stage, though, clay is best removed with sharper tools and the action becomes more sculptural as carving creates clearly defined surfaces and sharp edges. Detail

is best defined at this point before the clay becomes chalky and carefully sculpted work flakes away.

Hollowing

Aꜱᴏʟɪᴅ form dries out and shrinks unevenly both before and during firing, making it liable to crack or even explode in the fire or kiln. It is therefore necessary to make all but the smallest models hollow – a small hole will allow the passage of air as the object expands. Although the problem can be avoided by modelling on to a hollow form pre-shaped, for example, from a pinch pot or a slabbed cylinder, most forms must be hollowed out. This is carried out by cutting the leatherhard object in half and scooping out with a spoon or a looped wire tool before luting the pieces back together.

Lᴇғᴛ: *Simple, modelled tiger from Indonesia; probably intended as a child's plaything.*

Aʙᴏᴠᴇ: *Hindu votive horse with scratched decoration, eastern Nepal.*

Bᴇʟᴏᴡ: *A Zulu modelling clay heads sold as souvenirs to tourists.*

PINCHING

BERNARD LEACH, the great craftsman potter, described the pinching technique as 'the most instinctive and primitive way of making a pot'. It is employed all over the world as a way of making small pots or for beginning larger ones and is often the first technique taught to children in school. Although in essence simply modelling a globular form by pinching or pulling, pots of great refinement, such as Japanese raku tea bowls, may be constructed using this simple method of manipulating raw clay.

ABOVE: *Shaping pots by squeezing clay balls between the thumb and fingers, a quick and satisfying way of making hollow forms.*

BELOW, LEFT: *Pinched tea bowl made in the Raku family workshop in Kyoto, Japan. Hand-formed vessels are a popular accessory in the Tea Ceremony because of their simple unpretentiousness.*

BELOW, RIGHT: *Biscuit-fired thumb pots with added feet; made by the author.*

Making a pinched pot

PINCHED pots, also known as 'thumb pots', are begun with a piece of clay that can be easily rolled between the palms of the hand into a sphere. The ball is then rested in the hollow of one hand while the thumb of the other is pressed into it to within about a $1/4$ in. (5 mm) of the bottom. Starting at the bottom and ensuring that pressure is applied evenly, the clay is then pinched between thumb and fingers as

it is gently rotated, gradually working upwards. As the pot is pinched it becomes enlarged and the clay more compact. The heat and absorbency of the hands causes the clay to dry out so work must be quick before cracks begin to appear. Periodically, the pot may be put in a damp place to soften it a little and placed upside down to prevent flattening of the base – thumb pots are often constructed in batches moving from one to another as they become too dry to manipulate.

Altering shape

FOLLOWING the natural process a pot would just become wider and wider. To bring the form inwards the lip may be pleated and squeezed together or V shaped cuts may be made with a knife and the edges of the cut sealed over. Larger forms are often started with a thumb pot and expanded by adding coils to the rim.

PINCHING, AFTER AN EGYPTIAN TOMB PAINTING, 1900 BC.

44

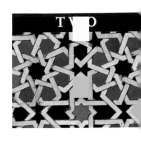

African techniques

IN sub-Saharan Africa throwing has been introduced comparatively recently and many spherical pots are built using the pinching technique. Traditional Venda potters in South Africa begin with a thick coil of clay formed into a doughnut shape which is then pulled up and squeezed into shape with the fingers, forming the top first and then inverting the work when leather-hard before pulling the bottom closed. Coils may be added to form a rim. During the 1950s the potter Ladi Kwali achieved celebrity in Europe as well as her native Nigeria through her collaboration with the English craftsman Michael Cardew who set up pioneering workshops in many parts of the world. Kwali began her pots with a lump of clay pressed into a calabash shell and then squeezed and pinched to pull up the sides. To reach the full height, coils of clay were added and smoothed, ultimately forming a virtually perfect sphere.

Hollow forms

IT requires great skill to close a thumb pot into a complete sphere, but the problem can be solved by luting together two leatherhard hemispheres. Air trapped inside will help the form maintain its integrity, but a hole must be pierced before firing. Hollow forms may be an end in themselves, such as the seed pots of the Pueblo dwellers of New Mexico, USA, or may provide the starting point for more elaborate pottery or sculpture.

ABOVE, LEFT: *Tiny pinched 'seed pot' by Lucinda Victorino, an Acoma potter from New Mexico, USA.*

ABOVE, RIGHT: *Weird fish, its body was constructed by the author by joining together two thumb pots.*

CENTRE, RIGHT: *Pinched pot by Hopi potter Bonnie Nampeyo, one of the many potters descended from the famous Tewa potter Nampeyo who developed the style of ceramic decoration known as Sitkyatki, which was based on ancient pots discovered near her home. Bonnie Nampeyo lives on the Hopi Reservation, Arizona, USA. The repertoire of bear's claw motifs and 'migration line' patterns executed in natural pigment has been handed down from mother to daughter in the Nampeyo family.*

BELOW, LEFT: *Mende potter squeezing the base of a jar into shape, Sierra Leone.*

BELOW, CENTRE; AND BELOW, RIGHT: *Reduction-fired thumb pots made in Swaziland for drinking beer.*

45

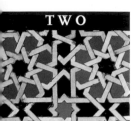

SLAB BUILDING

THE USE of slabs in creating ceramic forms dates back more than 10,000 years – it was one of the techniques employed during the Jomon Culture in Japan when the earliest known functional pottery was made. Simple but effective, the slab-building technique has subsequently been used for making both functional and decorative pieces – in the construction of sophisticated Chinese porcelain wares and for the sculptures of the Tiwi people of the Melville and Bathurst Islands off northern Australia who did not acquire pottery-making skills until the late twentieth century.

Making slabs

A NUMBER of methods, often in combination with each other, are used to form slabs. The first stage is to take a lump of clay and fling it down hard on to a solid surface. The Tiwi repeat this process, flinging the lump down again and again until the resulting slab is too large to lift and they then trample it out under their feet. To pound the clay flat potters in the Mexican state of Oaxaca employ a distinctive mallet, called an *azotador*, made from baked clay.

For a more even surface slabs can be rolled out using a cylindrical object such as a wooden dowel, a bottle or a rolling pin. To ensure an even thickness, a slat for the roller to rest on may be placed on either side. Rolling is carried out from the centre towards the edges, the clay being turned occasionally.

An alternative method is to cut slabs from a lump of clay using an implement known as a harp which consists of a wire kept taut by a metal frame. By adjusting the wire up or down slabs of different thicknesses can be cut and kept even by pressing the frame down on to the work surface as the wire is pulled through the clay.

At this stage the slab may be cut into shape to create tiles or the base for a relief plaque. The earthenware votive plaques made in Molela in the Indian state of Rajasthan use slabs for the background and also for the relief work, creating the raised figures of gods and heroes out of pieces of cut slab bent into a curve.

OPPOSITE, ABOVE, LEFT: *Chinese slab-built, porcelain vase.*

OPPOSITE, BELOW, LEFT: *Slab-built Iranian bottle decorated with oxide pigments in the Qajar style. The neck will have been coiled on to the slabs forming the body.*

OPPOSITE, BELOW, RIGHT: *Early 20th-century English ridge tile from the peak of a roof, formed from clay slabs.*

ABOVE, LEFT: *Tin-glazed earthenware tile from Puebla, Mexico.*

ABOVE, RIGHT: *Stoneware figure, by the author, mounted within a cut slab frame.*

LEFT: *Chinese porcelain, slab-built jar with underglaze blue decoration.*

RIGHT: *Plaque, from Molela in Rajasthan, India, consisting of relief figures mounted on a large slab.*

ABOVE: TIWI SLAB-
BUILT SCULPTURE,
MELVILLE AND
BATHURST ISLANDS,
AUSTRALIA.

ABOVE: JAPANESE
SLAB-BUILT BOTTLE
WITH *TENMOKU*
GLAZE.

Joining slabs

ONCE cut into shape, slabs are predominantly allowed to dry to the leatherhard stage before joining to ensure they will remain rigid, although soft slabs are employed if bending and pulling are required. Two slabs are joined together by luting, scoring and smearing with clay slurry before pressing together. Joints may butt up or be mitred. Once attached, exuded slurry must be wiped away and the surfaces cleaned up.

The most commonly formed slab pottery is four sided, although with mitred joints many sided forms can be built. Uses range from square vases and boxes to the hollow Roman box flue tiles fitted into central heating systems. Tiwi sculpture is built by cutting two identical slabs and building up several coils of clay between them.

Making cylinders

CYLINDERS are formed from plastic slabs that will bend without cracking. The slab is wrapped around a former covered with paper, to prevent sticking, and the edges are trimmed and luted together. Pipes and tubular pots are easily built in this way and semi-cylindrical items such as Chinese and Indian roof tiles are made from cylinders cut in half lengthways.

COILING

ABOVE: COILED BASE FOR A TOBACCO PIPE, YEMEN.

BEFORE THE invention of the potter's wheel, coiling was the most common technique for making pottery and remains the most widespread hand-building technique. It is generally recognized that baskets preceded ceramics and it is easy to see how basketmakers building their wares by coiling strands or bundles of fibre, stitching each new coil to the previous one, inspired early potters to apply the same technique to clay. The connection is particularly obvious when observing the similarity between pots and baskets in groups such as the Pueblo people of New Mexico, USA, or the Zulu of KwaZulu Natal, South Africa, where coiling is used in both crafts today.

ABOVE: *Congolese potters at work. The person in the centre is coiling, while the potter to the right is paddling a coiled form into shape. The potters to the left are scraping coiled jars smooth.*

Snakes

COILED pots are made from elongated, rolled out clay often compared to sausages, ropes or snakes. Among the Shipibo of northern Amazonia, Peru, the allusion is taken to extremes. They believe a snake at rest wraps itself into coils resembling a pot, maize beer brewed in clay vessels ferments with a hiss and when drunk delivers a sting. In West Africa, too, a myth tells how the Earth is held together by a cosmic serpent wrapped around it, an image found in many cultures.

To make a coil a lump of clay is first squeezed roughly into shape and then placed on a surface to which it will not stick. The potter leans over and rolls the clay back and forth with the hands, gradually spreading the fingers as the 'snake' writhes and wriggles, becoming longer and thinner until it reaches the right length and a consistent thickness. A number of coils can be fashioned at the same time, but care must be taken to ensure they do not dry out. The ideal length of a coil matches the circumference of the pot, while the thickness will relate to the size of the vessel and its intended purpose. Coils can also be formed by cutting strips from a slab or by squeezing large ropes with the hands.

Building a coiled pot

THE base of the pot can be formed by pinching or placing a pancake of clay in a mould which may be purpose built or improvised from a concave form such as an old broken pot or a piece of gourd. One coil at a time is attached, smeared carefully on to the clay below to ensure a good join; directly on top for a vertical wall; slightly staggered to draw the form in or out; at intervals to ensure an even, well-blended surface. Smoothing and scraping are carried out using a commercially made tool such as a metal kidney or a traditional one such as a corn cob or a calabash rind.

Many potters prefer to be able to turn the work as they go and employ a number of variations on the turntable or banding wheel. In Mexico, for example, the mould (*molde*) in which the base was formed is placed on a baked clay dome called a *volteador* so the work can be readily balanced and revolved on it.

Too much weight will cause the structure to collapse and so periodically it must be allowed to dry and harden (but not beyond the leatherhard state) before the addition of further coils. When joining new coils to leatherhard clay, the drier surface must first be scratched and coated with slurry to ensure a good join.

Since the days of the Anasazi some pots made by Pueblo people in the American Southwest have been smoothed only on the inside, giving them an appearance categorized as 'corrugated'.

ABOVE, RIGHT: *Large coiled water pot for ceremonial ablutions, Cameroon.*

LEFT: *Coiled jar by British potter Jane Perryman.*

OPPOSITE, BOTTOM LEFT: *Makarunga coiled yoghurt jars decorated with graphite, Zimbabwe.*

LEFT; AND CENTRE: *Coiled Acoma 'fineline' jar by Lillie Patricio, New Mexico, USA. Many Acoma pots are now slipcast and merely painted by hand; Shipibo coiled vessel for drinking maize beer, Ucayali River region, Amazon rainforest.*

BOTTOM RIGHT: *Navajo woman with coiled Acoma pots; photographed by Ben Wittick in the 1880s. High-quality Acoma pottery was a prized item traded with neighbouring tribes in the USA.*

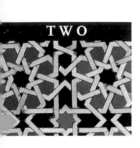

TWO

PADDLE AND ANVIL

T HE PADDLE and anvil technique consists of beating clay between a wooden bat (the paddle) and a mushroom-shaped stone (the anvil). The walls of pots made in this way are densely compacted and are therefore thin, but very strong.

Metalworking and pottery

A s both metalworking and pottery making require the use of fire, exponents of the two crafts have often been found in close proximity to each other in localities where there is a good stock of combustible materials. In parts of Africa, such as Cameroon, it is traditional for the men of a family to be metalworkers, while the women are potters. Certain techniques, for instance, casting and stamping are common to both, although their origins are not certain. Just as metal on an anvil can be beaten into shape with a hammer, clay can be beaten between a stone and a wooden bat. With both metal and clay the material is bent into shape (curved forms are the easiest to construct) and compacted which increases its structural integrity.

Working from scratch

I N Chulucanas in northern Peru the construction of a *tinaja*, the local water jar, begins with a *bolo*, a sausage of clay large enough to make the whole pot except the neck which is built up from coils of clay at the end. As if building a giant pinch pot, the potter pummels the *bolo* into a cone and then, working on his lap, begins slapping the outside with his right hand as he pushes his left inside to form a chamber. This crude form is set aside to dry and firm up. Drying times vary around the world according to heat and humidity, but the clay must still be malleable and is not allowed to reach the leatherhard stage. At this point the potter holds an anvil stone or sometimes simply his hand inside the cavity to resist the blows as he strikes the outside with a flat wooden paddle, turning the pot as he goes. Large pots are placed on the ground or on a stand and the potter walks around them backwards as he paddles. The whole process of drying and beating may be repeated two or three times before the final form is ready for the building of the neck.

ABOVE: USING A PADDLE AND ANVIL, AFTER AN EGYPTIAN DRAWING, 19TH DYNASTY.

A selection of paddles of different sizes and weights are kept to hand, lighter paddles are employed to smooth and refine the pot in the later stages.

In some regions such as Yemen the pot may be built up from a foundation to which lumps or rolls of clay are added and then beaten into position.

Paddling as a secondary technique

A PADDLE and anvil may be employed to compact and shape a pot which has been started using another technique – for instance, pinching, coiling or even throwing. In northern India water pots thrown on a wheel into an approximation of their final form are sometimes beaten into their final shape. This may require several stages of drying and paddling, resulting in pots as much as three times as large as at the thrown stage.

Decorative applications

IN Sarawak, Malaysia, the initial form of a pot begins with a lump of clay into which a stone has been pressed. The sides are raised by beating in the usual way, but the paddle may be carved with geometric designs and the impressions left by its impact create a textural pattern on the surface of the pot. Other examples of this technique can be found in South America and Central Africa.

ABOVE: *Brass water pot, from northwest India, showing the similarity between hammered metalwork and paddled pottery.*

BELOW: *Indonesian paddled jar darkened by the oxygen-reduced atmosphere of an open firing.*

OPPOSITE, TOP: *Paddled cooking pot from Myanmar (Burma); the pattern is created by a carved paddle.*

OPPOSITE, CENTRE: *Shipibo-Conibo chicha jar for maize beer; from the Peruvian Amazon. The thin coiled walls have been compacted by paddling.*

OPPOSITE, BOTTOM LEFT: *Paddled cooking pot made in Goa, India.*

OPPOSITE, BOTTOM RIGHT: *Coiled and paddled polychrome jar made between 1100 and 1300; excavated at the Tonto National Monument in Arizona, USA.*

THROWING

THE MANUFACTURE of a round pot on a swiftly spinning turntable or 'wheel' is known as throwing. It is a magical and hypnotic pottery technique, appearing, in the hands of a skilled potter, deceptively effortless. Pots can be thrown much faster than they can be coiled, but the process requires considerable practice and the patience of an apprentice. While coiling is a technique most often carried out by women, throwing is more often the province of men. Until the 20th century the wheel was virtually unknown in South America and is still seldom found in traditional societies south of the Sahara.

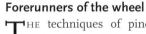

Forerunners of the wheel

THE techniques of pinching, coiling and paddling all involve the revolving of clay, in the hand, in the lap or on some simple device or, when making larger objects, the potter must walk around the clay. Many African potters begin their pots in a calabash shell placed on top of another shell inverted on the ground which allows one to turn easily upon the other. In New Mexico, USA, the bottoms of broken pots or specially made domes called *pukis* are used in the same way, while in Mexico the shaping of pots may take place on a baked clay disc or *molde* balanced and spun on a domed *volteador*. The 'slow wheel', turntable or tournette has been in use for millennia and was depicted on Egyptian tomb walls.

The wheel

THE true potter's wheel first appeared in China in the 4th millennium BC and simultaneously in Mesopotamia from where its use had spread to Egypt by 2400 BC. Early wheels were large solid discs balanced on a central pivot and were set spinning with the hand or with a stick inserted into a notch near the outer edge, a method still in use today in India and Japan. The momentum of a flywheel below the turntable keeps the wheel spinning for longer and makes it possible to propel the revolutions with a kick of the foot which can be even more effective with the use of a pedal and crank shaft. For centuries this was the preferred model in Europe and North Africa. The energy of the potter is conserved if the turning of the

ABOVE, LEFT: *Thrown Portuguese 'peasant' jar only glazed around the neck.*

ABOVE, RIGHT: *French-style kickwheel powered by the foot directly on the flywheel. This wheel is still employed by English potter Stephen Parry.*

BELOW, LEFT: *Indian potter using a wheel rotated with a stick.*

RIGHT: *Stoneware flower pot thrown by David Leach, Bernard Leach's son.*

OPPOSITE, BELOW, LEFT: *Egyptian potter throwing on a distinctive sloping kickwheel.*

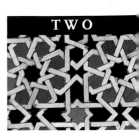

keeping the hands wet to avoid friction. He then draws the form upwards, creating a cone, makes a depression and begins to pull the walls gradually upwards. This is a skill best learned in the studio and not from a book such as this. With practice, all manner of hollow, rounded forms can be created on a wheel, some of which may be altered by squeezing, cutting and piercing or the addition of pieces of clay to form handles or spouts.

Once a thrown pot has dried to the leatherhard stage it may be returned to the wheel where it can be 'turned' to a more precise shape by shaving away superfluous clay with a strip or loop of metal. Turning produces sharp angles and is used for refining thickly thrown wares and, particularly, the underside of bowls and plates.

ABOVE: *Filling a thrown, tin-glazed jug, Tunisia.*

BELOW, CENTRE: *Thrown terracotta stand for incense sticks; made in Nepal.*

BELOW, RIGHT: *Moroccan thrown, tin-glazed jug from Safi.*

wheel is accomplished by another power source such as an assistant, water power or, in modern times, electricity. With the notable exception of Japan, wheels around the world revolve anti-clockwise.

Throwing a pot

ONCE a lump of clay has been thrown on to the wheel head the potter must fight centrifugal force and keep pushing the clay back to the middle or 'centring' it,

ABOVE, LEFT, FROM TOP TO BOTTOM: *Thrown bowl, made in Romania during the 19th century, decorated with slip and oxides; the underside of a Romanian bowl refined by turning.*

TWO

MOULDING

THE CREATION myth of the Kulin, an Aboriginal people who live in the Australian state of Victoria, tells how, after he had created all the other animals, Bunjil, the Great Spirit, spent a long time pondering how to make his masterpiece and finally took two sheets of bark which he carefully cut and carved into shape and then pressed soft clay into the indentations. Bunjil breathed life into the nostrils, mouths and navels of these inert forms and danced around them whereupon they rose and joined him – the first man and woman.

Pressing clay into a hollow form is a quick and easy way of producing many identical objects whether statuary, sections of pots or medallions with which to decorate them and the technique has been employed to make objects as diverse as pre-Columbian stirrup spout pots, Chinese tomb figures, Roman oil lamps and the mythological scenes on Wedgwood jasperware.

TOP; AND ABOVE: *English biscuit-fired mould for making clay plaques; tiles moulded with figures of Vikings; made by Thyssen Keramik, Denmark.*

Making moulds

To produce an object the correct way round moulds must be made in negative. Hard materials such as wood or stone may be carved in intaglio (the opposite of relief) which is a very skilled process, whereas soft materials such as clay or plaster may be formed around a matrix. A matrix may be a natural form or a man-made object identical to the final desired form except that it is larger to allow for the subsequent shrinkage of the clay during drying and firing. Clay moulds are formed by pressing the matrix into plastic clay and plaster moulds by pouring liquid plaster over the matrix. Plaster dries to a smooth, hard block, but clay moulds are best biscuit fired. For three-dimensional forms it is generally necessary to make a mould in several pieces so that it can be assembled and dismantled for repeated use.

Using moulds

WHATEVER material is used to make a mould, the process of employing a mould is basically the same. Soft clay is taken, either in slab form or in small lumps, and pressed down into the mould. The clay is allowed to harden a little and then carefully removed intact. To prevent sticking, the mould may be sprinkled with sand or, in Mexico, with ashes or dust. An advantage with clay and plaster moulds is that moisture is sucked out of the clay into the mould, shortening the hardening time. At the leatherhard stage separate sections may be luted together and extra detailing or modelling added.

Jigger and jolly

Now mainly used for mass producing plates and bowls, the jigger and jolly technique was used in the production of

OPPOSITE, BELOW, LEFT; AND OPPOSITE, BELOW, RIGHT: *Glazed tile, from Isfahan, Iran, moulded with the relief figure of a huntsman; raku chameleon formed in a two-piece mould at the Fenix Pottery in Strand, Cape Province, South Africa.*

NEAR RIGHT; AND FAR RIGHT: *A moulded religious plaque of the Holy Family of Christianity on the outside wall of a house in Mdina, Malta; moulded salt-glazed figurine acquired in Cochin, India, but probably made in northern Europe.*

BELOW, LEFT: *Two-piece moulds were used by the Moche people of Peru (AD 200–750) to make stirrup pots. Modern replicas like this are made in Lima using the same techniques.*

BELOW, RIGHT: *Moulded plaque of a Buddhist deity, Kathmandu, Nepal.*

Samian ware during the Roman Empire. A plaster mould, which is plain or, in the case of Samian ware, heavily impressed, is centred on a revolving turntable and soft clay is pressed on to the surface either by hand or with a metal armature. In jiggering the mould forms the inside, while in jollying it is used to form the outside.

Mass production

USING a mould saves considerable time and expense and sets of identical items can be easily and economically produced. It can also have a religious application in that the repeated production of religious images, particularly in Buddhist cultures, is believed to have a cumulative effect, the mould increasing in spiritual potency with each use.

Hump and hollow moulds

THE TRANSFORMATION of a rolled out slab of clay into a curved form is easily accomplished with concave or convex moulds. The rounded surfaces of a gourd or calabash, both the inside and the outside, make ideal natural formers, as does the base of a broken pot. Functional forms are still constructed using such moulds, just as they have been since ancient times, but in the developed world it is now more common for potters to construct their own moulds from plaster to suit their personal needs. Plates and shallow bowls are difficult to throw on a wheel and have therefore often been made using moulds.

Using hump and hollow moulds

A HOLLOW mould resembles a basin or dished indentation while a hump, or drape, mould resembles a giant mushroom. A hollow mould shapes the outside of a form, while a hump mould shapes the inside. Although most often rounded, hump and hollow moulds may be straight sided or irregular, and without sharp angles where the sides join the base. Both types of mould must be wider at the rim than at the base to allow a completed form to be removed.

The first task is to roll out a slab of clay larger than the mould. If the slab is rolled out on a piece of cloth or hessian it is easier to lift and place carefully over the surface of the mould. Gravity and the elasticity of the clay will help it to hug the mould, but the potter needs to encourage the process with a damp sponge or rubber kidney, gently smoothing away pleats and creases. As the clay begins to dry the edges may be trimmed back to the edge of the mould with a knife or wire.

In a concave hollow mould a new clay form may be left to dry as it will pull itself away from the mould as it shrinks. On a hump mould, however, the clay will shrink more tightly to the mould and must therefore be removed earlier to prevent cracking.

Decorating moulded forms

THE surface of a mould may be embossed or incised with designs that will show on the finished work. Patterns as delicate as textiles were, for instance, a common feature on the inside of Ding ware porcelain bowls made during the Chinese Song Dynasty (960–1279). Raised lines on the mould also left impressions on some 18th-century Staffordshire pottery made in England which served as guidelines for subsequent slip trailing.

Functional items used in English dairies, and those in the colonized world, in the 17th and 18th centuries were known as keeping room wares and were sometimes decorated with marbled or 'joggled' patterns created by swirling liquid slip. The slip was applied to a slab which was then draped, decorated side down, over a hump mould. Direct slip trailing, on the other hand, could be carried out on a plate or bowl while it dried in a hollow mould.

Extending forms

IN West and South Africa many potters begin their pots with a base shaped in a piece of calabash shell, while Native American potters often employ the base of an old broken pot. By using such makeshift formers or a plaster mould

height can be built up by adding coils or further slabs of clay to form the walls. Two moulded sections can also be joined together to create a spherical or carinated form.

Function may dictate the addition of handles, which can be joined at the leatherhard stage, or a foot ring which gives stability. With hump-moulded shapes a foot may be added while the clay is in the mould, but with a hollow mould the clay must be removed first.

OPPOSITE, ABOVE, RIGHT: *Oval and rectangular plaster hump moulds.*

OPPOSITE, BELOW, LEFT: *Slip-painted moulded dish from Oaxaca, Mexico, with three added feet. Similar pottery was used in Aztec times.*

ABOVE, LEFT; AND ABOVE, RIGHT: *Moulded dish decorated with marbled slip; English moulded plate with trailed and painted decoration.*

RIGHT: *Moulding the base of a jar over an old pot, Madagascar.*

BELOW, LEFT: *Slip-painted oval moulded dish made in Quinoa, Ayacucho Department, Peru.*

BELOW, RIGHT: *English moulded dish with trailed slip decoration; made by the author's mother.*

SLIP CASTING

APART FROM the skilled manufacture of the original matrix from which a mould is made the casting of slip in moulds is essentially a job for a trained technician. With the addition of deflocculants, such as sodium silicate or carbonate which reduce the amount of water necessary to make a fluid slip mix, drying speeds can be faster than with press-moulded plastic clay and the majority of industrially produced hollow wares such as teapots are now made by slip casting. Earthenware, stoneware and porcelain wares can all be made in this way.

Plaster of Paris moulds

THE origins of slip casting are obscure, but the technique was adopted by European factories during the late 17th century using moulds of biscuit-fired clay. Plaster of Paris was first made in France in the 1770s from gypsum mined in Montmartre. It was ground and heated to remove chemically bound water. Plaster was immediately seized upon as the ideal mould-making material as it retained the true, crisp form of the original and also absorbed water more quickly from the clay. Plaster moulds can be used to produce vast numbers of casts, but

eventually lose their crispness as the alkali in the slip eats away at them.

Just as in press moulding, while some wares are cast in one go in a mould assembled from several sections (often held together with tough rubber bands during casting), others are cast in several separate moulds and assembled after casting. The head and limbs of figurines, for example, are often cast individually, as are the belly, spout, handle and lid of a teapot. The distinctive feature of a slip-casting mould is the 'collar' or 'spare', which acts as a funnel and reservoir at the point where the slip is poured into the mould.

Casting

For casting, slip must be mixed to a creamy consistency so it can be poured freely. This is achieved by mixing either plastic or dry powdered clay with water, and is made easier with a device known as a blunger which sieves and paddles the mixture. After a final sieving to ensure there are no lumps, the slip is poured quickly into the collar of the mould which may be spinning on a turntable to ensure even distribution. Once the mould is full the slip is allowed to settle. As moisture is absorbed by the plaster, the level of slip drops and the excess can be poured away leaving a thin skin of clay adhering to the sides of the mould. The filling and pouring off process may be repeated several times until the skin is of the right thickness. When leatherhard, the clay form is removed from the plaster mould and allowed to dry. Separate sections may then be joined together and all the scars and joints cleaned up with a knife and sponge, a task known as fettling.

The Ute Mountain Pottery

Slip casting is so simple and quick that it is an ideal technique for commercial production as is demonstrated at the Ute Mountain Pottery at Towaoc, Colorado in the USA. Although the Ute tribe has no ceramic tradition of its own, a pottery was set up in 1971 to aid the tribal economy which is mainly supported by cattle ranching and a casino. The slip-cast earthenwares produced are inspired by the traditional pottery – particularly wedding vases – of neighbouring tribes and also by contemporary forms such as coffee mugs. Decoration is applied using designs derived from nature and Ute beadwork patterns.

PRE-FIRED DECORATION

LEFT: *Bowl, from Swat in Pakistan, painted with slip.*
ABOVE, LEFT: *Dish painted with oxides on slip, Pucara, Peru.*
ABOVE, RIGHT: *Sgraffito dish, Pucara, Peru.*
RIGHT: *Navajo vase with appliqué motif, Arizona, USA.*
BELOW, LEFT: *Goat-shaped vessel with impressed and appliqué decoration, Oaxaca, Mexico.*
BELOW, RIGHT: *Jug with appliqué designs, Swat, Pakistan.*

PRE-FIRED DECORATION

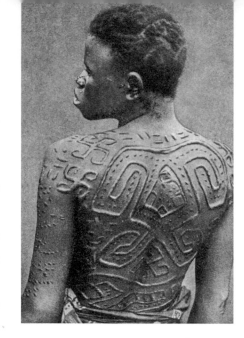

ANALYSING THE decoration of a pot's surface is frequently the best method of diagnosing its geographic and chronological origins and often the status of its owner too. A number of decorating techniques can be employed before wares are submitted to the fire and although these may later be coated with glaze they are not dependent upon it for their vitality. Some patterns are added to pottery while it is still yielding, altering the surface by adding or subtracting clay, but others are added in the form of vegetable, mineral or even animal derived pigment, smeared or painted on to the absorbent dry surface.

ABOVE; AND BELOW: *Scratched petroglyphs on cliffs at Chaco Canyon, New Mexico, USA; probably inscribed between AD 850 and 1250; reduction-fired pottery, with pre-fired decoration, from around the world.*

DESIGNS DICTATED BY TECHNIQUE

MANY MARKS are accidentally made by tools or fingers during the construction of pottery and although they may be subsequently smoothed away they do suggest decorative possibilities, inspiring, for example, the frequent ornamentation of wheel-thrown pottery from all over the world with patterns of incised horizontal rings. Some Acoma potters in New Mexico, USA, have adopted an ancient 'corrugated' technique used by the Mimbres culture of New Mexico a thousand years ago, emphasizing rather than erasing the imprints of their thumbs on coiled jars. Tools, on the other hand, may be used to create patterns from the potter's imagination, but are limited by their rigidity or shape. Designs impressed with a wooden comb, a popular technique in southern Africa, appear as rows of attractive dots, but are restricted on the whole to straight rows.

LEFT: POT DECORATED WITH A WATER SERPENT COMMON TO MUCH PUEBLO POTTERY, NEW MEXICO, USA.

OPPOSITE, ABOVE, RIGHT, FROM TOP TO BOTTOM: *Skin decorated with scarred tissue, Belgian Congo (now the Democratic Republic of Congo); figure for averting headaches, decorated with patterns of scarring, Kubobo tribe, Democratic Republic of Congo.*

CULTURAL DESIGNS

PAINTED DESIGNS are less restricted by the nature of tools and may be as curvilinear or irregular as the artist desires. Painted patterns are therefore likely to draw upon a repertoire of traditional motifs that are also used for textiles, wood carving or body decoration in the form of scarification or tattoos. The same patterns are drawn by the Shipibo-Conibo people of Amazonian Peru on their pottery and their textiles – the patterns have their origins in the past and are variously interpreted as representing the skin of the anaconda, the carapace of a turtle or even a map of the stars. The patterns painted upon the pots of Berbers in Morocco also appear in tattoos and can be traced back to the time when Mediterranean culture was dominated by the Phoenicians.

THE FUNCTION OF DECORATION

TODAY, IN the acculturated West we see little more than aesthetic issues in decoration. Once motifs predominantly had a deeper meaning and their depiction served a magical purpose, protecting the user from malignant forces or indicated the affiliation and status of their owner. The cultural store of signs and symbols now also serves the function of expressing the maker's pride in their ethnic origins. Today, the manufacture and decoration of pottery in New Mexico by individuals, families and tribal groups is one of the most successful of Native American economic ventures. The forms and designs employed are predominantly traditional or draw their influence from the rich heritage of the ancient cultures of the American Southwest.

ABOVE, LEFT: *Slip-painted jar with traditional motifs; made at San Ildefonso Pueblo, New Mexico, USA, by Cynthia Starflower, one of many potters related to internationally renowned Maria Martinez.*

LEFT: *A member of the Hopi tribe painting jars with a brush made from chewed yucca stem, Arizona, USA; photograph taken by Roland Reed in 1910.*

ABOVE, RIGHT: *Earthenware animals decorated with the traditional linear designs of the Shipibo-Conibo people of the northwest Amazon in Peru.*

RIGHT: *Traditional linear designs painted on a large textile by the Shipibo-Conibo people of northwest Amazonia.*

APPLIQUE

THE WORD appliqué is more often associated with sewing than ceramics, but it describes a technique in which a pattern or design can be built up in relief by attaching pieces of clay. In Mexico the technique was popularized by Teodora Blanco Núñez, a potter from Oaxaca who died in 1980. Reviving a pre-Hispanic technique, she decorated her pots and figurines with raised floral motifs which imitated embroidery and gave the style the name bordado (Spanish for embroidered).

ABOVE: *Wedgwood Jasperware dish with applied moulded sprig of a mythological scene, Staffordshire, England. The earliest examples of Jasperware date from 1775.*

Technique

ADDING pieces of clay is a simple matter, although the two surfaces to be joined need to be of similar consistency and moistness. Joining by smearing is possible when the clay is soft and this is the best time to add features such as ropes of clay that must be sufficiently soft and malleable so they can be twisted and bent into position. Lumps of clay may also be added and modelled or carved into shape. To keep pre-formed details crisp, however, it is better to join them as the work firms towards leatherhardness – at this point it is necessary to scratch the surfaces and apply slurry as glue. After joining, further detail can be built up or scratched away. The work should be kept damp for about a week to allow the moisture to even out before drying slowly or the applied features may dry out more quickly and fall off.

Pellets

THE use of pellets or small balls of clay to add detail was popular in Iron Age Iran (*c.* 1000–800 BC) and may have been

ABOVE: *'Tenderness', an early 19th-century genre scene by Walton of Staffordshire, England; moulded with applied details.*

NEAR RIGHT: *Skeleton with appliqué details made for the Day of the Dead, an ancient festival, in Oaxaca, Mexico.*

ABOVE, RIGHT: *Chinese jar with added sprigs depicting the Eight Immortals of Chinese mythology.*

intended to imitate the rivets used in the construction of metal vessels at that time.

Zulu potters in South Africa still use pellets on many of their vessels. Nowadays, they are simply pressed on to the surface, but were once applied like rivets, pushed through a hole drilled in the vessel and flattened on each side. A number of explanations are given for patterns made with these pellets which in Zulu are called *amasumpa* or warts. While some say that the dots refer to wealth in cattle, others say

details known as sprigs. These may be modelled by hand or formed in a mould made from plaster or baked clay. Fine examples of this method are the English salt-glazed hunting jug, made in London from the 18th century onwards, and the elaborate árbol de la vida (tree of life) which is a popular image in Mexican folk art. Delicate sprigs depicting classical scenes also feature on Jasperware, the most popular product of the Wedgwood factory in Stoke-on-Trent, England, which was first produced in 1775.

THREE

ABOVE, LEFT: *Earthenware 'teapot' or wine jar, from the Indonesian island of Lombok, with added decoration in the form of a lizard.*

ABOVE, RIGHT: *Small salt-glazed 'hunting' jug with moulded sprigs; made in London during the 19th century. Sprigs usually depicted hunting or drinking scenes.*

RIGHT: *Small Zulu beer pot, from KwaZulu Natal, South Africa, decorated with pellets and fired in an oxygen-reduced atmosphere.*

that they are based on the ritual markings on a woman's body or the raised scars caused by the insertion of medicines into a cut in the skin. In Uganda the bumps on terracotta figures of the guardian spirit Mbirhlengda are supposed to refer to the terrible skin diseases with which he sometimes punishes wrongdoers.

Byzantine pottery of the 9th century AD, known as petal ware, was decorated by attaching balls of clay to the damp surface and smoothing down on one side to create an effect like fish scales, feathers or flowers. This technique was a legacy of Roman potters in Asia Minor and has been a popular method for creating surface texture ever since.

Motifs and sprigs

WHILE detail may be built up on the surface of the clay, it is also a common practice to apply pre-shaped

INCISING

AN UNFIRED clay surface is easily marked or scratched and can even be scarred by fingernails during the act of shaping. It is a yielding material ideal for incised or engraved decoration and many ancient peoples saw the possibilities of expressing on clay the repertoire of patterns they had built up scratching on rock walls. Potters, however, have the advantage that mistakes can be erased by smoothing out the forgiving, plastic surface.

Technique

CLAY is most easily scratched with a tool when soft, but is inclined to drag when it sticks to the point of the tool. If the clay has reached chalky dryness any attempt at scratching will result in chips and flakes breaking away. The sharpest lines are achieved as clay approaches the leatherhard stage, but even then the scratch can be furrowed as it throws out the waste.

Tools can be made using all kinds of objects, from sharpened sticks or bones to needles and knives, but sharp, fluid lines are best achieved employing, as the Chinese and Koreans do, implements cut to a square point like a chisel. Bamboo is an ideal material for making these tools – it is hard but easily cut – so the perfect implement for any specific job can be quickly crafted as the need arises. Another widely used tool is a comb as it can scratch several grooves into the clay at the same time. Combs are frequently used for decorating the surface of thrown wares, scratching lines as a leatherhard pot is turned slowly upon the wheel or turntable.

Motifs

INCISING or graving is a linear technique and is therefore used for depicting outlines or geometric patterns. The similarity of the techniques means that in any specific culture many patterns are common to ceramics, rock carving, metal engraving, woodcarving and the scarification or tattooing of skin. Straight lines and flowing forms are most easily achieved – a graving tool cannot be moved as deftly through clay as a brush across the surface. For contrasts in intensity, which suggest tone, hatching can be used by making closely packed lines parallel to one another or sets of overlaid scratches crossing each other at an angle.

Simple pictograms inscribed into clay tablets were used in Sumeria from about 3100 BC to identify the contents of storage jars. Originally depicting the contents, such

ABOVE: MISSISSIPPIAN CADDOAN VESSEL WITH INSCRIBED PATTERN, USA, 1200–1600.

RIGHT: INCISED CALCIFORM BEAKER, SUDAN, 4TH MILLENNIUM BC.

NEAR RIGHT: *Slip-painted water jar with inscribed pattern, Luena River area, west Zambia.*

FAR RIGHT: *Contemporary inscribed vessel, Thailand.*

BELOW, INSET: *Mexican terracotta flower pots, with incised decoration, for sale in Santa Fe, New Mexico, USA.*

as fish or grain, these gradually became stylized into ideograms that provided the basis for the first writing system.

Variations

INCISING produces monochromatic designs which are revealed by the play of light across their surface. As can be seen on pots made by the Mississippian Caddoans of the USA between 1200 and 1600, burnishing the surface can increase the contrast because the colour of the grooves will remain dull. It is also possible to inlay the grooves with clay of a different colour – a technique used to great effect on Korean celadon wares during the Koryo Dynasty (918–1392).

A scratched surface can also provide an effective abrasive. Since Aztec times, Mexicans have grated their chilli peppers in a *molcajete*, a bowl with an incised bottom, while roughened clay blocks are made in Turkey for scraping dead skin from the feet.

OPPOSITE, ABOVE, RIGHT: *Inscribed Indonesian jug for serving rice wine.*

OPPOSITE, BELOW, LEFT: *Modern copy of an incised and painted stirrup pot dating from the time of the Paracas Culture in Peru (1000–300 BC).*

OPPOSITE, BELOW, CENTRE: *Cream jug, with scratched decoration, made by the English potter David Leach in the 1950s.*

OPPOSITE, BELOW, RIGHT: *Straits Chinese teapot, with incised drawing, made in Indonesia.*

Carving

Also known as 'excision' (cutting out), carving is used on clay to create a design in relief below the original surface. Clay carving is often found in regions that also have a tradition of carving in wood or stone and, sharing the same concept, employs the same or similar tools and skills. In many Islamic countries, such as Egypt and Iran, carving can be seen on stone, plaster and wood and so clay is just another medium. Intaglio carving (in negative) is sometimes used in the making of clay moulds.

Above: *Terracotta tile moulded from a carving copied from an English Medieval woodcut.*

Below, left: *Terracotta pot with fluted decoration, Thailand.*

Below, right: *Faceted bowl made by Japanese potter Takeshi Yasuda in the 1980s.*

Above: Bottle with moulded and carved decoration, Egypt, 11th century AD.

Opposite, above, left: *Carved blackware pot (reduction firing) by Adelphia Martinez, San Ildefonso Pueblo, New Mexico, USA.*

Opposite, below, left: *Greek plate with a carved and scratched design.*

Technique

Carving is carried out on clay surfaces that have been made thicker than is normally necessary, whether by coiling, throwing or slabbing, and is best done when the clay is leatherhard so that clearly defined edges can be produced. Knives and chisels are used to cut the clay away in thin shavings; at times gouges may also be used to cut U or V shaped channels, for instance, when cutting the veins of a leaf. The illusion of depth is enhanced by undercutting the main forms, creating extra shadow. Carving in clay is most effective with confident, sweeping cuts and so, as mistakes are difficult to fix, it is best to mark out the design on the surface of the clay first.

Faceting and fluting

Faceting and fluting are techniques most often used to alter thrown forms. Facets are flat faces which normally run vertically down the surface of a pot and create a geometric form, predominantly hexagonal or octagonal.

Carefully measured guidelines are first marked out on the surface and clay is then sliced away with a knife or more effectively with a harp fitted with a tight wire.

Concave flutes run parallel diagonally or vertically rather like the grooves on a Greek column and are cut out with a round-ended tool such as a gouge or, ideally, a clay plane.

Carving in pre-Columbian America

THE carving of stone was a major art form among the ancient cultures of the Maya, the Toltecs and the Aztecs in Central America and low-relief carving was also employed on some high status pottery such as funerary urns. Deeply carved designs, frequently depicting jaguars, were executed on the black, reduction-fired pottery of the Cupisnique people (800–600 BC) of the Lambayeque River region of northern Peru.

Carving in the Rio Grande

POTTERY carving in a chunky style, surprisingly similar to the Lambayeque wares, began in northwest New Mexico, USA, during the late 1920s when the Tafoya family of Santa Clara Pueblo began to carve their pots with traditional motifs such as bear claws, kiva steps and clouds; by 1931 the technique had been taken up at San Ildefonso Pueblo where the most typical motif remains the water serpent.

Carving in Eastern Europe

IN Eastern Europe there is an old tradition of vernacular wood carving which has no doubt influenced the carving of clay vases and jars which are now being produced at crafts cooperatives in Romania. The patterns on these are crisply carved and have bold, floral motifs, reminiscent of the local embroidery, emphasized by a textured background created with a blunt punch.

ABOVE, CENTRE; AND TOP RIGHT: *Romanian carved vase blackened by reduction firing; carved vase, from Romania, fired in an oxygen-rich atmosphere.*

RIGHT: *'Wedding vase' fired in an oxygen-rich atmosphere by Clarissa Tafoya, Santa Clara Pueblo, New Mexico, USA.*

BELOW: CARVED AZTEC FUNERARY URN, TENOCHTITLAN, MEXICO.

THREE

PIERCING

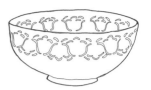

THREE

MANY CERAMIC objects require perforations if they are to serve their purpose and these holes must be cleanly cut. This can be achieved most easily when clay is in its leatherhard state as it will not be pulled out of shape or chipped by tools. Even the most functional holes can be made in a pleasing arrangement and the effects produced by light and shade and by negative and positive have inspired more complex designs, applying perforations as a decorative technique in their own right.

Functional holes

HOLLOW forms must always be pierced before firing to allow the expanding air inside to escape – for this purpose a small hole, carefully placed out of sight, is adequate. Items used for sprinkling or pouring demand a cluster of holes like those found in salt cellars or on the tops of jars containing fragrant pot pourri. Where the spout of a teapot is joined on holes are often pierced in the belly – large enough to allow the passage of liquid, but small enough to prevent the flow of tea leaves.

Larger, less restrictive holes are made in lamps and lanterns so the light can be seen; if the holes are arranged to do so patterns can be cast on to walls and ceilings. Air bricks set into a wall as ventilation can also be pierced with aesthetic consideration and enhanced with modelled detailing.

Used purely for decoration, holes range from pinpricks to flowing patterns resembling fretwork. One popular form of Chinese export ware, also produced in Iran during the 17th and 18th centuries, is decorated with pierced patterns often referred to as rice grains. The tiny elliptical holes become filled with glaze during firing, allowing the passage of light but not foodstuffs.

Making holes

LEATHERHARD clay can be punctured in a number of ways using improvised or

ABOVE: Chinese spoon with perforations sealed by glaze.

BELOW: French tin-glazed 'basket' with perforations to enhance the 'interweaving'.

specialized tools. The smallest holes can be made with a needle or any convenient pointed object, whether metal, wood, bone or plastic. Larger holes are kept crisp by removing clay rather than just pushing through it. This can be accomplished with a drill or a punch made from a hollow tube, although many studio potters use a device designed originally for removing apple cores.

ABOVE, LEFT: *Chinese-style slip-cast elephant with pierced decoration; made in Thailand for export.*

ABOVE, RIGHT: *Double-skinned teapot with lead glaze and pierced decoration, Leeds, England.*

Invented during the 18th century, probably the most successful British ceramic product was creamware, which had a white earthenware body made from Devon clay and ground flint. The Leeds factory produced a distinctive range of creamware which was decorated with lattice-like patterns of holes.

Cutting shapes

THE making of larger holes is sometimes known as fenestration ('the making of windows'). To cut out straight-sided shapes a thin bladed craft knife can be used, but it is poor for cutting tight curves – a more effective instrument is a wire employed in a similar way to a carpenter's fretsaw. Passed through a hole drilled

through the clay wall, the wire is pulled along a pre-marked line while exerting even pressure with both hands. This technique has been used in China for decorating trays and ceramic seats and is now much imitated in other parts of South-East Asia.

CENTRE, RIGHT: *Pierced Nepalese lamp, or incense burner, shaped like a fish. The appertures have been pierced with a sharp bladed knife.*

LEFT: *Stoneware lamp made in Britain by a studio potter during the 1970s. Piercing has been executed using a tube-shaped implement.*

RIGHT: *Incense burner with perforations – a nightlight can be placed inside, Cornwall, England. Aromatherapy and alternative therapies have added another stock item to the repertoire of many studio potteries.*

IMPRESSING

M ANY ACCIDENTAL indentations are made during the construction of a pot – by fingertips, the tools that define its shape, a mat or basket upon which it has stood. These vestiges can be found upon some of the most ancient pottery and have, with many other impressions, inspired techniques for the deliberate decoration of clay. For a potter's mark to be clear the clay must be yielding, but to avoid smudging it must no longer be so sticky that it adheres to the tool as it is withdrawn. It is important that the force of an impression is countered from the inside to prevent a pot being distorted.

Cords

T HE first known functional ceramics were made in Japan 12,000 years ago and the culture that produced them has been named Jomon (Japanese for cord marking) because of the impressed patterns with which much of them were decorated. Cords have also been employed in other regions, for example in Britain during the Bronze Age, using very similar techniques. Many markings were simply produced by pressing a twisted or plaited

cord into soft clay, while others were made by whipping the surface or rolling the cord across it. Patterns resembling basketry were created by wrapping cord around a stick, square in section, which was rolled over the clay. On Jomon pottery cord markings were often combined with many other scratched, stamped and appliqué patterns.

Dots and dashes

T HE simplest mark to make is the dot, impressed with an implement – metal or wood, a reed or a bone – sharpened to a point. Patterns can be built up easily from many dots arranged in clusters or lines. Dashes are produced using a tool

TOP LEFT: *Stamping patterns on to leatherhard clay, Cameroon. The roulette is also frequently used to impress pots in this part of the world. The cleanest impressions are made by pressing into leatherhard clay.*

TOP RIGHT: *Chicken-shaped whistle decorated by impressing the surface with a stamp, Guatemala.*

CENTRE, RIGHT: *Sherd of vessel with incised and stamped patterns, Wales, 6th or 7th century AD. Impressions have been made using a tool with a straight edge.*

LEFT: *Earthenware oil jar decorated by pressing applied bands of clay with the thumb, North Africa.*

with a rectangular tip. By cutting notches in such a tip a 'comb' is created which will stamp out a short row of dots with each impression. A stylus with a wedge-shaped tip was used in Sumeria 5,000 years ago for the writing of cuneiform (which means wedge shaped). Natural objects may also be used – fine, crenellated lines, for example, can be produced with the edge of seashells.

identical images can be produced by carving motifs upon a cylinder and rolling it over the clay. Carved stone cylinder seals were used in Mesopotamia, while roulettes made of clay were employed in the production of Roman Samian ware. Today, in West Africa elaborately carved wooden roulettes remain one of the principal tools for applying ceramic decoration.

Circles and crescents

ROUND indentations can be made with the fingertip, a stick or any object with a rounded tip. Should pressure be applied evenly employing a hollow object such as a bone or a metal tube, the result will be a ring, but if an object is pressed down at an angle so that only part of it makes contact a crescent will be produced. Sometimes it is difficult to distinguish crescents made with a tube from those made by the fingernails, although most potters prefer to keep theirs cut short to avoid accidental scratches.

Stamps and roulettes

IT is possible to produce more sophis-ticated patterns by impressing the surface with one or more stamps made of fired clay or carved wood, a technique also employed by potters to stamp their signatures upon their wares. A row of

TOP RIGHT: *Maker's mark stamped on the lid of a Chinese teapot. Chinese stamps and seals give information about the maker and the date of manufacture.*

RIGHT: *Terracotta wall sconce with modelled and stamped decoration, Nepal.*

BELOW, LEFT: *Oil jug with impressed pattern, Swat, Pakistan. The bands were incised while the body of the jug was on the wheel.*

BELOW, RIGHT: *Terracotta fish with stamped scales, Thailand.*

SLIP

SLIP IS a mixture of clay and water prepared by soaking and sieving until it has reached an even creamy consistency. Applied as a coating over the surface of a pot, it may be used to achieve a smooth finish, to decrease porosity or to alter the colour of a pot's surface. Slip applied to biscuit and stoneware to which gum or flux has been added to improve adhesion is known as an 'engobe'.

Slip colour

SLIP made from the same clay as a pot is known as a 'self' slip, but often slip of a contrasting colour – made from a different clay or altered by adding pigment – is used to decorative effect. White slips are generally made from kaolin (china clay), while red and black are produced by adding haematite, blue by adding cobalt and green by adding copper oxide.

Applying slips

A NUMBER of techniques can be employed for completely or partially coating a surface with slip; all the techniques demand that the recipient surface has dried enough to remain rigid, but is still damp enough to ensure adhesion. Slip can be smeared over the surface with the hands, or a rag, or painted on with a soft brush. Many potters in the American Southwest still apply their slip with a rabbit tail. It is also possible to dip an item into a tub of slip or to pour slip over it – such methods are more commonly used in Europe and the Far East.

Terra sigillata

ROMAN finewares were often coated with slip made from clay rich in illite (a member of the mica family) which fired

ABOVE; AND RIGHT: *Five-hundred-year-old clay colouring smeared on the Temple of the Sun at Pachacamac, near Lima, Peru; foot of Samian ware bowl excavated in Britain, 4th century AD.*

to a rich orange-red sheen in an oxygen-rich atmosphere. The platelets of the clay lie very flat and parallel to the surface, giving an exceptionally smooth, dense surface. Wares covered with this slip are known as terra sigillata ('decorated earth') as they were often decorated with small, densely packed raised motifs. The title 'Samian ware' is often given to similar products from Gaul and Britain produced during this period.

Marbling

THE utilitarian bowls and dishes used in British and colonial farmhouse kitchens during the 17th, 18th and 19th centuries were given a random 'marbled' or 'joggled' surface. These wares were moulded from slabs that were first given a coating of slip before one or more slips of a contrasting colour were trailed on top. The slab was then lifted and tilted and swirled until a pleasing effect had been achieved. Marbled wares were also produced on Islamic pottery in imitation of pottery imported from China where marbling had been a decorative technique since the T'ang Dynasty (618–906). The patterns resembling ripples or fast-changing clouds were popular among the Taoist people who believed they symbolized the free flowing of Ch'i (Vital Energy).

Mochaware

THE distinctive English mochaware made during the 18th and 19th centuries in Staffordshire and the West Country was created by dropping a diffusion of hops or tobacco on to damp slip and allowing it to run, dividing into veins to create the semblance of a tree. The technique was revived in the 1960s by Roger Irving Little at the thriving Boscastle Pottery in Cornwall.

ABOVE: *The process of applying slip to a jug at Boscastle Pottery, Cornwall, England (from top to bottom): coating the jug by dipping in a bucket of slip; applying the mocha mix to a slipped surface; the jug after the mocha has spread across the slip.*

OPPOSITE, LEFT; AND OPPOSITE, INSET: *Moulded dish with marbled slip decoration, England; applying a coating of slip by dipping, Iraq.*

OPPOSITE, BELOW, RIGHT: *Zia water jar, by Eleanor Pino Griego, decorated with burnished and painted slip, New Mexico, USA.*

ABOVE, RIGHT; AND RIGHT: *Earthenware jar, Tuscany, Italy. Dipping can be used to apply both slip and glaze; mochaware vessel by Rupert Andrews, England, 1970s.*

THREE

SLIP TRAILING

S LIP TRAILING is a technique where thick slip is used as a medium for drawing, leaving a raised line. With the exception of yellow and brown wares produced at Fushina in Shimane Prefecture in Japan, it is almost exclusively found in Europe.

Technique

THE traditional tool for pouring slip was a 'can' made from clay or a sheep's horn. Quills of different sizes could be fitted to the spout as required and the flow of the slip was controlled by covering or uncovering a hole with the thumb which allowed the inflow of air. During the 20th century it became more common to use a nozzle attached to a rubber bulb – the flow of slip was easily controlled by pressure when it was squeezed. Modern potters have improvised, using syringes or recycled plastic bottles. Whatever the tool employed, drawing must be carried out with flowing movements, keeping a consistent speed to ensure an even line.

Slip trailing traditions and styles

S LIP trailing was sometimes used on Roman pottery as a form of raised decoration and was often applied in the same colour as the background. This is known as barbotine work and was a feature of Castor ware which was produced in England during the 2nd century AD and decorated with flowing plants and hunting scenes.

Slip trailing is very much a folk art and reached the height of its popularity on European tableware used by the lower classes during the 17th century; the gentry at this time were eating from porcelain plates and dishes. The Portuguese style is jewel like with animals and plants depicted using large numbers of dots, while the French style that still flourishes in Beot is much more geometric and formally arranged. In Hungary patterns are free flowing and depict bold floral motifs resembling the local embroidery.

The English tradition

I N England the main centres of slipware production were London, Wrotham in Kent and Harlow in Essex. Many of the

ABOVE, LEFT: *Hungarian vase with elaborate trailed and painted decoration.*

ABOVE, RIGHT: *Fragments of Roman pottery with barbotine decoration; excavated at Barcombe, Sussex, England.*

LEFT: *Tool for slip trailing – a rubber reservoir is squeezed to express slip at a controlled rate.*

RIGHT: *Portuguese plate with a pattern formed from dots of slip.*

ABOVE, LEFT: *Slipware charger in the 17th-century style; by Harry Juniper of Bideford, Devon, England.*

ABOVE, RIGHT: *Three plates with geometric designs of trailed slip, from Beot, France.*

BELOW, LEFT: *Plate, with slip-trailed fish, by Ben Lucas of Welcombe Pottery, Devon, England.*

RIGHT: *German cups and saucers with feather-combed slip decoration.*

THREE

finest pieces have survived as they were commemorative and intended for display on dressers and not for daily use. Some of these recorded births or marriages, while others were inscribed with drinking rhymes or religious invocations. After the English Civil War (1642–46) the most impressive slip trailing was produced in Staffordshire, most notably by Thomas Toft whose huge plates were generally graced with naïve depictions of King Charles II and the royal family. Slip trailing had dwindled by the 19th century, but interest was revived by the experiments of Bernard Leach at St Ives in Cornwall during the early 20th century.

Feather combing

An alternative method of decoration is 'feathering' or 'feather combing' which is part of the European repertoire, and was also known to the Chinese, appearing on Song Dynasty bowls in the 3rd century AD in patterns resembling wood grain or peacock feathers. A series of parallel lines are first trailed over the surface and then the tip of a quill is drawn lightly across them repeatedly, leaving no trace but dragging the trailed lines into a series of peaks.

LEFT: PLATE WITH TRAILED SLIP PATTERN BY BERNARD LEACH, ENGLAND.

SGRAFFITO

THE TERM sgraffito or sgraffiato is derived from the Italian word for scratch and refers to a technique in which designs are etched or incised through a layer of slip to reveal the contrasting colour of the clay beneath.

History

EXPONENTS of the Black Figure style (700–550 BC) in Ancient Greece decorated their work with lively naturalistic scenes painted with black slip on a cream or red background. Fine lines delineating muscles and drapery were created by scratching through the black slip to the lighter base colour.

ABOVE, RIGHT: *Sgraffito tile by David Leach, England, 1950s. David Leach and his father, Bernard Leach, experimented with many traditional decorative techniques.*

BELOW, LEFT: *Sgraffito plate from Szentendre, Hungary. Lines have been scratched through both the slip and the glaze.*

BELOW, CENTRE: *Portuguese plate with sgraffito applied through the glaze.*

BELOW, RIGHT: *Red-slipped jar where the decoration was engraved after firing, Belem, Brazil.*

Sgraffito was probably developed as a decorative technique in its own right by the Copts in Egypt during the 5th and 6th centuries AD and subsequently spread to Byzantium, Central Asia and, by the 11th century, China, most probably disseminated by trade along the Silk Route. Unlike Black Figure vases, these wares were generally made from a red earthenware coated with a lighter coloured slip so that etched lines appeared dark. The etched line became the dominant feature and the subsequent coats of glaze were generally clear or splashed randomly over the surface.

Technique

FIRSTLY, the clay surface is coated with an even layer of slip of a contrasting colour to the body and both are allowed to approach the leatherhard stage. Chisel-shaped tools cut from wood or bamboo are then used to draw out the design, wider tools being employed for broader lines. Pressure on the tool should be sufficient to cut down through the slip layer and merely

skim the surface beneath. A skilled hand may begin to approach the subtleties of brushwork or calligraphy, but the rigours of the discipline generally dictate a bold, somewhat naïve style. On occasion, scratching details through layers of coloured glazes can produce a similar effect.

American sgraffito

THE enthusiasm for Native American pottery has provided a regular income for its makers and consequently the time to experiment with new styles and techniques. Since the 1960s potters living in the Pueblos of New Mexico have developed their own version of the sgraffito technique where the surface of the pot is

scratched or carved away after firing. To accomplish this it has been necessary to embrace modern technology and use not only surgical steel scalpels, but also dentists' drills and even laser cutters.

Champlevé

During the 11th century AD artisans in the Persian Empire developed a form of sgraffito once known as *gabri* ware because it was associated with fire-worshipping Zoroastrians who are also known as Gabri. Produced in the Garrus district of western Iran and inspired by metal-engraving techniques, this procedure involved carving away not only lines, but also areas of the background. Designs included human figures, animals and inscriptions in the Kufic script. The

ground was generally dark while the raised areas were coloured with green or brown lead-based glaze. Now known as *champlevé*, from the French word for a raised field, the same technique became popular in Europe from the 14th century, although in Britain the glaze employed was generally honey coloured.

ABOVE, LEFT: *Contemporary jug in the North Devon sgraffito style; by Harry Juniper of Bideford, England.*

ABOVE, RIGHT: *Pot with pattern etched after firing; made by Wilma L. Baca of Jemez Pueblo, New Mexico, USA.*

RIGHT: *Jar, from Lombok, Indonesia, with a sgraffito pattern inspired by Chinese motifs.*

I F THE correct materials are used, designs painted on to raw or biscuit-fired clay will become fused permanently to the surface, providing decoration that can survive for millennia. Pottery from the Samarran culture (6300–6000 BC) in Mesopotamia, for example, was decorated with bold red and brown designs that remain clearly delineated today.

THREE

Pigments

S OME vegetable extracts are used in paints, but most will only survive a low-temperature firing. Kabyle pottery from Algeria uses decoctions of lentiscus, century plant and juniper. Most often pigments are composed of natural earth colours and produce a range of muted tones of black, brown, red, yellow and white. Kaolin (china clay) is a common source of white and ochres provide reds and yellows. The palette is extended considerably by the addition of mineral oxides. Iron oxide is the most widely used, producing – when used in different strengths and depending on the atmosphere in the kiln – yellow, red or black. Bright colours are also available with cobalt providing blue, copper providing green, cinnabar (mercury sulphide) providing vermillion red and manganese providing purple and black, and so on. While the extraction of oxides from rock could be a time-consuming task, iron oxide has often been obtained by scraping the rust from old, exposed metal.

Slip

W HEN used for painting pottery, slip – as a colour in its own right or mixed with oxide pigments – is used more thinly than when it is used for dipping or trailing. Thin 'separated' slips are acquired by 'levigation' which involves allowing the liquid clay mix to stand in a bucket or vat until the heavier particles have sunk to the bottom so that the thinner slip on the surface can be skimmed off. Deflocculants such as wood ash may be added to create a colloidal suspension in which particles are separated to keep the mix fluid. Slip used

by the Ancient Greeks contained wood ash as well as urine or sour wine to stabilize the particles.

Preparation and application

M INERAL pigments must be painstakingly ground into a fine powder, a task accomplished with a mortar and pestle or on a saddle quern such as the *mano y metate* still used in Central America to grind flour. The powdered colour can then be mixed with a slip, the clearest colours being achieved when using a white slip, or they may be mixed with a binding agent such as gum arabic. Laguna potters in New Mexico, USA, make their black paint by mixing haematite (an iron oxide) with the juice of wild spinach or yucca.

A base coat of slip is often applied before designs are painted on. Many potters work freehand, although guidelines drawn with pencil or charcoal will burn away in a firing. The most accurate designs are executed with a brush, often

TOP; ABOVE; AND RIGHT: *Roof decoration painted with earth colours, Ayacucho, Peru; inside of a Corinthian-style cup, dating from the 5th century BC, painted with oxides, Greek colony in southern Italy; earthenware Berber vessel, from southern Morocco, painted with designs inherited from the Carthaginians and Phoenicians.*

OPPOSITE, BELOW, LEFT: *Dish with slip-painted, traditional Aborigine designs, Walkabout Community, Northern Territories, Australia.*

improvised using a chewed stick or, in the case of the Acoma and other Puebloan peoples in the USA, a chewed yucca stalk. The best brushes are those made from animal hair in China and Japan which can achieve a fine, controlled line while carrying a considerable amount of pigment, allowing the execution of bold, flowing designs.

BURNISHING

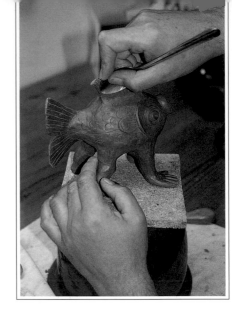

BURNISHING IS a very simple method of endowing a clay vessel with an attractive sheen. It is used most often for decorating low-fired pottery and has roots in the distant past – examples survive from over 7,000 years ago in the Near East – and it is still commonly employed where traditional techniques have not been supplanted by more advanced technologies such as the use of high-temperature kilns and glazes. Many examples of burnished pottery, for example, are still being manufactured in sub-Saharan Africa and among the indigenous peoples of the American Southwest.

The advantages of burnishing

NOT only is a burnished surface shiny, it is also compacted by the rubbing process which results in denser, stronger walls that are more impervious. These qualities are enhanced when the surface is first coated with a fine slip. Burnishing is, understandably, often used on water jars for both decorative and practical purposes.

Smoothing and scraping

TO achieve the best shine the clay surface must be as smooth as possible. When clay is still damp irregularities and the marks made by tools or fingers can be easily smeared and smoothed. While many craftsmen employ a commercially produced kidney-shaped piece of rubber,

others must improvise – Mexican potters, for instance, use a piece of leather or felt from an old hat and in Uganda the Nyoro use a scrap of bark cloth. As the clay dries out, a more aggressive tool may be utilized to scrape the surface – for example, a metal kidney, a cut-down hacksaw blade or, in Africa, a piece of calabash rind. Acoma potters in New Mexico, USA, often achieve an even surface with a piece of sandpaper.

ABOVE, LEFT; AND ABOVE, RIGHT: Smooth stones from the American Southwest, typical of many used for burnishing pottery; burnishing leatherhard clay with the back of a spoon.

BELOW, LEFT; AND BELOW, RIGHT: Incised and burnished water pot, Mozambique; burnished jar from Mata Ortiz, Chihuahua, Mexico. Mata Ortiz decoration is inspired by pottery, excavated at Casas Grandes, made by Mogollon-Anasazi potters (1300–1500).

Burnishing

Burnishing is best carried out when the clay is on the drier side of leatherhard. A smooth, hard object with a slightly convex surface is rubbed repeatedly over and over the clay until it becomes shiny. Stones smoothed by a river are the most widespread implement, but a bone or the back of a spoon may be adequate. In Argentina some potters prefer to use a light bulb!

San Ildefonso black on black

Maria Martinez, who subsequently became one of the world's most respected potters, spent her whole life in the humble surroundings of San Ildefonso Pueblo beside the Rio Grande in New Mexico, USA. In 1919 she and her husband, Julian, developed a distinctive new style using only simple, traditional technology. The style attracted the attention of art dealers and has since provided many Puebloan potters with a good income. Simple traditional forms were hand built from local clay and then carefully burnished with a smooth river stone. Using slip made from the same clay, a design, typically of a water serpent or fanned out feathers, was then painted over the top but left unburnished. In their backyard, when enough wares were ready, the Martinez family covered them with pieces of scrap metal, such as hub caps and old car parts, and built a fire from animal dung in which temperatures of up to 760°c (1400°F) could be achieved. The heap was then covered with powdered dung, creating a reducing atmosphere which turned the pots black. The result was monochrome pots where the bodies were shiny and the painted areas matt.

ABOVE, LEFT: *Reduction-fired pot in the Maria Martinez style by Manuel Adakai of Utah, USA. The lighter colour is achieved by painting in slip over the burnished background. Adakai is of Navajo and Santa Clara extraction.*

ABOVE, RIGHT: *Reduction-fired burnished pot with sgraffito decoration; from the Indonesian island of Lombok.*

ABOVE: ANGLO-SAXON BURNISHED JAR WITH STAMPED DECORATION (AD 400–650).

FIRING

FAR LEFT: *Japanese Imari porcelain plate.*
ABOVE, LEFT: *Turkish earthenware yoghurt pot.*
ABOVE, RIGHT: *Votive elephant fired in reduced atmosphere, Bangladesh.*
NEAR LEFT: *Earthenware water pot, Acatlan, Puebla, Mexico.*

NEAR RIGHT: *Ash-glazed stoneware jug by Stephen Parry, England.*
FAR RIGHT: *Raku 'Moongazing Hare' by John Hine, England.*

FIRING

THE BEAUTY of clay as a material is that in its raw state it is easy to work and shape and yet once it has been exposed to the heat of a fire it becomes hard, resilient and permanent.

ABOVE, LEFT; BELOW, LEFT; BOTTOM LEFT: *Unloading porcelain from a cellular kiln, Kyoto, Japan; loading a pit kiln, Baghdad, Iraq; earthenware pottery for sale at a fair outside Delhi, India.*

CHEMICAL CHANGES

UNFIRED CLAY, however expertly manipulated, is vulnerable as it will still become flaccid and collapse when too wet or crack and crumble when too dry. When exposed to dull red heat over 600°c (1112°F) an irreversible chemical change takes place in which all moisture is expelled from the clay and it becomes ceramic, the particles fusing together permanently like stone. Even when ground down into sandy grog, fired clay no longer becomes plastic when mixed with water and in this state its only use to the potter is as a temper for opening the body of the clay.

FUEL

THE CHOICE of fuel for firing pottery is dictated by the combustible materials available in the vicinity of the workshop. The Pueblo potters in New Mexico, USA, such as the world famous Maria Martinez of San Ildefonso, traditionally fire their wares in small clamps fuelled with sun-dried cow chips, huge Cretan storage vessels called *pithoi* are often fired with crushed olive stones, while in the Mexican state of Puebla fuel may include maize husks and cactus spines and the domed *mantou* kilns of northern China once employed coal. Today, firings in North Africa are sometimes fuelled by old car tyres.

Although often recently superseded in developed countries by electricity, the most efficient and widely used fuel is wood and many potteries once maintained their own woodland to ensure adequate supplies. Before use, all timber must be thoroughly dried to prevent moisture entering the kiln atmosphere and ideally it should be resinous as this will provide the greatest heat. In China and Japan pine is often chosen, while in northern Peru a steady heat over 950°C (1742°F) is achieved with zapote wood, but the hottest fires are fed with algarrobo and can reach 1100°C (2012°F).

The great industrial sites of ceramic production develop where there is an ample supply of both clay and fuel – the great Chinese porcelain centre at Jingdezhen, for example, is located beside hills rich in kaolin and is surrounded by forests of pine trees.

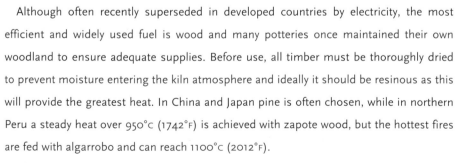

LEFT: STOKING
A MUD BRICK UP-
DRAUGHT KILN,
AFTER AN EGYPTIAN
TOMB PAINTING,
1900 BC.

ACCIDENTS

A FIRING IS a risky and potentially disheartening undertaking as many disasters can occur. One danger is the rapid expansion of moisture locked in the clay body which causes explosions – pots must therefore be thoroughly dried out and heated slowly. Explosions can also be caused by the expansion of trapped air bubbles which can be avoided by proper preparation of the clay with wedging and kneading and by the making of a small perforation in all hollow forms. Sudden changes in temperature caused by draughts can cause pop-outs or dunting in which chunks of a pot may split off. Many problems can be avoided by enclosing the firing and raising and lowering the heat gradually.

The heat itself can also cause problems. If the firing temperature is not high enough a clay vessel will not fuse properly and will remain crumbly or flaky. On the other hand, if the temperature is excessive (particularly in a glaze or 'glost' firing) all wares in contact with each other may become fused together in an inseparable mass.

ABOVE; CENTRE, LEFT; BOTTOM LEFT; AND BELOW, RIGHT: *Raw, biscuit-fired and glazed pots in the studio of Stephen Parry, Norfolk, England; thumb pots damaged by too sudden an increase in temperature during firing; wares fused together at a temperature too high for the clay body; Tunisian water jar. The firing was too cool for the surface to fuse properly, leaving it crumbly and brittle.*

OPPOSITE, TOP RIGHT; AND OPPOSITE, ABOVE, RIGHT: *Wood-fired earthenware pot decorated with slip, Oaxaca, Mexico; Cretan pithoi fired using crushed olive stones for fuel.*

87

OPEN-AIR FIRINGS

FOUR

There is archaeological evidence in Hungary and France that our forefathers were using hearths 350,000 years ago and it has been surmised that the altered state of clay, hardened by fire, was probably the inspiration for the first use of ceramic technology. Firing clay in an open fire is a technique still commonly found in sub-Saharan Africa, the Americas, India and South-East Asia. No permanent structure is required, only sufficient stocks of fuel.

LEFT: *Figure of the Hindu god Ganesh; made from slabs of clay and fired in the open using wood and dung, India.*

RIGHT: *Painted Day of the Dead candlestick from Oaxaca, Mexico; fired with wood for fuel.*

Technique

A FIRE has to be constructed carefully to ensure that heat builds up gradually and is spread evenly. The air must be dry, with no wind which could cause sudden changes of temperature, possibly resulting in the cracking of the pots. Fuel is laid on the ground, often in a shallow pit, the pots are stacked carefully on top and then covered with more fuel and finally a covering of sherds from old broken pots. Fuel varies according to the local flora and fauna. Zulu women, for instance, lay their pots on a bed of aloe leaves and then cover them with dried grass; in northern Peru the fuel of choice is zapote wood which burns with a steady heat; while in New Mexico, USA, potters traditionally employ dried cow dung gathered in the summer. Once lit, the temperature may rise to 800°C (1472°F) within half an hour and the pots may be fired within an hour. They then need time to cool gradually before being removed from the ashes.

Maria Martinez (1884–1980) of San Ildefonso Pueblo, New Mexico, now considered one of the world's greatest potters, employed a method that allowed a little more control. Firstly, the pots were laid on a grate over a bed of dry sticks and covered with sheets of scrap metal such as old car hubcaps – to protect the pots from contact with the flames produced by the layer of

cow chips placed as fuel over the top. Finally, the whole mound was covered with powdered dung to induce reduction.

Clay and temper

THE rapid rise in temperature that occurs with a bonfire causes the moisture content of the clay to boil and expand rapidly which often makes the pot explode. To avoid this, pots are built from a clay body that has been mixed with a mineral or organic temper which keeps passageways open through which the steam may escape.

The results

SUBJECT to unpredictable forces, firing in the open, even by experienced technicians, may involve the loss of a large proportion of the pots submitted and those that survive are often fragile and friable due to the low temperatures achieved. Potting is therefore an important part of daily life, keeping up with the constant demand for replacements and often, as a result of constant practice, a high degree of skill is achieved building pots with thin, compact walls.

Open firings may be employed to produce both an oxidizing and a reducing atmosphere and the colour of the clay may vary between bright red and black. Because of the problems of keeping the flow of heat and oxygen even the colour may be patchy. The random scorching caused by contact with flames, known in New Mexico, USA, as 'fire clouds', is often appreciated for its beauty and in many places attempts are sometimes made to encourage this happy accident by the careful positioning of pots or the introduction into the fire of materials such as pine cones that will cause flashing as they ignite.

BELOW, RIGHT: *Reduction-fired container, from Burkina Faso, fired in the open. West African firings are traditionally communal and may include hundreds of pots.*

ABOVE: *Bricks being stacked for firing in the open, Bissau, India.*

BELOW, LEFT: *Blackware pot fired with dried cow dung by Cynthia Starflower, a member of the Martinez family, San Ildefonso Pueblo, New Mexico, USA. During firing Puebloan potters protect their pots from the flames with pieces of scrap metal. The heap of pots and fuel is generally about a metre (3 feet) across.*

Kilns

LEFT: LOADING AN EGYPTIAN KILN, AFTER A TOMB PAINTING, 1900 BC.

A KILN is a technical advance in the firing of ceramics as it allows greater control of the temperature and the atmosphere. Heat can be increased gradually which ensures that less pots are broken and higher temperatures can be reached, producing stronger wares. The flow of air and hot gasses can also be controlled which prevents sudden dangerous gusts and spreads heat evenly around pots packed inside the kiln, while command over the quantity of oxygen present allows the mastery of the colour changes brought about by oxidation and reduction. Although a low-temperature firing in the open may take less than an hour, a high-temperature firing in a large kiln, such as a Japanese climbing kiln into which 100,000 pots could be packed, might take as long as two weeks.

ABOVE: *Wood firing, cross-draught kiln built for his own use by Stephen Parry, Norfolk, England.*

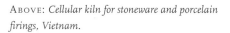

Early kiln technology

To prevent damage caused by draughts simple firings are often carried out in a pit, surrounded by a wall – a method still used in southern India – or in a 'clamp' covered with a roof-like layer of broken clay sherds as in Nigeria or pieces of scrap metal as in New Mexico, USA. Combining these elements results in a simple kiln with pots stacked inside a permanent structure. In Ancient Egypt pots were loaded from above on to a perforated grate before the top was sealed with sherds or clay.

Bottle kilns and bank kilns

THE bottle kiln in use by Roman times tapers towards the top, rising into a chimney that creates a strong up draught which sucks heat up through the firing chamber. By introducing hot gasses from the fires higher up the chamber and sucking them out into the chimney through a flue near the bottom, a down draught is created which holds the heat in the kiln for longer.

During the Warring States period (403–221 BC) the Chinese discovered the

ABOVE: *Cellular kiln for stoneware and porcelain firings, Vietnam.*

BELOW, LEFT: *English potter Philip Leach by his electric kiln used mainly for earthenware firings.*

LEFT: *Electric powered kiln. Spy holes for observing the stage of firing are visible in the door.*

TOP RIGHT: *Brick-built bottle kilns at the Royal Porcelain Factory in Copenhagen, Denmark.*

BELOW, LEFT: *Pyrometric cones used during an earthenware firing. The one on the right has melted showing the temperature exceeded 1010°C (1850°F), while the left cone remains erect showing the temperature did not reach 1060°C (1940°F).*

efficiency of a kiln formed from a cave or elongated chamber dug into a bank fed with fire at the bottom and a flue at the top. This system was soon superseded by a brick chamber built sloping up a bank. This climbing kiln became known as the 'dragon kiln', a long structure with flames and smoke pouring out of holes along its sides, in which the powerful draught could raise temperatures to over 1200°C (2192°F), allowing the manufacture of stoneware. In the 5th century Korean prisoners of war built the first Japanese cellular kilns (*ana-gama*), which are domed chambers built over a channel cut up a slope. The later *noborigama* was comprised of a number of these in succession. Stoneware fired in these chambers acquired an accidental layer of falling wood ash that created a simple but attractive glaze.

Kiln furniture

FIRINGS with solid fuel require constant supervision and the experienced eye can judge the state of heat and the atmosphere by the colour and texture of the smoke and flame. Modern electric kilns are fitted with gauges and metres, but it is possible to judge the kiln temperature by observing pyrometric cones through a spy hole. These are used in sets of three, each becoming soft and bending at a different heat.

Wares must be stacked inside the kiln so that there is a free flow of heat and so

CENTRE, RIGHT: *Props for kiln shelves. Shelves reduce the need for contact with glazed surfaces.*

BOTTOM RIGHT: *An experimental wood-firing kiln and results; built by Harry Juniper and other Devon potters, England.*

OPPOSITE, BELOW, RIGHT: *Cells of a wood-fired climbing kiln at Bizen, Japan. Japanese kilns are often large enough to fire several thousand pots at one time and are easily capable of achieving stoneware temperatures.*

that surfaces coated with glaze do not fuse together. Shelves and racks made from refractory clays may be used, while individual items can be spaced out by balancing them on three-legged 'stilts'. Pieces requiring protection from the flames may be placed in a ceramic container called a saggar.

EARTHENWARE

Pottery using clay that matures when fired to temperatures of around 950–1150°C (1742–2102°F) is known as earthenware. At this heat the clay becomes hard, but because it does not become fully vitrified it remains relatively porous. As suitable clay is widespread and the required temperatures are not difficult to achieve, earthenware pottery is the most widely used ceramic medium in the world.

Decoration

Earthenware is produced by so many different peoples that the style of decoration varies enormously, including the alteration of the surface with scratches and impressions and the application of designs using slips and glazes which bond well with the semi-porous surface. The exploration of these possibilities has led to the development of many notable ceramics such as the slipware of northern Europe and sgraffito decoration in Iran. The exciting pallet of mineral colours available to the practitioner firing at earthenware temperatures has also been responsible for both the brightly painted 'peasant' pottery of the Mediterranean and the sophisticated Turkish tiles created in Iznik from the end of the 15th century.

Above, left: *Jar from Transylvania, Romania, 19th century.*

Above, right: *Earthenware teapot, by Frannie Leach, decorated with slip and oxides, Devon, England.*

Use

Easily and cheaply produced, earthenware is used to make a vast range of functional everyday ware including vessels for drinking, carrying or storing liquids and pots for cooking and serving food. The semi-porous quality of the body allows a degree of evaporation to occur which ensures that liquid contents are kept cool and even pots that have been glazed to prevent leakage may be left unglazed around the neck for this purpose. The open pores also allow the quick passage of air and moisture,

an advantage as a pot is less likely to crack when heated over a fire or in an oven.

Terracotta

IN use since ancient times, the term terracotta (a corruption of the Latin terra cocta meaning baked earth) is used to describe unglazed articles that have been fired to temperatures within the earthenware range. Generally a warm red in colour, terracotta has been widely employed as a medium for sculpture, garden ornaments and flower pots as well as bricks and architectural detailing.

Biscuit

ALTHOUGH it is possible to glaze and fire raw wares in a single firing, nowadays it is more common to employ an initial firing to give some strength and porosity before the application of a coat of glaze. This process, known as a biscuit or bisque firing, involves taking the temperature of the kiln to around 980–1100°C (1796–2012°F), depending on the clay used. The use of the French word biscuit (twice baked) indicates that this is the first of two firings if the work is going to be glazed or may possibly be a reference to the clay's crispy texture. The term can also be used to describe items that have been fired once in this way, but remain unglazed, as in the case of the faces and hands of dolls or moulds like those sometimes employed by the Romans for making lamps.

OPPOSITE, BELOW, LEFT: *Large English earthenware crock.*

OPPOSITE, BELOW, RIGHT: *Pottery for sale in Cairo, Egypt.*

TOP LEFT: *Berber pottery for sale in southern Spain. Even today traditional Berber and other North African potters work almost exclusively in earthenware.*

RIGHT: *Moulded terracotta vessel from the Netherlands.*

LEFT: *Biscuit-fired hare modelled by the author.*

RIGHT: *Earthenware pottery in the streets of Mexico.*

RAKU

RAKU IS a very exciting technique in which the firing of a glazed pot may take as little as an hour or two. Unusually the pots are introduced to a kiln that is already hot and removed directly from the heat as soon as the glaze has melted and matured.

The Tea Ceremony

DURING the 16th century the philosophy of Zen Buddhism and the Tea Ceremony were an important influence on Japanese ceramics – although very stylized, they focused the attention of the participants on the beauty of the simple and natural. Tea masters and enthusiasts collected accessories that reflected these qualities. The great master Sen no Rikyu (1522–91) enlisted the skills of a tile maker named Chojiro to model and fire tea bowls. The quickly fired results were chunky, hand-formed cups dipped in a red or black glaze that had the rustic charm desired. The thick walls protected the hands from the heat of the tea, while the bubbly glaze felt pleasant against the lips. The results were so successful that Toyotomi Hideyoshi, a leading statesman at the time, named this new pottery Juraku ware after one of his palaces, and in 1598 he gave a seal to Chojiro in the shortened form 'raku' which he adopted as his family name. Raku means joy or ease. The Raku family pottery still thrives in Kyoto fifteen generations later. The technique was also explored by other contemporaneous craftsmen of the day such as the multi-talented Honami Koetsu.

Studio pottery

THE influential British potter Bernard Leach spent many years in Japan and claimed that his fascination with clay was the result of attending a garden party in Tokyo. While a small raku kiln was heated up, the guests were invited to decorate unglazed pots. These were dried by the kiln, quickly fired and then used for drinking tea, all in just one hour. Having subsequently studied ceramics in Japan for a number of years, Leach introduced raku to the Western world when he returned to England in 1920. It has been a favourite technique of studio potters ever since because of the range of effects that can be achieved, including the wide spectrum of colours that can be produced with glazes fired at low temperatures. The firing is so short that it requires the minimum of equipment and the cost of fuel consumed is low.

ABOVE, RIGHT: *Stephen Murfitt, an English ceramist, wears protective clothing while removing a large raku pot from his top-loading kiln.*

Technique

IN a normal firing the contents of a kiln are warmed up slowly to dry out all the chemically combined water in the clay, a process which also causes some shrinkage. Increasing the temperature too quickly can produce cracks as the pots shrink too fast or explosions caused by trapped moisture that cannot escape. The sudden temperature changes of a raku firing would prove disastrous without appropriate precautions – they involve mixing the clay body with ground mineral tempering, such as quartz, sand or grog, in a ratio of about two to one. This reduces the amount of water locked in the clay and also opens the structure, allowing a free passage of air and moisture. Today, objects intended for a raku firing are generally further protected by an initial biscuit firing. The pots are introduced into the heated kiln using a pair of tongs and fired in the range of 800–1100°C (1472–2012°F) and are removed with the tongs as soon as the glaze has matured.

By transferring the pots, while hot, into a reduction bin filled with sawdust or shavings a range of decorative effects can be achieved including lustre, crackled glaze and smoke blackening.

OPPOSITE, LEFT: *English raku vessels by Stephen Murfitt. The lustre finish is achieved by reduction during a post-firing immersion in a bin of sawdust.*

OPPOSITE, BELOW, CENTRE; AND OPPOSITE, BELOW, RIGHT: *Raku tea bowls with thick glaze; made in Japan at the Kyoto workshop of the Raku family.*

ABOVE, LEFT; AND ABOVE, CENTRE: *Moulded raku leopard and moulded raku meerkat; both made at the Fenix Raku Pottery in South Africa. Bright colours are achieved easily at the low temperatures used for raku.*

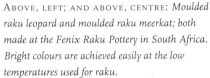

NEAR RIGHT; FAR RIGHT; AND BELOW: *Seal of the Raku family to be found stamped on the base of their products; raku hare by Larson Rudge, England. The unglazed areas of most raku is typically gritty because of the coarse clay required to resist thermal shock; small raku hare by British potter John Hine.*

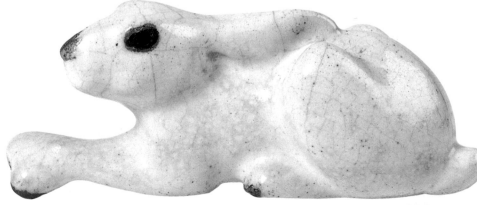

95

STONEWARE

RESEMBLING THE colour and texture of rock, stoneware is made from refractory clays fired at a high temperature of 1200–1400°C (2192–2552°F). At this heat the clay becomes vitrified with a high density making it impervious to water and hard enough to strike a spark from steel. Stoneware has a muted, natural colour with only a few exceptions such as the red clay products of Yixing in China imitated in 17th-century England by the Elers brothers.

ABOVE; AND LEFT: *German salt-glazed stoneware with blue underglaze decoration; Dutch stoneware gin bottle.*

BELOW, LEFT: *Unglazed red stoneware pottery from Yixing, China.*

BELOW, RIGHT: *Elegantly restrained thrown stoneware bowls from Vietnam.*

Stoneware clays

SECONDARY clays are used for stoneware as they are low in fluxes such as alkali, calcium and iron oxides, which lowers the melting point, and rich in impurities such as silica or alumina that fuse with the clay and allow the body to vitrify without collapsing when fired at a high temperature. These particles may be revealed as differently coloured, gritty specks on the surface.

Stoneware in the East

IT was during the Zhou Dynasty (10th to 3rd centuries BC) that stoneware first appeared in China as the result of developments in kiln technology which increased the draught and improved heat retention meaning higher temperatures could be reached. Firings lasted several days rather than the hours that had been sufficient for earthenware. Many of these early stonewares were built and decorated

to resemble the bronzes of the period – they featured carved or incised motifs and the application of moulded sprigs. Other pots were decorated with simple glazes achieved by sprinkling the surface with wood ash or feldspar which subsequently melted and flowed over. Chinese techniques spread gradually across the East and culminated in the Chinese stonewares of the Song Dynasty (960–1279) and the celadon glazed wares of the Koryo Dynasty (918–1392) in Korea.

Stoneware in the West

IN Germany's Rhineland, with its sandy grey clay and plentiful supply of wood for fuel, pottery was being fired to temperatures above 1300°C (2372°F) by the middle of the 14th century as a result of a new style of horizontal kiln with a lower stoke hole. As the usual lead glazes could not stand the heat, many of the early German wares were left unglazed,

FOUR

but were decorated, like early Chinese stoneware, with carved, applied or stamped motifs. The first glazing on German pots was achieved with salt which coated the wares with a thin transparent film and was often used over the old relief decoration. The introduction of the lucrative new stoneware technique in England was accompanied by fierce litigation when the patent awarded by King Charles II to John Dwight in 1671 was infringed by rivals such as the Elers brothers eager to cash in on the demand for tough tableware.

Glazing

BEING vitrified and therefore waterproof, stoneware does not require a glaze and may be left plain, coated with slip or tinted with oxides. However in the search for

ABOVE: *Collection of English salt-glazed stoneware bottles for ink and soft drinks.*

RIGHT: *Large stoneware teapot with oxide decoration, Denmark. The colour of this teapot changes in a most attractive way as it is filled with boiling water.*

added colour, glaze may be added to the biscuit-fired body which generally results in muted tones as only blue and red remain vibrant when fired at a high temperature. Stronger tints for stoneware firings are now available commercially, but in the past bright colours were achieved with a subsequent lower temperature enamel firing below 900°C (1652°F).

PORCELAIN

IN HIS travels around China Marco Polo (1254–1324) encountered translucent white ceramics which reminded him of a cowrie shell called *porcellana* ('little pig') from which the name porcelain is derived. Suitable for thin walled, translucent vessels, porcelain is one of the most highly regarded and copied of all ceramics.

FOUR

ABOVE; AND BELOW: *Chinese porcelain plate with transfer-printed dragons; hard-paste porcelain dish with underglaze decoration, made at the Meissen factory in Germany.*

Porcelain in China

THE method of making porcelain had been perfected in China by the time of the T'ang Dynasty (618–906). Along with other high-temperature fired, hard stonewares it was referred to as tz'u, and was prized by aesthetes less for its translucence than for the clear ring with which it resounds when tapped. The body consists of china clay, which is also known as kaolin after its original source at Gaolin ('high hill'), combined with china stone or petuntse (a corruption of the Chinese baidunze), a ground feldspar. Using the technology of the dragon kiln this mixture could be fired to very high temperatures (1300–1450°C [2372–2642°F]) which achieved a hard glassy finish. The secrets of this lucrative technique were kept closely guarded. The finest porcelain was arguably made during the Song Dynasty (960–1279), but the most famous wares were produced at Jingdezhen during the Ming Dynasty (1368–1644), many decorated by painting under the glaze with cobalt blue or copper red (the only colours known at the time that would remain true when fired to high temperatures). Later Ming wares were decorated with the wider palette available with overglaze enamels.

During the Koryo Dynasty (918–1392) porcelain was made in Korea and it was a Korean potter (known in Japan as Kanae Sanpei) who, in 1616, first discovered china clay in Japan, initiating porcelain production at Arita where the construction of blue and white ceramics continues to this day.

Working with porcelain

WITHOUT the addition of a more plastic clay, porcelain is difficult to throw

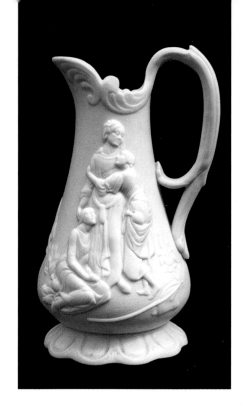

LEFT; BELOW, LEFT; AND BELOW, CENTRE: *Moulded soft-paste vase made in England from a mould dated 1847; bone china cup with hand-painted decoration, England; Chinese porcelain dish with cobalt blue decoration.*

RIGHT; AND BELOW, RIGHT: *German hard-paste drinking vessel with transfer decoration and pewter fittings; porcelain bowl by studio potter Elspeth Owen, England.*

OPPOSITE, TOP RIGHT: *Imari porcelain plate with painted and stencilled decoration, Japan.*

OPPOSITE, CENTRE, RIGHT: *Chinese porcelain plate made for export; it imitates the Japanese style popular between 1860 and 1890.*

and model and it is, therefore, more often formed by moulding or slip casting. Although porcelain is vitreous and needs no glaze it may be used in combination with underglaze or overglaze painting for decorative effect. Chinese figurines of Buddhist deities made for export in Tê-Hua were often coated in a thick, transparent white glaze called 'blanc-de-chine'.

Porcelain in the West

THE demand for porcelain from the East exceeded supply and potters in Europe and in Islamic countries struggled to copy porcelain for hundreds of years. Attempts included 'stonepaste' or 'soft paste' versions using mixtures that were low on clay, but contained a large amount of ground quartz that vitrified at temperatures below 1150°C (2102°F). In England during the 18th century glassy quartz with ash from animal bones was replaced by an alkali-rich mixture that produced a vitreous product known as bone china. It was very popular for domestic wares and became an important export item.

The recipe for 'true' or 'hard paste' porcelain was eventually discovered during the 18th century in Germany by a chemist, Ehrenfried von Tschirnhausen, and an alchemist, Johannes Friedrich Böttger, leading to the establishment of the first European porcelain factory at Meissen where there was a suitable source of clay. The secret eventually spread to other parts of Europe, carried by disaffected German workmen.

OXIDATION AND REDUCTION

FOUR

THE MOST obvious change to take place during a firing is the hardening of the clay body and the vitrification of the glaze, but other reactions occur which relate to the amount of oxygen present in the immediate atmosphere.

Controlling the atmosphere

IN an electric kiln heat is produced without the consumption of oxygen, but in gas and solid fuel firings it is used up as the fuel burns, making it necessary to ensure an effective draught and flow of air. If the amount of oxygen is restricted then the oxygen present in the clay is sucked out to fuel the burning. In open-air firings, which are common in most of Africa and the Americas, this is achieved by covering the fire and pots with a layer of ash or dung and in enclosed kilns air vents are closed. Watching the flames during a firing tells an experienced ceramist about the state of the atmosphere. Bernard Leach explained this procedure by comparing the kiln to an oil lamp with a glass chimney in which the flame normally burns bright and yellow, but if the chimney is covered and the oxygen supply diminished then the flame becomes smoky.

Changes to the clay body

THE unrefined clays used by traditional potters, such as the Zulu in South Africa, are made up of organic impurities which are rich in carbon. In an oxygen-rich atmosphere the fired clay reaches a pink or red colour as a result of the presence of iron ore, but in a reduction firing the result is grey or black. The colour change is caused by the carbon that would burn away in an oxidized firing, but remains to colour the clay in a reduced atmosphere. The principle is the same as in the making of charcoal when, cooked in a sealed atmosphere, wood is deprived of oxygen and burns away leaving behind pure black carbon. Kitchenwares from La Chamba, Colombia, which are reduced to black in burning dung, are now available from kitchen suppliers all over the world.

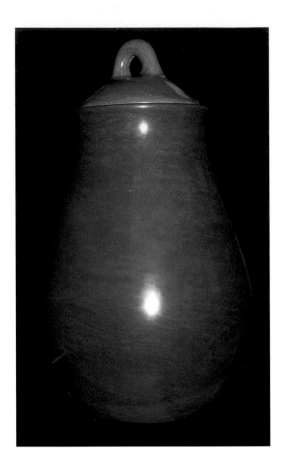

ABOVE: *Lidded jar by Jason Ebelacker, Santa Clara Pueblo, New Mexico, USA. The jar has been coated in a red slip, burnished and then fired in an oxygen-rich atmosphere. The iron ore content has turned red just as iron turns rusty red when exposed to air.*

BELOW, LEFT; AND BELOW, RIGHT: *Gourd-shaped water bottles from Perak, Malaya. The one on the left was fired in an oxygen-rich atmosphere and the one on the right in a reduced atmosphere. Iron retains its metallic greyness when not exposed to air and so the iron oxide in the clay turns to black or grey when the fire is deprived of oxygen.*

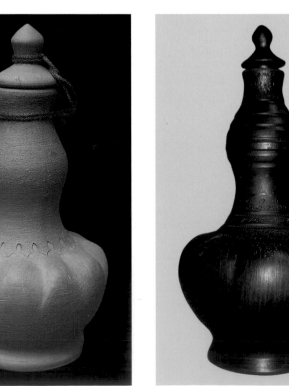

Changes to oxides

BOTH the clay body and glazes can be coloured with oxides that produce different colours in different atmospheres. Iron as a metal is grey but when corrupted by air turns into red rust (iron oxide). During an oxidized firing the oxide creates the colour – either yellow, red or brown according to the amount present – but in a reduction firing when the oxygen is removed the oxide reverts to iron and gives a grey or black hue. Small amounts of iron

ABOVE: *Oxidized and reduced pottery for sale in Old Delhi, India.*

are present in the reduction-fired celadon wares of China and Korea which are a soft greenish grey. Another good example is copper which in its metallic state is orange-red, but when exposed to air tarnishes to green verdigris (copper oxide). In an oxidized firing copper oxide produces green tones, but in reduction provides a rich red known as sang de boeuf or ox blood.

Black Figure wares

THE slip-painted vases decorated by Athenian craftsmen during the 6th and 5th centuries BC required a combination of both oxidation and reduction during the same firing in a kiln in the range of 850–1000°C (1562–1832°F). Iron-rich clay was used for both the body and slip. At the peak of the firing the oxygen was reduced by closing vents and stoking the fire which made the iron-rich clay turn black. At this heat, potash in the finely grained slip caused it to fuse and become impervious to oxygen. As the kiln cooled vents were opened and the atmosphere became oxidizing once more and the body turned red, but the impervious slip remained black.

ABOVE: *Celadon bowl with the jade-like green achieved in a reduced atmosphere, Chinatown, Hanoi, Vietnam.*

LEFT: *Carved vase fired black in a reduced atmosphere, Romania.*

ABOVE, RIGHT: *Pueblo potter with reduction-fired wares, New Mexico, USA.*

BELOW: *Cookware turned black by reduction in burning dung after firing, La Chamba, Tolima, Colombia.*

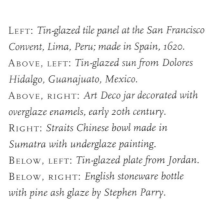

LEFT: *Tin-glazed tile panel at the San Francisco Convent, Lima, Peru; made in Spain, 1620.*
ABOVE, LEFT: *Tin-glazed sun from Dolores Hidalgo, Guanajuato, Mexico.*
ABOVE, RIGHT: *Art Deco jar decorated with overglaze enamels, early 20th century.*
RIGHT: *Straits Chinese bowl made in Sumatra with underglaze painting.*
BELOW, LEFT: *Tin-glazed plate from Jordan.*
BELOW, RIGHT: *English stoneware bottle with pine ash glaze by Stephen Parry.*

GLAZES

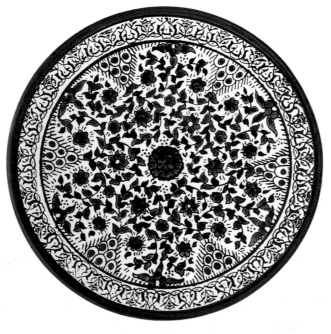

GLAZES

A GLAZE IS a coating that vitrifies in the kiln and provides the underlying clay with a smooth glassy finish. A glazed pot is both waterproof and easy to clean. By manipulating the glaze mix, its application and subsequent firing, many purely decorative effects can be created and as a consequence glazes are often used not only on earthenware, but also on stoneware and porcelain which do not actually require a waterproof coating since they are dense and vitrified in themselves.

ABOVE: *Flint, a common source of silica which provides the glassy element of a glaze.*

LEFT: *Quartz, a source of silica.*

BELOW, LEFT: *Rust, a readily available form of iron oxide.*

BOTTOM: *Cornish casserite, a tin-bearing ore; iron ore; and galena, a form of lead.*

HISTORY

B Y THE 4th millennium BC the Egyptians had developed techniques for glazing faience or fritware which they called *thenet* ('shining' or 'dazzling'). Observing how during firing the efflorescence of copper and silica of the quartz-based body created a shiny blue or turquoise coating, Egyptian potters began applying a glaze slurry to the surface by dipping or brushing.

It was in Mesopotamia that glazes were first used on a clay body. By the Bronze Age (1600 BC) techniques were in use that exploited the low melting point of alkali present in the ashes of desert plants which were combined with crushed quartz. Typical glazed pottery was blue or green as a result of the presence of small quantities of iron oxide and copper. These early glazes were often crackled as they expanded and contracted at a different rate from the clay body. It was also in Mesopotamia, Babylon and Syria that the properties of lead as a glaze material were first recognized.

Apart from in the Islamic North, glaze has never been used on traditional pots in Africa, but waterproofing has been improved by burnishing or varnishing with plant extracts. The same is true of the Americas, although in around AD 1300 the Ancient Puebloans of New Mexico and Arizona experimented for a time with lead glaze paints on their decorated wares.

OPPOSITE, ABOVE, LEFT: *Glazed pots drying before firing, Urubamba, Peru. Urubamba is the Pablo Seminario workshop.*

OPPOSITE, BELOW, LEFT: *Chinese slip-cast temple dogs with cobalt coloured glaze. Temple dogs are placed strategically outside shrines and temples to protect them from the enemies of the faith. Sometimes ceramic versions are made with multi-coloured glazes applied in overglaze enamels.*

Glaze ingredients

To perform effectively a glaze requires three basic components – flux, silica and alumina. Obtained from materials such as lead, salt, limestone or ashes, flux lowers the melting point of the mixture, causing it to flow across the surface. High-temperature glazes for use on stoneware or porcelain generally require less flux. Silica, obtained from hard, heat-resistant minerals such as flint or quartz, forms the glass. Viscosity, thickness and stability are provided by alumina derived from sources such as clay, feldspar or tin oxide. To mix a predictable, consistent glaze it is necessary to follow a recipe, carefully measuring out the ingredients which are first dried and ground into powder. In the East, however, potters often use less carefully prepared materials and the resulting glazes frequently feature specks and irregularities that give individual character.

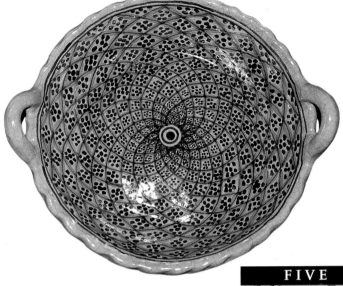

ABOVE, RIGHT: *'Talavera' style dish from Dolores Hidalgo, Guanajuato, Mexico.*

RIGHT, FROM LEFT TO RIGHT: *Dipping porcelain in glaze, Royal Porcelain Factory, Copenhagen, Denmark; verdigris or copper oxide on a copper coin; naturally occurring 'float' copper from Michigan, USA.*

Colour

Although affected by the colour of the underlying clay body, the main colouring agents in glazes are metallic oxides. Until the 17th century the most commonly used pigments included cobalt for blue, copper for green (or red in reduction), tin for white, manganese for purple, antimony for yellow and iron for reds and browns. Most potters now buy powdered oxides from a ceramic supplier, but in the past iron oxide was often scraped from old metal in the form of rust and copper oxide was obtained from the verdigris on tarnished copper.

GLAZE APPLICATION

O NCE THE dry ingredients have been mixed with water and sieved to remove lumps, glaze can be applied to the clay surface in a number of ways which range from the purely random to the tightly controlled. The method used dictates the required consistency of the mix – spraying, for instance, requires more water and finer sieving. Although it was once common practice to use lead glazes on a green (unfired) body, today it is more usual to biscuit fire wares before glazing.

Methods of application

T HE random falling of ash which formed a glaze on oriental pottery was sometimes enhanced by sprinkling ashes directly on to the upper surface before firing. European potters making slipware, on the other hand, generally created their lead glazes by sprinkling powdered galena (lead ore) on to the damp surface of green wares.

Glaze can be poured over pots and the excess caught in a bucket beneath. Coverage can be controlled by turning the pot beneath the flow, but Chinese potters of the T'ang Dynasty (618–906) enjoyed the effects of randomly poured glaze, often in several colours, dribbling down the surface.

Dipping a pot, held in tongs or between the fingers, into the glaze is a widely employed technique, used to great effect in Japan where one half of a bowl may be dipped in one colour before it is revolved and the other side dipped in another.

A thin coverage is achieved when glaze is applied with a brush or smeared on with a cloth. Localized coverage can be controlled by stippling with a brush or sponge.

Modern potters are able to give pottery a thin even or graduated coating by spraying on the glaze. The fine spray is potentially a health hazard and demands the use of a face mask and extractor fan.

Clay surfaces that will be in contact with other wares or parts of the kiln during a firing should be kept clean of glaze to prevent them fusing together.

TOP; AND ABOVE: *Applying glaze with a brush at the Ute Mountain Pottery, Colorado, USA; maiolica plate with hand-printed design, Tuscany, Italy, 19th century.*

FIVE

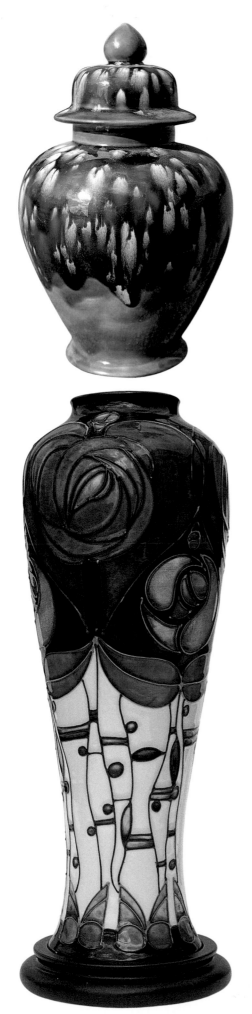

Controlling the glaze

IN 11th-century Seville in Spain the problem of containing glaze within specific areas was accomplished by applying barriers of manganese and grease that burnt off during the firing, a technique known as *cuerda seca* ('dry cord'). Another Spanish method, *cuenca*, used from the 16th century onwards, contained the glaze in depressions stamped into the clay. Tube lining, a feature of 20th-century Moorcroft pottery, which is made in England, contains the glaze with lines of trailed slip. Stencils and resists may also be employed.

Crackle

COMPATIBLE bodies and glazes must have the same rate of expansion and contraction. If the glaze shrinks more slowly than the body as it cools it will flake off, but if it shrinks more quickly it will craze. In the East great care is taken to exploit this knowledge so that glazes with a fine crackle can be produced. In particular, green celadon wares with crackle glaze were highly prized for their resemblance to jade. Crackling is also a common feature of rapidly cooled raku pottery.

ABOVE, LEFT; AND ABOVE, RIGHT: *Chinese jar with glaze poured and dribbled over the top; Chinese teapot with crackled glaze.*

LEFT; AND BELOW, RIGHT: *Lamp base with glaze colours kept separate with lines of slip, Moorcroft, England; tile with colours kept separate using the* cuerda seca *technique, Andalucia, Spain.*

OPPOSITE, BELOW, LEFT; AND OPPOSITE, BELOW, RIGHT: *Hand-painted maiolica plate with sponged border, Malta; Japanese rice bowl – half the bowl has been dipped into the glaze bucket.*

UNDERGLAZE PAINTING

BY PAINTING on to a clay surface before glaze is applied, a hardwearing finish can be achieved with the decoration fused to the protecting layer of glaze. Among the most famous wares painted under the glaze are the blue and white porcelain vessels made in China at the end of the 14th century during the Ming Dynasty. They were inspired by Persian wares painted with cobalt blue, known in the East as Mohammedan Blue.

Technique

WITH underglaze painting metallic oxides are painted on to an absorbent surface either in an unfired state, whether plastic, leatherhard or dry, or after biscuit firing, the background sometimes being intensified or altered with a coating of slip first. The ground oxide pigment is mixed with water and applied with a brush, although flow and adhesion can be improved with the addition of gum or glycerine. The Japanese traditionally employ a mixture of tea and seaweed extract. Colour can also be made opaque by adding clay, or tin or zinc oxides. Painting needs to be confident and bold as once colour has soaked into the clay it cannot be erased.

Earthenware

ALTHOUGH at lower temperatures it may be necessary to add a flux such as lead or borax, there are many oxide pigments that can be used on earthenware pottery, providing a palette of strong colours, notably the brilliant blue of cobalt oxide. By the 13th century, building on a Persian tradition of oxide and slip painting that stretched back several centuries, potters in Kashan were producing beautiful blue and white wares on which the cobalt's tendency to run was restricted by painting outlines in black slip.

The zenith of Islamic underpainting was reached with the flowing motifs that appeared in Turkey on Iznik pottery during the late 15th century. Over a base coat of white slip, Iznik potters typically

ABOVE: *Earthenware saucer with underglaze designs, Jerusalem, Israel.*

BELOW: *Sixteenth-century tile with underglaze decoration, Iznik, Turkey.*

ABOVE, RIGHT; AND RIGHT: *Underglaze-painted stoneware pot from Swankhalok, Thailand, which was a flourishing ceramic centre between 1350 and 1512; jug with slip and oxide decoration under the glaze, Romania, late 19th century.*

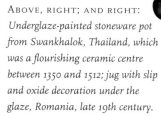

painted carnations and tulips in bouquets and scrolling patterns combined with Chinese motifs. The colours were particularly clear and bright, painted in a polychrome palette using green, cobalt blues, manganese black and purple and a vibrant copper-based turquoise. The problem of finding a good red was solved by the addition of a thick scarlet derived from Armenian bole. Encouraged by the patronage of the Ottoman court, all manner of vessels and tiles were produced at Iznik to grace the mosques and the palaces of the nobility until the demand for such a vast output led to a decline in quality in the late 17th century.

Stoneware

At higher temperatures oxides will fuse to the clay body without the addition of flux – instead a stiffener such as silica may be added to prevent the pigment flowing. Inspired by Persian blue and white ceramics, Chinese potters of the Ming Dynasty (1368–1644) imported vast quantities of cobalt to decorate their porcelain – it is one of the few oxides that produces a strong colour when exposed to the heat required for stoneware and porcelain firings. Producing red is a difficult process achieved by firing copper in a reduction firing. For polychrome decoration, outlining was executed in blue and red underglaze painting, while other colours were added later in a lower temperature enamel firing. In Japan blue and white wares have been produced in Arita since china clay was discovered there in the early 17th century. Polychrome wares are still produced, using cobalt underglazing with added enamel colour, and are known as Imari (after Arita's port).

ABOVE, LEFT: *Bowls with cobalt blue patterns under the glaze, Arita, Japan. The lower bowl is decorated with a design known as octopus scroll.*

ABOVE, RIGHT: *Plate with Islamic calligraphy painted in oxides on slip background, Ferghana, Uzbekistan. A large number of plates produced in Islamic countries are for inspiration rather than practical use.*

BELOW, LEFT: *Bowl with underglaze blue designs; made for export in Macau, China.*

BELOW, RIGHT: *Dutch plate with underglaze decoration in the Chinese style.*

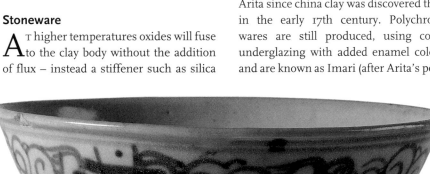

TRANSFER PRINTING

ALTHOUGH INVENTED by an Irish engraver, John Brooks, the process of transferring images on to pottery was pioneered in Liverpool, England, by printers John Sadler and Guy Green. In 1756 they revolutionized the production process, printing 1,200 tiles in six hours. Sadler had first experimented with printing from woodblocks before developing an improved method which involved using an engraved copper plate to print designs on to a sheet of tissue which was then transferred on to clay. At this time there was an enormous demand for tea wares in the 'Chinese' style and so the predominant colour used for transfer printing was cobalt blue, providing a cheap earthenware alternative to expensive porcelain. The process was quickly adapted throughout Europe.

The process

USING tracing paper and carbon paper a design is first copied on to a sheet of copper and then engraved following the outlines and shaded with a system of lines or dots. Some control of hue is possible at this point as deeply cut lines will hold more ink and therefore print a deeper colour. The copper plate is then covered in pigment mixed from metallic oxides, flux and printing oil and rubbed in well. Next, the surface is wiped clean, leaving a residue of colour in the engraved lines. A sheet of fibre-free tissue coated with soft soap, which prevents the pigment sticking, is then placed on the plate and passed

FIVE

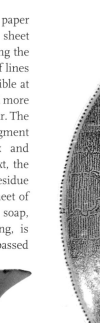

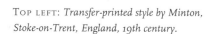

TOP LEFT: *Transfer-printed style by Minton, Stoke-on-Trent, England, 19th century.*

ABOVE, RIGHT: *Nineteenth-century transfer-printed lid for Gentleman's Relish, England.*

LEFT: *Harvest jug with transfer-printed illustration of a folk song, England, 18th century.*

OPPOSITE, ABOVE, LEFT; ABOVE, RIGHT; BELOW, LEFT; AND BELOW, RIGHT: *Transfer-printed mug sold in England to celebrate the Coronation of King George VI in 1937; sake jar with decal of a sumo wrestler, Japan; plate with blue and white transfer decoration, Spakenburg, the Netherlands; multi-coloured plate illustrating the tale of Ruslan and Ludmilla, Russia.*

between rollers to print the design. Next, the tissue is placed on to the biscuit-fired surface of a plate or pot and rubbed down vigorously until the pigment has adhered to the clay and then the tissue is soaked with water and sponged off, leaving the image behind. Once dry and secured by hardening off in the kiln at 680–700°C (1256–1292°F) the ware is dipped in glaze and fired again at 1060–1100°C (1940–2012°F).

Transfers can be used on earthenware, stoneware or porcelain and were originally applied under the glaze, but can also be applied over it. Sometimes extra colours are added by hand painting details in enamels, but in 1840 a system of polychrome printing was developed in which three or four separate transfers were made, one for each colour and one for the outline, and applied one over the other on to the biscuit-fired surface, taking great care that all registered properly.

William De Morgan

THE great British ceramic designer of the Aesthetic Movement of the 1870s and 1880s was William De Morgan, who developed his own painstaking method of transferring designs on to tiles. The original was placed under a sheet of glass and the design was traced by hand on to a sheet of tissue paper laid on the other side. Colour pigments were applied to the tissue which was then fixed to the tile, dusted with powdered glaze and fired. The paper burnt away during the firing, leaving the design fixed to the tile. De Morgan produced a large quantity of beautiful, although expensive, tiles – many inspired by Islamic wares and often featuring a palette of blues, turquoise and greens.

Modern techniques

SCREEN printing and lithographic engraving are used to create many modern designs which are often transferred to the clay as a decal which floats off its backing when wet. Attached to the glazed surface and given a low firing, decals are bright and colourful, but susceptible to wear.

LEAD GLAZE

ABOVE: LEAD-GLAZED JAR, T'ANG DYNASTY (618–906), CHINA.

THE FIRST lead glazes are credited to the Assyrians or Babylonians in around the 7th century BC and dramatic lead-glazed brick friezes were a feature of many buildings of that era. By the first century AD glazes using lead as the flux were employed by the Chinese and the Romans and since then they have been one of the most widely used of all ceramic finishes. The brightly coloured majolica of the late 19th century (not to be confused with the maiolica by which it was inspired) is comprised of lead glaze. In pre-Columbian Central America glazes were unknown, although the Toltecs were able to achieve a metallic finish on some of their pottery by using plumbate (lead-rich) clay.

FIVE

The dangers of lead

LEAD-GLAZED vessels have been used all over the world for cooking and the storage of water and it was not until the 19th century that people became aware of the dangers of lead poisoning. This was mainly the result of factory workers inhaling galena (lead ore) powder, but there is also a risk when using under-fired wares as acids from lemon juice, tomatoes or coffee can release toxins. Firing at a higher temperature or substituting lead bisilicate for galena reduces the danger. During the 19th century borax was some-times used as an alternative.

Using lead

LEAD is ideal for use as a glaze flux at lower temperatures as it reaches the optimum fluidity during an earthenware firing. Potters working in the European slipware tradition sprinkled undiluted lead in the form of galena powder on to damp, unfired pots. During the firing the dust melted and flowed, creating a thin transparent film. The practice in the East, which is now far more common, was to glaze biscuit-fired pottery by dipping it into a liquid glaze made from lead, silica – such as sand – or feldspar and clay. The lead used by potters in Yemen is obtained from old car batteries.

Colour

LEAD can be employed to make a clear glaze, but in the 18th century English potters were fond of the warm honey

OPPOSITE, CENTRE: *Frieze of majolica tiles, 19th century, Dorchester, England. Majolica wares were often moulded in relief and coated with thick glaze.*

OPPOSITE, TOP RIGHT: *Lead-glazed jar, Sabah, Malaysia.*

OPPOSITE, BOTTOM: *Slip-painted bowl with lead glaze, Kashgar, Xinjiang Uygur Autonomous Region, China.*

ABOVE, LEFT: *French jug with lead glaze over slip-trailed decoration.*

ABOVE, RIGHT: *Lead-glazed sgraffito jug in the English North Devon style; by Harry Juniper of Bideford.*

BELOW, LEFT: *Portuguese lead-glazed plate with traditional slip-trailed decoration under the glaze.*

BELOW, RIGHT: *Nineteenth-century* sancai *(three colour) statuette of the God of Longevity, China. Sancai glazes often appear to have been poured randomly over the surface and allowed to dribble.*

tones that were created by the chemical reaction of sulphur in the clay during an oxygen-rich firing. Colour is generally dictated by the clay body or slip beneath the glaze (often it is applied over trailed slip or sgraffito designs), but it has frequently been tinted green by the addition of copper oxide. Reds and browns can be produced by adding iron-bearing clay.

Sancai ware

DURING the Han Dynasty (206 BC– AD 250) Taoist alchemists carried out considerable research into the properties of lead and developed a serviceable glaze once knowledgeable artisans arrived from the Middle East. A long period of political upheaval after the end of the Han era meant the trade in lead to China was disrupted, but the T'ang Dynasty (618–906) brought stability and with it the return of trade and a flourishing of the arts. Chinese potters employed their replenished stocks of higher grade lead to develop a new style of decoration known as *sancai* (three colour) ware that was used on moulded white earthenware funerary goods such as figurines, camels and horses. Often regardless of naturalism, runny lead silicate glazes tinted green, brown and amber with copper and iron oxides were poured and dribbled over the figures.

TIN GLAZE

T HE ADDITION of tin oxide to a lead or alkaline glaze makes it white and opaque, providing an ideal surface for elaborate painted 'in glaze' decoration. The principle was known in Babylon in the 6th century BC where lead glazes were opacified with antimony, but for a thousand years the secret was virtually lost.

FAR LEFT: *Painting designs on to a white glaze ground, Tunisia.*

NEAR LEFT: *Tin-glazed vase from Safi, one of the major sites of pottery production in Morocco.*

History

T HE reign of Harun al-Rashid (ruled AD 786–809/AH 170–193), Abbasid Caliph of Baghdad, in what is now Iraq, was seen as a Golden Age for Islamic culture and trade – a number of tales from *The Thousand and One Nights* were set during this time. White T'ang porcelain and stonewares were exported from China along the Silk Route, making such an impression that many attempts to imitate them were initiated. Some such as the stonepaste and painted slipwares were beautiful in their own right, but the most far-reaching impact was made by the rediscovery of the tin-glaze technique which was still employed in Egypt.

Over the centuries tin-opacified wares have spread far and wide, acquiring different appellations along the way. The Italians first saw such wares imported from Majorca and therefore named them maiolica, while the French were taught the technique by Italian potters emigrating from Faenza and called it faience.

When introduced to England by ceramists fleeing religious persecution in the Netherlands, it was referred to as delftware after the Dutch pottery centre of Delft.

Technique

Tin-opacified glazes, sometimes known as tin enamels, are created from lead oxide with the addition of ten per cent tin oxide made by heating the metals. Heating or 'fritting' partially vitrifies the metal making the risk of poisoning from the toxic lead much lower. The metals are then repeatedly ground and reheated and finally mixed with water to form a creamy mixture into which biscuit-fired pottery is dipped.

Colour is added with a brush, applying oxides that may have been mixed with a little gum, glaze or flux to help them adhere. There is a wide choice of oxides available that remain true to colour in an earthenware firing and consequently tin-glazed wares are generally bright and colourful. The finished painted wares are subjected to an earthenware firing in the kiln. Tin remains inert, and therefore opaque, up to 1150°C (2102°F), but for a higher firing zircon can be used as an alternative.

Styles and motifs

The decoration of pottery at the time of Harun al-Rashid was dictated by the precepts of Islam and consisted largely of beautiful calligraphic inscriptions praising God or quoting the Koran. As the technique spread west along the north coast of Africa the designs remained virtually devoid of representational motifs, but flowing geometric shapes, sometimes suggestive of vegetation, became more common and remain the most usual style of Moroccan decoration to this day. To the north and east plants, birds and animals were more commonly depicted and even, in Iran, exquisite human forms were painted in lustre over the opaque ground.

Cobalt oxide, with its strong blue, was used for the first time as a ceramic pigment on Abbasid tin-glazed pottery and in their

Right: Tin-glazed plate with copious amounts of cobalt blue; made in Jordan.

Below: Tin-glazed plate from Fes, decorated in the blue and white style typical of this part of Morocco.

Opposite, top right: Mosaic tiling in the Bin Yusuf Medersa, Marrakesh, Morocco.

Opposite, bottom right: Tin-glazed plate, from Cyprus, inspired by the Turkish Iznik style.

turn envious Chinese and Japanese potters were inspired to imitate the ceramics of Iraq, prompting a massive trade in cobalt east along the Silk Route. The mining of tin for glazes, on the other hand, provided a healthy income for estates in Cornwall and Devon in the west of England.

MAIOLICA

SOUTHERN EUROPE has a long history of pottery decorated with tin glazes – the colourful plates and bowls of Spain, Portugal and Italy, with their bright floral designs, trace their ceramic ancestry back to Islamic potters who settled in Iberia during the Moorish occupation (711–1492). By the 1450s tin-glazed pottery from southern Spain, enhanced with lustre, had become extremely popular in the courts of Italy and, transported via the island of Majorca, became known as maiolica.

Spain

THE Moorish potters who brought tin-glazed pottery into Spain were continuing a stylistic tradition that could be traced back across North Africa to Iran and their work typically included depictions of birds, animals and arabesques. However, as the Christian and Islamic cultures influenced one another the Hispano-Mooresque style developed, calling on a repertoire of twining foliage, heraldic beasts and coats of arms.

RIGHT: *ISTORIATO PLATE, DERUTA, ITALY, 16TH CENTURY.*

By the 17th century the most influential centre was at Talavera de la Reina where bright, clear designs were dominated by blue. Pottery exported from here to Spanish colonies inspired imitators in the New World and was so influential that pottery produced today at Dolores Hidalgo in Guanajuato, Mexico, is still made in the 'talavera' style.

Today, a considerable amount of tin-glaze pottery is produced in Spain and Portugal, but is now used more by the lower classes than the nobility and is painted in a vibrant 'peasant' style with brightly coloured flowers built up by dynamic brushwork.

Italy

ORIGINALLY copying imported Spanish wares, Italian tin-glaze painting took on a life of its own during the Renaissance in the 16th century as the artistic ambitions of all craftsmen were stretched to their limits and many production centres grew up including those at Faenza, Deruta, Castel Durante and Urbino, all of which developed distinctive styles. The most respected artisans of the day were painters and the tin-glaze surface provided

TOP LEFT; AND CENTRE: *Two hand-painted, tin-glazed tiles, Portugal.*

LEFT: *Contemporary maiolica plate painted in the 16th-century style, Deruta, Italy. Maiolica plates have commonly featured biblical, mythological and historical scenes executed with great skill particularly as at the time of application the pigments do not resemble their final colours after firing.*

a great opportunity for them to display their virtuosity. Decoration gradually became more colourful and complex, the white ground often disappearing completely beneath the painting. Italian maiolica painting culminated in the *istoriato* style, with its elaborate paintings of biblical episodes and scenes from the myths of Classical times, which flourished during the 15th century. At this time the status of the artist/craftsman rose so much that signatures began to appear on many painted ceramics.

ABOVE, LEFT: *Mexican tin-glazed jar in the 'talavera' style; made at Dolores Hidalgo, Guanajuato.*

ABOVE, CENTRE: *Tiles, depicting peasant life, outside a shop in Cordoba, Spain.*

ABOVE, RIGHT: *Hand-painted plate in the floral 'peasant' style, Andalucia, Spain. Within the restrictions of abstracted floral pattern, plates and bowls from southern Spain and Majorca are produced in a vibrant range of colours and designs.*

BELOW, LEFT: *Maiolica jug, Deruta, Italy. Maiolica wares are still made, as they have been for the last 600 years, in Italian towns such as Deruta and Faenza.*

RIGHT: *Maltese maiolica plate.*

Technique

THE tin-glazed pottery of Italy employed basically the same techniques used in the Islamic world. Biscuit-fired items were dipped into a glaze mix composed of water, ground tin and lead oxides, and potash obtained from burning the lees in wine barrels, combined with quartz sand. The decoration was painted with a brush on to this white coating using metallic pigments and then, protected by saggars, the wares were fired up to 1000°C (1832°F) in a wood-fired kiln. Lustrewares were given a further firing at a lower temperature in a reducing atmosphere.

FIVE

TIN GLAZING IN NORTHERN EUROPE

FOLLOWING THE trail of exported goods, potters from Spain and Italy found a ready market for their products as they fled their homelands from the late 15th century onwards in search of greater financial rewards or better working conditions. After centuries of pottery dominated by homely, earthy colours under thick lead glazes, the arrival of brightly painted, tin-glazed wares to the countries of northern Europe opened the way for the development of a lighter, more sophisticated style of painted decoration that has since been produced all over Europe, from Denmark to Hungary.

Faïence

FRENCH tin-glazed wares are referred to as faïence, named after Faenza, one of the main Italian centres of maiolica production, although both Italian and Spanish potters were responsible for its introduction. By the mid-16th century French craftsmen were producing their own tin glaze in styles that were later subject to the influence of both Delft and Chinese porcelain. During the 18th century they also experimented with vivid enamel pigments fixed in an extra, low-temperature firing known as 'petit feu' as opposed to the usual high-temperature 'grand feu'. Today, production of tin-glazed pottery continues, as it has since the 17th century, in the Brittany town of Quimper. Typical wares are decorated with naive paintings of sprays of flowers and rustic figures.

Fayence

GERMAN tin-glazed pottery is known as fayence, also after the Italian town of Faenza. It was stove makers in Nuremberg and the South Tyrol who, at the beginning

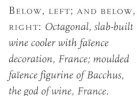

FIVE

BELOW, LEFT; AND BELOW, RIGHT: Octagonal, slab-built wine cooler with faïence decoration, France; moulded faïence figurine of Bacchus, the god of wine, France.

ABOVE, RIGHT: Faïence plate with rolled up edges, Quimper, Brittany, France.

OPPOSITE, ABOVE, LEFT; AND OPPOSITE, ABOVE, RIGHT: Jug with paddled sides and fayence decoration, Germany; Delft 18th-century ginger jar with Chinese-style landscape, the Netherlands.

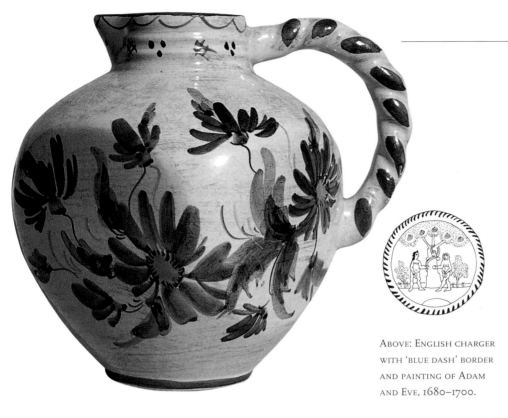

ABOVE: ENGLISH CHARGER WITH 'BLUE DASH' BORDER AND PAINTING OF ADAM AND EVE, 1680–1700.

of the 16th century, adapted their expertise at lead glazing on relief tiles to the new technique and, earning themselves the nickname 'white potters', created work decorated in a combination of Gothic and Renaissance styles. In turn, tin glazing spread from Germany to Switzerland and into Eastern Europe, to Hungary, Moravia and Slovakia.

Delft and delftware

TIN glazing was introduced to the Netherlands during the 16th century and from 1630 to 1750 its production was dominated by the town of Delft. At this time the polychrome palette was supplanted by blue and white as potters sought to emulate imported Chinese porcelain decorated with cobalt blue. These ceramics were known as 'kraak' wares after the sailing vessels on which they arrived. Delft is particularly famous for its tiles, intended for use on fireplace surrounds or for covering entire walls. These 'Chinese' scenes were soon replaced by more European subjects including flowers, animals, windmills and illustrations of biblical stories. The designs were often copied on to the blanks by rubbing pumice through a master copy perforated with pinpricks.

In England vast numbers of blue and white tiles were produced in the Dutch style, known as 'delftware', for use in kitchens and dairies. Decorative plates were also made in a 'chinoiserie' style and polychrome chargers were painted with scenes in a folk-art style depicting, for instance, Adam and Eve or informal portraits of the ruling sovereign. From England both product and technique were exported to the USA and the colonies.

CENTRE, RIGHT; AND BELOW, RIGHT: *Delft tiles with typically Dutch landscape, 18th or 19th century; late 18th-century delftware teapot with transfer-printed design, Ferrybridge, England.*

LUSTREWARE

ABOVE: *Nineteenth-century lustreware vase from Morocco.*

RIGHT: *English 19th-century factory-made lustreware jug.*

BELOW: *Hispano-Mooresque lustreware plate combining Christian and Islamic styles, Spain, probably 15th or 16th century.*

THE SUBTLE sheen of lustrewares is created by light reflected off metallic particles suspended in the glaze. The effect is opulent, providing a cheaper alternative to gold and silver tablewares, but requires considerable time and skill.

The technique

EARLY lustre was made by grinding salts of silver or copper and mixing them with fine clay as a carrier. Diluted with vinegar this solution was painted over a glazed surface that had already been fired and was then fired again in the region of 720–790°C (1328–1454°F), a temperature at which the glaze would soften without melting, allowing the metallic particles to stick and form a thin film. The reduction of oxygen in the kiln ensured that the particles ended up as shiny metal rather than dull metal oxide. After firing, the clay carrier was cleaned off to reveal the soft glow.

Islamic lustreware

CERAMIC lustreware was a development of lustre painting on glass in Egypt and Iraq during the 8th and 9th centuries AD. To begin with lustre was painted on to a tin-glazed surface already painted with a number of colours, but during the 11th century potters in Iran, Egypt and Syria began using a stonepaste body that resembled porcelain. The most breathtaking lustrewares were painted between the 12th and 14th centuries in Rayy in Iran and subsequently at Kashan after the sack of the former by the Mongols. Designs were painted in a monochrome coppery brown lustre and depicted moon-faced figures surrounded by calligraphy and flowing arabesques.

European lustreware

THE art of lustre painting spread with Islam along the north coast of Africa and was introduced by the Moors from Morocco into southern Spain where the main centre of production was established at Malaga and Manises. The Hispano-Mooresque style combined Islamic and Christian styles and motifs, but after the expulsion of the Moors in 1492 it was dominated by foliage and heraldic devices executed in copper-derived gold lustre, sometimes with the addition of cobalt blue. The beginnings of maiolica production in Italian towns such as Deruta were inspired by imports of highly prized Spanish lustrewares which had been painted on a tin-glazed base.

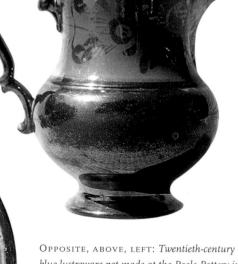

OPPOSITE, ABOVE, LEFT: *Twentieth-century blue lustreware pot made at the Poole Pottery in Dorset, England. Lustre has been employed mainly to highlight design and pattern, but more recently has been enjoyed as decoration in its own right.*

OPPOSITE, ABOVE, RIGHT: *Four lustreware tiles made by a contemporary English studio potter; similar to late 19th-century Arts and Crafts designs.*

OPPOSITE, BELOW, LEFT: *English lustreware form by Norfolk studio potter Stephen Murfitt who specializes in raku-fired lustreware. After firing, Murfitt encourages reduction by taking his pots from the kiln and placing them in a bin of sawdust.*

Industrial lustre

Dᴜʀɪɴɢ the late 18th century European potters developed ways of applying metallic films to factory products using platinum or gold in a suspension of oil and resin. Fired in an oxygen-rich kiln, the burning off of oil and resin caused enough reduction to fix the lustre. Although the results were often scintillating, they lacked the confident beauty of earlier Islamic and Spanish wares.

ABOVE: LUSTRE TILE BY WILLIAM DE MORGAN, ENGLAND, 1880s.

Lustre and the studio potter

Wɪᴛʜ the rise of aesthetic conscious-ness and the Arts and Crafts Movement of the 19th century, many European craftsmen began to explore lost arts and techniques. Among these was William De Morgan, friend and collaborator of William Morris, who was fascinated by the East and the production of lustrewares. During the 20th century many individual studio potters followed his lead, often combining lustre with raku firings. Today, Cambridgeshire potter Stephen Murfitt makes high-quality raku wares, achieving reduction for his lustre by immersing hot wares straight from the kiln into a bin of sawdust.

ABOVE: THIRTEENTH-CENTURY LUSTREWARE BOWL, IRAN.

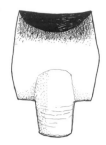

BELOW, LEFT: *Vessel, by Michael Gaitskell,
with iron-based glazes – brown* kaki *and black*
tenmoku, *England.*

BELOW, RIGHT: *Stoneware pottery with dolomite
glaze by Michael Gaitskell, Somerset, England.*

BOTTOM RIGHT: *Mugs from 'Made in Cley',
Norfolk, England. The one on the left is* tenmoku
and the one on the right is celadon.

OPPOSITE, ABOVE, LEFT: *Japanese sake jar and
cup with* tenmoku *glaze.*

W HEN FIRED at temperatures over 1200°C (2192°F) most clay becomes hard and impervious, if somewhat gritty. Although a waterproofing layer is not essential, glazes are still applied to many stoneware and porcelain items to add decorative interest or to make them easier to clean and pleasant to touch. Like high-temperature kilns, stoneware glazes were developed in the Far East and were originally applied to unfired clay, although it is now general practice to subject wares to an initial biscuit firing before glazing.

Glaze ingredients

A LL glazes are composed of flux, silica and alumina, but at high temperatures most materials will melt with less flux. Rich in lead flux, the majority of glazes used on earthenware become too runny at extreme temperatures and are therefore unsuitable for stoneware – instead there is a higher proportion of alumina and silica obtained from ground clays and stones which will give the glaze body.

Colour

A LARGE number of colourful commercial pigments designed for use on stoneware are now available, but the traditional palette is a subtle range of 'natural' creams and browns provided by natural clay and stone such as dolomite which will produce an opaque, matt glaze the colour of oatmeal. The bright tones of oxides become

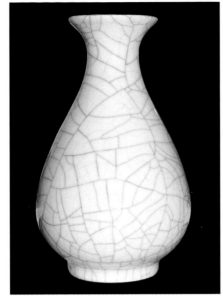

unstable at high temperatures, with the notable exception of cobalt which remains a clear blue. The pigments are particularly limited for use on porcelain fired at 1300–1450°C (2372–2642°F), but the white body shines through transparent glazes which gives the colour a particular intensity.

Iron glazes

SOME of the strongest colours in the natural range are created because of the presence of iron. The Japanese *kaki* (persimmon) glaze is so called because of its rich rust-red colour. The addition of 10 per cent wood ash turns *kaki* into a deep black glaze called *tenmoku* after T'ien-mu, a sacred mountain in China.

Special effects

SKILFUL control of glaze, temperature and the atmosphere in the kiln can produce a number of special effects. The Chün glazes of northern China, for instance, were endowed with an opalescent glaze shimmering with silica particles obtained from rice-straw ash. Oxidized Chün is a cream colour, but when reduced it takes on soft blue tints ranging from lavender to purple. Reduction is also crucial in the production of celadon 'greenwares' which were a speciality of Korean potters during the Koryo Dynasty (918–1392). The name, however, is taken from Monsieur Celadon, a character in a French play who always wore green. The colour in both Chün and celadon glazes is the result of the reduction of the tiny amounts of iron present. Specialities of the Song Dynasty

(960–1279) included 'hare's fur', an iron glaze streaked with rust-brown, and 'oil spot', a lustrous black glaze flecked with metallic, silvery spots.

Many techniques have evolved from the accidents of the past, but the imperfections in clay and glazes and the problems of controlling a kiln mean that a firing is an adventure and opening the kiln may still reveal unexpected marvels.

ABOVE, CENTRE; ABOVE, RIGHT; AND BELOW: *Chinese vase with crackled white glaze; jug with Chün glaze over blue tinted slip by Michael Gaitskell, Somerset, England; spherical Chinese bottle with impressed design under translucent celadon glaze.*

ABOVE: BOWL WITH 'OIL SPOT' GLAZE, CHINA, SONG DYNASTY (960–1279).

Ash glazes

WHEN CHINESE potters of the Zhou Dynasty (10th to 3rd centuries BC) carried out the first stoneware firings they observed the effect of ash falling on pots. It was, however, in Japan that this technique was most thoroughly explored after stoneware technology was achieved thanks to the introduction of the *ana-gama* cellular kiln from Korea during the 5th century. During the 16th century the rise in popularity of the Tea Ceremony under the guidance of Sen no Rikyu and Kobori Enshu, with its Zen aesthetics and demand for 'natural' wares, stimulated the manufacture of ash-glazed pottery with unpredictable, irregular surfaces and subdued colours. Due to the influence of Bernard Leach, wood ash glazes have become part of the stock in trade of modern studio potters in the West.

The properties of ash

THE ashes of wood and other vegetable fibres are rich in alkaline materials such as potash, lime and magnesia that, in the heat of a kiln, become runny and vitrify to form a shiny crust. Ash can be used in its natural state or in glaze mixes, such as *tenmoku* or celadon, as a flux enabling other ingredients like clay or oxides to flow over the surface of the clay.

Natural ash glazes

JAPANESE *ana-gama* kilns are wood fired and as the wood burns the strong draughts drag the ash into the firing chamber where it falls unevenly on to the surface of the contents, creating a 'natural'

glaze. The best results are achieved on pots with a wide body, increasing the available surface area upon which the ash can accumulate. To avoid an accretion on the inside of vessels they can be fired upside down. To encourage the ash build up in specific places some control is achieved by the careful placing of wares in the kiln, near the stoke hole for instance, or straw may be packed between pots in the kiln before firing. To avoid the ash, areas may be masked out by covering them with small cups or pots. Other controlled effects include winding straw around pots to create streaks or sprinkling them with ash to make spots known as *goma* (sesame seeds).

LEFT; AND BELOW, LEFT: *Controlled pine ash glaze on an English jug by Norfolk potter Stephen Parry; natural ash glaze on a jar fired at the firebox end by Dorset potter Tim Hurn, England.*

RIGHT: *Ash glaze dribbling down a sake bottle from Shinano, Nagano Prefecture, Japan.*

RIGHT, INSET: *Large Chinese ash-glazed plant containers.*

OPPOSITE, ABOVE, LEFT: *The fire mouth of a Japanese* ana-gama *cellular kiln at Bizen.*

OPPOSITE, BELOW, LEFT: *Stoneware jar fired in a Bizen kiln with the natural ash glaze and crude shape typical of many tea wares.*

OPPOSITE, BELOW, RIGHT: *Natural ash glaze on a large water jar from Burma (Myanmar).*

The first Japanese ash glazes were known as Sue wares – Sue means offering – because they were used as ritual grave goods, but modern kilns, including those at Bizen, Shigaraki and Tokoname, now produce storage vessels and tea wares.

Deliberate ash glazing

ASH glazes are made by washing and sieving burnt plant fibres and then mixing them with clay or pulverized glaze stone such as feldspar. Pots are dipped in the glaze and allowed to dry before firing in the kiln. A subtle range of colours can be achieved by using different kinds of ash. Walnut ash, for instance, will yield an off-white finish, while oak produces a smooth pale blue or green.

The deliberate use of ash as a glaze ingredient can be observed on the pottery of Hagi in Yamaguchi Prefecture where they use straw or the wood of the *isu* tree to create a creamy glaze. It is highly regarded for tea cups as the colour changes when it absorbs the tea, a process known as *chanare* which means becoming accustomed to tea.

SALT GLAZE

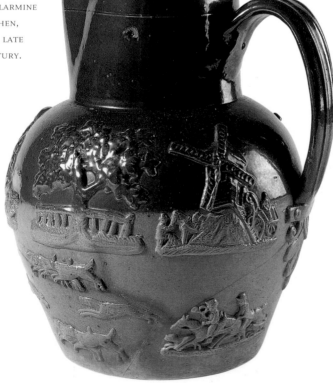

FOR SEVERAL centuries salt glaze was the only European glaze suitable for stoneware and was an almost exclusively European tradition which only appeared in a few other locations, including parts of Malaysia. It is a unique finish as it is thin, transparent and tightly fused to the body of the pot. Different colours and effects, such as the diagnostic 'orange peel' finish, are achieved not by the glaze, but by the colour of the clay body or slip beneath or by underglaze painting.

History

IN North Africa, salt water is added to plastic clay to diminish the risk of spalling (surface flaking during firing). It also lightens the colour of the body, but no true glaze is formed as it would require the vaporizing of the salt at a high temperature.

By the end of the 14th century potters in Germany had acquired the technology that enabled them to fire to stoneware temperatures, but the lead-based glazes of the time could not stand the heat. Legend tells that it was the result of firing kilns with wood from barrels which had been employed for transporting salted fish that led to the discovery of salt glaze during the 15th century. The Rhineland, with its rich deposits of clay, was the main centre of manufacture and once the technique was perfected strong vessels, often decorated in low relief, were produced.

During subsequent centuries exports inspired the building of stoneware kilns for firing salt-glazed wares across northern Europe and the first British stoneware kiln was set up in London during the 17th century. Jars, mugs and bottles were made for everything from gin to ginger beer and during the late 19th century the technique

was deemed ideal for the manufacture of sanitary ware. Fears about the toxic fumes produced in the process led to its decline in the mid-20th century.

Technique

WHEN salt glazing it is vital that the contents of the kiln are stacked in such a way that heat and fumes can circulate freely and evenly. The temperature is raised to around 1200°C (2192°F) and then common salt is introduced. A 15th-century German wood-fired kiln had a capacity of about 30 sq m (36 sq yards) and would have required about 100–150 kg (220–330 lbs)

ABOVE: *Salt-glazed jug with impressed decoration, Las Alpujarras, Spain.*

BELOW, LEFT: *English bowl, by Rowena Kinsman, glazed with soda (sodium bicarbonate), a less toxic alternative to salt.*

LEFT: BELLARMINE JUG, FRECHEN, GERMANY, LATE 16TH CENTURY.

FIVE

of salt which was shovelled into openings in the side and the roof. (Bernard Leach recommended 1lb of salt for every cubic foot of kiln space.) The salt immediately vaporized and coated everything with a glassy film.

Unfortunately clouds of highly toxic sulphuric acid fumes are produced during this process and as early as 1556 the authorities in Cologne, Germany, banned firings in populated areas. The health risks are such that salt is seldom used anymore and modern potters are more likely to use a solution of soda crystals (sodium bicarbonate) which produces a similar finish, but is much less dangerous.

Modelling

Germanic utensils had been decorated with faces since 900 BC and among the new salt-glazed wares one of the most popular was the *Bartmannskrug* or bellarmine jug which bore a moulded mask named after Cardinal Bellarmine (1542–1621), a controversial figure in his day. Since it is so thin a salt glaze makes an excellent coating for modelled surfaces as no details are blurred. In England it was used on London-made harvest jugs decorated with moulded sprigs depicting hunting and drinking scenes as well as on three-dimensional objects such as the naïve Staffordshire 'pew groups' made during the 18th century.

BELOW, LEFT: *Two Dutch salt-glazed jugs with decoration in underglaze cobalt blue. Salt glazing is a technique found almost exclusively in northern Europe.*

RIGHT: *A German salt-glazed jug with a moulded hunting scene thrown into relief by underglaze blue applied to the recesses.*

OPPOSITE, BELOW, CENTRE: *Jug with moulded face, made by the English Doulton factory in 1929.*

OPPOSITE, BELOW, RIGHT: *Made by Bourne of Lambeth, London, between 1830 and 1840, this salt-glazed 'hunting jug' has applied sprig decoration.*

OVERGLAZE ENAMEL PAINTING

ENAMELS ARE applied over a fired coat of glaze and then fired at a low temperature. As an extra firing is involved the cost to the potter is high, but the painterly finishes possible with the range of bright colours available have often been considered worth the extra time and expense.

Technique

THE pigments used over the glaze are made, like underglaze colours, from metallic oxides, but as the required firing temperatures are low the palette available is more vivid. The oxides are blended with silica and a flux such as soda, potash, borax or lead, and the mixture is then fritted (fired to glass and then ground into powder). When used for painting, the powder is traditionally mixed with fat, oil, aniseed oil or oil of cloves, but today commercial preparations thinned with water are available. Using a squirrel hair brush, very delicate painting is possible and for this reason decoration is often carried out by an artist rather than the potter. Colour can also be applied by spraying, sponging or dusting on to a damp ground. To show the colours off to their best advantage, an underlying white base is most effectively provided by a white body such as porcelain, or a coating of slip or tin glaze. To avoid the discolouration caused by smoke and fumes, firing takes place in a muffle kiln or electric kiln in an oxygen-rich atmosphere. Temperatures required are in the range of 700–900°C (1292–1652°F) – hot enough for the enamels to fuse to the softened base glaze.

Islamic enamel painting

OVERGLAZE painting was first developed in the Persian towns of Rayy and Kashan during the late 12th century. *Minai* painting on shallow bowls and containers of thrown stonepaste resembled miniature painting of the period with exquisitely detailed narrative scenes of myths and courtly tales and flowing arabesques. The early *haft rang* (seven colour) style was outlined under the glaze with cobalt blue, manganese purple or copper green, while later work was executed over the glaze with black, chestnut, red, yellow, green and white with gold leaf. The *minai* style came to an abrupt halt with the Mongol invasion of 1224. In the Sultanabad region the *lajvardina* style of the early 14th century used black, red, turquoise and white enamels on a cobalt blue ground.

BELOW, LEFT; BELOW, RIGHT; AND OPPOSITE, ABOVE, LEFT: *Vase with enamelled decoration, Gouda, the Netherlands; earthenware jug with overglaze painting in imitation of Japanese Kakiemon porcelain, England, 19th century; Chinese Ming Dynasty bowl with overglaze decoration in the* doucai *style, c. 1700.*

Enamel painting in China and Japan

IN China enamel painting on porcelain began during the 15th century with the *doucai* (fitting colours) style which was precisely painted on small wares using a palette of thinly applied apple green, red, aubergine and lemon yellow. The *wucai* (five colour) wares of the 16th century were much more crudely wrought with red or black outlines overpainted with red, blue, turquoise, yellow green, aubergine and black. Famille verte painting, dominated by greens, was produced until the 18th century, while famille rose, dominated by pink, was produced in vast quantities after 1720 for export to Europe – it was sometimes commissioned for large, monogrammed dinner services.

In Japan the credit for developing enamel painting (*akae*) is given to Sakaida Kakiemon who began producing wares decorated with landscapes, tigers, dragons and birds, predominantly of orange reds, at Arita. At Imari, named after Arita's port, large quantities of export wares with underglaze cobalt outlines overpainted with designs derived from brocades and lacquerwork were produced. Imari was much copied in Europe and stimulated the production of enamelled wares at Sèvres in France and Meissen in Germany during the 18th century.

RIGHT; TOP RIGHT; AND FAR RIGHT:
Japanese slip-cast vase with lively overglaze painting made for export to Europe; Japanese plate made at Arita during the 1890s using the distinctive Imari palette of enamel colours and underglaze blue; women decorating porcelain with enamels at the Royal Porcelain Factory in Copenhagen, Denmark.

FIVE

BLUE AND WHITE

BLUE AND white is the most popular ceramic colour combination of all, decorating tables and dressers all over Europe, Asia, the USA and North Africa. It is the subject of an epic tale of adventure and industrial espionage, spanning continents and stretching back for more than 2,000 years. The hero of the story is cobalt.

Cobalt

FOR centuries the strongest colour in the ceramic palette has been an intense blue obtained from ground cobalt oxide. Cobalt blue stands out from other pigments which, on the whole, are much earthier and has the distinct advantage that, unlike other oxides, when exposed to high temperatures in a kiln it remains true, whether in an oxidizing or reducing atmosphere. This means potters using a firing at any temperature or any method of glazing – earthenware, stoneware or enamel – and using it under, in or on the glaze, can produce strong blues. Blue and white is, therefore, probably the most popular of any ceramic decorative format.

The history of blue and white china

BLUES derived from cobalt were being used to colour glass, stonepaste and pottery at the time of the New Kingdom (1550–1069 BC) in Ancient Egypt. Since then pottery painted with cobalt has been traded or smuggled, imitated and adapted all over the world, inspiring both artistic masterpieces and technological

LEFT, FROM TOP TO BOTTOM: *Saucer with underglaze blue painting, made in China for export to Europe; blue and white export plate with landscape decoration, recovered from the wreck of the Diana which sank in the Malacca Straits in 1817; English transfer-printed Willow pattern plate, the design was inspired by the landscapes on Chinese export porcelain.*

BELOW; AND BOTTOM: *Chinese tea bowl and saucer, export wares recovered from the wreck of the Tek Sing which sank in the South China Seas in 1882; English 19th-century soup tureen with transfer-printed Willow pattern decoration.*

European consumers' demand for porcelain was insatiable as it was seen as the most fashionable accessory to the great Chinese export of tea drinking. Feverish efforts to manufacture a comparable money-spinning product were responsible for the development of soft-paste porcelain, bone china, creamware and true hard-paste porcelain. These products are now referred to in common parlance as 'china', in homage to the country whose wares they were originally intended to emulate.

breakthroughs. The first porcelains imported into the Middle East during the 8th century AD were relatively devoid of colour or pattern. Islamic potters attempting to produce a similar body developed stonepaste and tin glazing upon which they executed designs in cobalt blue dominated by calligraphy and swirling floral designs. Traded back along the Silk Route, accompanied by raw cobalt, these wares inspired craftsmen in China to adopt the style on porcelain, while incorporating Chinese themes. They produced what are regarded as some of the world's finest ceramics – the blue and white wares of the Ming Dynasty (1368–1644) which were made at the imperial factory in Jingdezhen. By the 17th century blue and white porcelain was being produced at Arita in Japan and soon both the Chinese and Japanese were exporting huge quantities of porcelain painted with cobalt to Europe.

Willow pattern

THE difficulty of meeting the demand for blue and white china was eased by the development of transfer printing in 18th-century England. Many designs for tablewares have since been produced in matching sets, but without doubt the most popular is the Willow pattern. Motifs from a number of authentic Chinese designs – a bridge, pagoda, willow tree and swallows – were combined by Staffordshire engraver Thomas Minton in the 1780s to produce a pattern that appeared Chinese, while satisfying the aesthetic preferences of the English. The plate illustrates the tale of the lovers Chang and Koong-Se who, fleeing from their disapproving homes, were transformed into swallows. Although charming, this spurious folk tale was invented to give credence to the Willow pattern design.

TOP LEFT; AND TOP RIGHT: *Novelty teapot with two chambers, decorated with a 'Chinese' landscape painted in underglaze blue, 19th century; one of a series of transfer-printed plates depicting colonial buildings in the USA. It is printed on ironstone, a resilient material used for tablewares in Britain and the USA.*

CENTRE, RIGHT; LEFT; AND RIGHT: *Chinese, slab-built, porcelain jar with cobalt blue underglaze painting; blue and white tin-glazed Delft plates proudly displayed in a Dutch home; tin-glazed plate painted in 'peasant' style, Andalucia, Spain.*

LEFT: *Detail of English enamelled tray with gilded highlights.*

ABOVE, LEFT: *Jar with 'negative painting', Chulucanas, Peru.*

TOP RIGHT: *Chinese plate with wax-resist calligraphy.*

RIGHT: *Jar with gilded highlights by Barbara Hawkins, Port Isaac, Cornwall, England.*

BELOW: *Resin-coated bowls by Guarani Indians, Ecuador.*

ALTERNATIVE FINISHES

ALTERNATIVE FINISHES

BEFORE THE invention of glazes a great variety of methods were used to make fired vessels beautiful or to render them waterproof. In many places these techniques are still employed, sometimes out of necessity, but often because traditional finishes are not considered inferior to what the developed world has to offer. There are other techniques, such as the use of resists and of gold, that have their origins in ancient unglazed wares, but have been adapted for use with glaze.

SOOT

SOOT IS a substance that adheres naturally to the surface of articles fired with smoky fuels – for instance, wood or dung, as in a bonfire or pit firing. The black finish, known as carbon smoking, bears a resemblance to the results of reduction, but only affects the surface. This effect can be enhanced or simulated by polishing a pot with soot mixed with a greasy substance. In southern Africa, for instance, the Swazis and Zulus use animal fat or vegetable pulp which they then burnish to a high sheen with a smooth pebble. Soot is also widely used as pigment for linear painting.

ABOVE, LEFT: *Reduction-fired pinch pot for drinking beer, polished with fat and soot, Swaziland.*

RIGHT: *Wheel-thrown water jar with a coating of limewash, Tunisia.*

BELOW, LEFT: Dhabu *for housing the spirit of a dead Bhil tribesman, Kutch, Gujarat, India. After firing in the open the* dhabu *has been coated with limewash.*

OPPOSITE, CENTRE, RIGHT: *Pot with impressed decoration and graphite polishing, Lobedu tribe, Zimbabwe.*

OPPOSITE, BOTTOM LEFT: *Polishing plates with beeswax at a pottery in Urubamba, Peru. Beeswax gives the wares a soft sheen and pleasant fragrance.*

LIMEWASH

A CONTRASTING FINISH is the matt white produced with a coating of limewash, a solution made by mixing water with ground limestone. This mix is often applied to paint both buildings and pots. In Gujarat, India, spirit houses and votive animals are painted a stark white in this way, while in Yemen it is used as a base for geometric designs nowadays rendered in commercially manufactured inks such as Quink.

GRAPHITE

PARTICULARLY GLOSSY shine can be achieved with powdered graphite. So luxurious is this finish that among the Buganda in Uganda, the technique was used only on the gourd-shaped vessels reserved for royalty. Here, potters apply a mixture of graphite and peanut butter to leatherhard pottery and then burnish it with barkcloth and smooth stones. Elsewhere in central, eastern and southern Africa the graphite may be applied before or after firing and is sometimes mixed with other fatty substances including butter and blood. While the Buganda prefer an all over finish, further south in Zimbabwe and South Africa, Makarunga and Venda potters reserve the graphite for details and bands of pattern which contrast attractively with the red terracotta of their pots.

ABOVE, RIGHT: Coiled urn for storing yoghurt drink; decorated with ochre and graphite, Makarunga tribe, Zimbabwe. Makarunga pottery is produced, exported and sold by a tribal cooperative. This piece was for sale in New Mexico, USA.

CENTRE, LEFT: Pierced and incised form with graphite polish; made by Harry Juniper, Devon, England.

MICA

GLITTERING SCALES of the mineral mica appear in clay-bearing granite. Mica-rich clays were used for cooking pots in Iran 3,000 years ago and are still used in Turkey and New Mexico, USA, to produce literally scintillating pots. Mica powder was dusted on to the damp surface of unfired pottery in France and Britain during the Iron Age and applied in slip during Roman times. It is also used in slip by Hausa potters in Nigeria. Once fired, the surface glitters with a bronze glow.

Tiles produced for over seven hundred years in Kikuma on the Japanese island of Shikoku are made from a blend of local clays into plain tiles or moulded finials shaped like fish or demons. When dry, these are coated with mica and burnished before firing. The finished tiles are endowed with a silvery grey lustre which gives a distinctive character to the roofs of Ehime Prefecture.

PAINT

BY APPLYING paint or pigment to a clay form after it has been fired a decorative
layer, which is not integrated into the clay, is created. Paint is available in a wide
range of bright colours and is easier to control than slips or glazes and the outcome
is not subject to the unpredictability of firing. The savings in time and materials also
save money.

ABOVE, LEFT: *Painted candlestick made to
celebrate the festival of the Day of the Dead,
Oaxaca, Mexico.*

BELOW, LEFT: *Painted tourist souvenir of a
lorry carrying produce to market, Ayacucho, Peru.
Similar brightly painted lorries and buses are also
available in Bolivia and Colombia.*

The uses of painted clay

VULNERABLE to wear and tear, painted
ceramics are generally intended
for decorative or ceremonial rather than
functional use. Sometimes the application
of colour may be part of a religious
ceremonial, as with the green markings
made from piñon pitch mixed with
copper that appear on some of the pots of
the Acoma and Laguna in New Mexico,
USA. More often paint is used because
of its ease of application and the range
of colours available. Many folk art
pieces from around the world, such as
Mexican Day of the Dead scenes or
Brazilian figures of popular heroes

and footballers, are brightly painted with
commercial paints.

Techniques

FAKED clay, particularly after a low-
temperature firing, is an absorbent
material best primed to prevent pigments
flowing uncontrollably. In Yemen a base
of limewash is used before painting with
Quink ink in yellow, purple, blue, green,
red and black, while in Belize replicas of
pre-Columbian Maya pottery are painted
over a base coat of plaster. An alternative
method is to control the flow of pigment
by mixing it with resin or glue. In northern
Nigeria Shani potters decorate their fired

ABOVE: *Traditional three-footed dish decorated
in the folk art style using modern acrylic
paints which, unlike the slip-painted patterns
of former times, make it purely decorative and
prevent its use in the kitchen.*

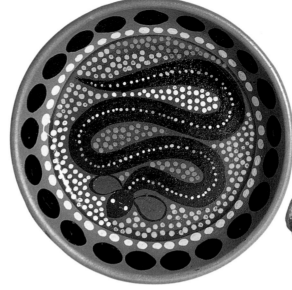

wares with a mixture of bonemeal and gum arabic and in Europe acrylic or powder paint is sometimes mixed with PVA glue. In Fengxiang moulded Chinese toys are primed with undercoats containing boiled soot or brick dust over which bright decoration is added using colours mixed with glue or egg white which imparts a lustrous sheen.

Decorating

THREE-DIMENSIONAL forms are usually painted in a fairly naturalistic style, colouring the clothes and skin of figures, for example. This technique is exploited to the full in the gaily vibrant painting of genre scenes that re-create everyday adventures such as bus journeys by potters in Peru, Bolivia and Colombia. The decoration on Fengxiang toys, however, has little to do with real life, but explodes with dynamic pattern.

Clay as a canvas

THE flat surface of a tile or pot is a blank canvas upon which the artist may execute designs from the depths of his or her imagination or drawn from a traditional repertoire. Mexican potters in Oaxaca decorate their three-footed bowls with traditional motifs painted with acrylics, but their grandmothers and distant forebears, such as the Aztecs, painted the same designs with slip. Australian Aborigines in Queensland, to whom pottery is a new craft, sometimes use acrylics to execute designs which until recently were painted on bark.

ABOVE, LEFT: *Tourist souvenir, from Belize, made in the traditional way with painting on a base coat of plaster.*

ABOVE, CENTRE: *Aborigine design depicting the Rainbow Serpent; acrylic paints on pottery by Virginia Grogan of North Queensland, Australia.*

ABOVE, RIGHT: *'Allstar and the Magic Carpet' made by the author and painted with acrylics mixed with PVA glue.*

BELOW, LEFT: *Painting jars with enamel paints, Cusco, Peru.*

BELOW, RIGHT: *Contemporary designs painted on a traditionally shaped money pot from Umbria, Italy.*

SIX

137

RESISTS

A LARGE NUMBER of hands appear in the pictograms painted by prehistoric peoples on cave and rock walls around the world. While the meaning of these images is conjectural, it has been proposed that a positive hand represented life and a negative hand represented death. A positive image is produced by covering the hand in pigment and pressing it directly against the rock and a negative image can be created when the hand is placed on the rock and pigment sprayed over it, covering only the surface that is not masked by the hand. This principle of 'negative painting' can also be applied to the decoration of pottery, masking out areas and colouring only the background with a coating of slip or glaze.

ABOVE, LEFT; AND ABOVE, RIGHT: Stoneware bowl with stencilled dragons made by Straits Chinese craftsmen in Sumatra; negative painting on a bowl from River Curaray, northeast Peru.

BELOW, LEFT: Small jug with a wax-resist illustration from the story of Don Quixote; painted by Pablo Picasso between 1957 and 1959.

BELOW, RIGHT: Earthenware jug with wax resist; made at the Rye Pottery, England, in the 1950s or 1960s.

Wax

WITHOUT question the most widely used resist in the field of ceramics is wax. Having been used for centuries by master potters in the Far East to repel glaze, it was introduced to the studio potters of the West by Bernard Leach and Shoji Hamada during the 1920s. In Ecuador potters of the Carchu culture (1200–1500) were using wax to mask designs from slip and it was also a technique known to craftsmen of the Middle Mississippi Culture, USA, which died out three hundred years ago.

Whether it is on raw or fired clay and whether it is employed to resist slip or glaze, the technique of using wax is basically the same and is virtually identical to the batik technique used in textile decoration in South-East Asia. Beeswax or, more often, thinned paraffin wax is heated in one pan placed in another containing hot water – this avoids exposing the wax directly to heat and a possible fire risk. Once the wax is melted it is fluid enough to be applied with a brush but, as it cools rapidly, it is best to work with quick, bold brushstrokes. Both Japan and China have a tradition of painting based on simple brushstrokes which leads to a confident vocabulary of stylized designs such as fish and bamboos, and free-flowing calligraphy.

Stencils and templates

CHINESE potters of the Song Dynasty (960–1279) would sometimes place a leaf upon the damp clay of a pot before they dipped it in slip. As the slip dried, the leaf could be pulled away to reveal its shape in negative. By cutting templates or stencils from paper both negative and positive patterns could be created in the same way. The expertise acquired by Chinese artists cutting silhouettes from paper and Japanese craftsmen cutting stencils used to print resist paste on to textiles was also applied to the creation of attractive designs on pottery. Much more recently the enterprising Navajo of the American Southwest, who

OPPOSITE, NEAR RIGHT: Beaker, from Ecuador, with wax-resist patterns based on traditional Carchu designs, 1200–1500.

OPPOSITE, FAR RIGHT: Japanese sake bottle with wax-resist calligraphy.

ABOVE, LEFT: *Jar from Chulucanas, Peru, with patterns made using a clay resist. The technique is only employed in this area.*

ABOVE, RIGHT: *Plate with paper resists; made by English potter Tamsin Hull.*

constantly explore new disciplines, have begun using stencils to create multi-coloured designs employing motifs drawn from their own lifestyle, their experiences as horsemen, their traditional dwellings and the rocky landscape.

Clay

A UNIQUE application of the masking technique has been employed in the Andes for hundreds of years and continues to thrive in Chulucanas in northern Peru. Both figurative and abstract patterns are marked out, using slip or damp clay, on to the surface of pottery that has already been fired. A second firing in a smoky reducing atmosphere turns the exposed surface black, but – when cool – the masking slip or clay is wiped or chipped away to reveal patterns in the paler colour produced in the oxygen-rich atmosphere of the first firing.

GLOSSY COATINGS

A NUMBER OF coatings can be used as alternatives to fired ceramic glazes, providing surfaces that are waterproof, shiny and easy to keep clean. Naturally occurring bitumen was used in Mesopotamia at the time of the Samarran culture (6300–6000 BC) to mend holes and repair cracks in pottery. During the Sassanian period (AD 226–637) jars for transporting oil and wine were routinely waterproofed with the same material. Most glossy coatings, however, have vegetable origins.

Vegetable glazes

IN Africa south of the Sahara, where low-temperature firings without glazes are the norm, pots are often taken from the fire and rolled immediately in particular leaves or coated with a juicy decoction. The plant juices flow readily across the surface, filling the pores of the clay and making the surface waterproof, shiny and often tasty. The pots of the Nupe in central Nigeria, for example, are given a mahogany-coloured coating by basting them with the juice of locust-bean pods. Pots made by Kongo women around the estuary of the Zaire River in the Democratic Republic of Congo (formerly Zaire) have a dramatic wood-grain effect achieved by the volcanic bubbling of juices splashed on to the hot pots. In Darjeeling, in India's West Bengal, 'glaze' made from a mixture of mango bark and other plant extracts mixed with soda and slip is applied.

Resin

RESIN, the sticky exudations of trees, makes an ideal waterproofing material. The Navajo of the Four Corners country of the American Southwest use the pitch of the piñon pine as a coating for both baskets and pottery. The pitch is heated and smeared over the pots with a rag while it is still hot from the fire, endowing the pots with both lustre and aroma. In Morocco patterns are applied to water jars using a finger dipped in *qutran*, the boiled down resin of the thuya tree, which is used more to flavour the contents than as a waterproof coating. The coiled pottery of the Amazon, from the headwaters in the Andes to the delta in Brazil, is given a glossy post-firing crust of resin. In the Peruvian Upper Amazon the plants that yield this resin, belonging to the genera *Protium* and

Hymenea, are a valuable source of income to the local peoples. Another important extract is gum arabic which is exuded by acacia trees native to Arabia. Gum arabic is exported in bulk and used as far away as Central America to give an attractive sheen to the pigments with which it is mixed.

Varnish and polish

SOME resins are carefully boiled and refined to produce transparent varnishes. Traces of lacquer, most probably for waterproofing, were found on Japanese pottery made during the Late Jomon period (2000–1000 BC). Lacquer is the resin of an oriental tree and has inspired the manufacture of modern imitations – varnishes which have all kinds of decorative and protective uses, including the sealing of Mexican folk art.

Substances used to polish materials other than clay, furniture polish for example, can also be applied to ceramics. In Urubamba, in Peru, at the Pablo Seminario workshop, the air is redolent with the smell of the beeswax rubbed on to the surface of contemporary style pottery.

SIX

LEFT: BUBBLY RESIN GLAZING, ZAIRE RIVER, DEMOCRATIC REPUBLIC OF CONGO (FORMERLY ZAIRE).

OPPOSITE, ABOVE; AND OPPOSITE, BELOW: *Navajo vessel coated with the resin of the piñon pine, Arizona, USA; coiled bowl with organic temper, painted and resin coated, Asurini, Para, Brazil.*

ABOVE, LEFT; RIGHT; AND BELOW, LEFT: *Pottery, polished with beeswax, for sale in Urubamba, Peru; three-chambered jug, derived from ancient ritual vessels, varnished with resin over slip painting, Kabyle, Algeria; Mexican modelled candlestick with painted and varnished decoration.*

GOLD

GOLD IS a mineral associated worldwide with the sun, the gods and wealth. Many attempts have been made to achieve a shining metallic finish on ceramics and all manner of wares, including pottery, have been touched up with gold. The effects range from tawdry to opulent. Experiments carried out applying gold to ceramic surfaces culminated in gilding processes which were developed in 18th-century Europe. These are sometimes referred to as lustreware, although this term is more accurately applied to the iridescent finish produced by suspending metallic powders in glaze.

ABOVE, LEFT; AND BELOW, LEFT: *Mid 19th-century inkwell with gilded designs, Coalport, Shropshire, England; enamelled and gilded plate made for export in the 1890s, Japan.*

Gold leaf

KNOWN as gold leaf, sheets of gold – beaten until incredibly thin and light – have been used to embellish craftwork for millennia in both the East and the West. European craftsmen employed it on ceramics until the 1720s as a glazed surface makes an ideal, impervious base. The area to be gilded was painted with size made from linseed oil, gum arabic and mastic which was allowed to dry before the leaf was applied to the surface and burnished. A beautiful sheen was achieved, but unfortunately was easily worn away.

Lacquer

LACQUERWORK was an early attempt to transmute base crafts into gold – the technique was attributed to the Chinese emperor Shun (2258–2206 BCE). Grave goods dating from his reign have survived. They have traces of lacquer intact and include items made from wood, bamboo, metal, textiles, paper, pottery and porcelain. Lacquer is a transparent resin derived from the sap of the lac tree (*rhus vernicifera*) which can be coloured with pigments such as cinnabar, chromium, cadmium or gold dust and then applied in many layers to a smooth, primed surface to produce a lustrous sheen. This technique was still being used on ceramics during the 20th century, but is vulnerable to wear.

Gold powder

IN the 18th century a hard-wearing golden shine was achieved very successfully using gold powder. The problem had been getting the gold to adhere to the surface of

ABOVE, LEFT: *Contemporary Turkish jug, a copy of ancient Mesopotamian forms. The gold enamelling was a modern addition.*

BELOW, LEFT: *Hard-paste porcelain plate with gilded detailing, Limoges, France.*

the glaze, but it was found that gold dust could be suspended in various substances that allowed the mix to be painted on but burnt away in a low firing of around 700°C (1292°F). At this temperature gilding could be conveniently combined with overglaze enamels. A muffle kiln was used to protect the wares from the adverse effect of the flames. Experiments had been sponsored by different factories in Europe such as Meissen, Sèvres and Wedgwood and a number of different suspensions were employed. Sèvres, for instance, used evaporated vinegar and garlic.

From 1750 British factories in Chelsea, Worcester and Derby mixed gold with honey and oil of lavender. After firing it was burnished and cleaned with vinegar and white lead to produce a glossy surface hard enough to be tooled or chased. Elsewhere a varnish made from crushed amber was employed. Mercury gilding was devised by metalworkers and used from the late 18th century – the process requiring the gold to be dissolved in aqua regia (thirty parts hydrochloric acid to ten parts nitric acid) and precipitated with mercury, but unfortunately it produced toxic fumes. The use of liquid gold, a suspension of gold in oils containing sulphur, was pioneered by Meissen in the 1830s and has since become the normal industrial technique for gilding.

ABOVE, RIGHT: *Porcelain teapot with enamelling and copious gilding, Japan. Large quantities of gilded wares were made for export in the Satsuma Province during the 18th and 19th centuries.*

BELOW, RIGHT: *Jar with gilded fish painted by Barbara Hawkins at the Port Isaac Pottery, Cornwall, England.*

SIX

EMBELLISHMENT

ONCE A potter has completed their task, the techniques of other craftsmen may be called into play. Decorative additions to the ceramic surface sometimes demand the expertise of a metal smith or the dexterity of a basketmaker, but at other times they may simply be stuck on with glue or tied on with a piece of string.

Metal

WITH their mutual need for fire and fuel, potters and metalworkers have often collaborated on projects. Porcelain bowls made at the Ding kilns of northern China from the 11th century onwards were fitted with a copper rim that hid the rough lip caused by firing upside down. In the Moroccan cities of Fes and Meknes bowls are sometimes fitted with filigree white metal strips which emphasize the designs of the glaze and some drinking mugs from Germany and Eastern Europe have hinged lids made from pewter. Among the Nupe in central Nigeria gourd-shaped coiled pots were taken to

a brass smith who would convert them into prestige articles by fitting them with hammered metal plates.

Inlay

THE inlaid decoration of ceramics generally takes place after the completion of the firing process, avoiding the problems of melting inserts and incompatible rates of expansion and contraction. A recess may be made in the soft clay before firing or it can be cut out afterwards with a fine drill. On the Indonesian island of Lombok pots are now inlaid with pieces of bone, plastic or mother of pearl, a decorative technique found more

often on the woodwork of Indonesia and Melanesia. Pottery made by the Swazi in southern Africa to sell to tourists includes clay saucers inlaid with patterns of brightly coloured glass beads pressed into the low-fired clay. At various Pueblos in New Mexico, USA, including Santa Clara, craftsmen are now experimenting with coral, shell and turquoise glued with epoxy into recesses etched into the clay with a dentist's drill.

Basketry

BASKETRY has often been used, from Britain to Bali, as a protective layer around pots, but is today being used to

OPPOSITE, ABOVE, RIGHT: *Rivets used to repair a valuable Hispano-Mooresque lustreware plate.*

LEFT: *Itinerant china mender rivetting plates, Rothiemurchus, Scotland, early 20th century.*

RIGHT: *Enamelled whistling astrological charm with silk cord and beads, Taiwan.*

CENTRE, LEFT: *Design of dyed straws, Mexico City, Mexico.*

ABOVE: AZTEC CHICKEN-SHAPED VESSEL, TEOTIHUACAN, MEXICO.

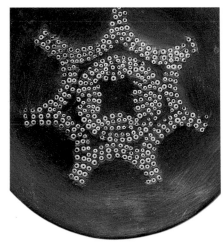

LEFT: *A Devon jug encrusted with seashells, England.*

ABOVE, RIGHT: *Pattern of beads pressed into clay, Swaziland.*

OPPOSITE, BELOW, LEFT: *Tin-glazed plate with white metal decoration, Fes, Morocco.*

OPPOSITE, BELOW, RIGHT: *Incised bowl with lip and handle woven from savannah grass, Ghana.*

make a number of decorative edges. Traditional indigenous materials are employed – in Lombok vases and plates are edged with woven strips of split rattan, while in Ghana rims and handles are built up from the local savannah grass twisted into cord.

Glue and string

A SIMPLE technique is to attach objects on to the surface with an adhesive substance. The art of *popote* in Mexico City involves painstakingly sticking tiny coloured straws on to a wax-covered board, but it is now also used on clay. In India the simple clay lamps made for the festival of Diwali may be brightly painted with sparkling sequins and metallic ribbons glued on and in English seaside towns holiday souvenirs were once made of local pottery encrusted with seashells.

On occasion small objects such as beads may be attached with a cord or string. This might not only be functional – to hang the object round the neck or on a wall, but can also be purely decorative. African sculptures frequently have attached items both as decoration and as offerings to protective spirits – Sao figures from Chad, for example, are encircled with strings of glass beads, while the *nkisi nkonde* made by the Bakongo in the Congo River basin are covered with snares for bad spirits.

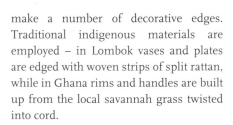

SIX

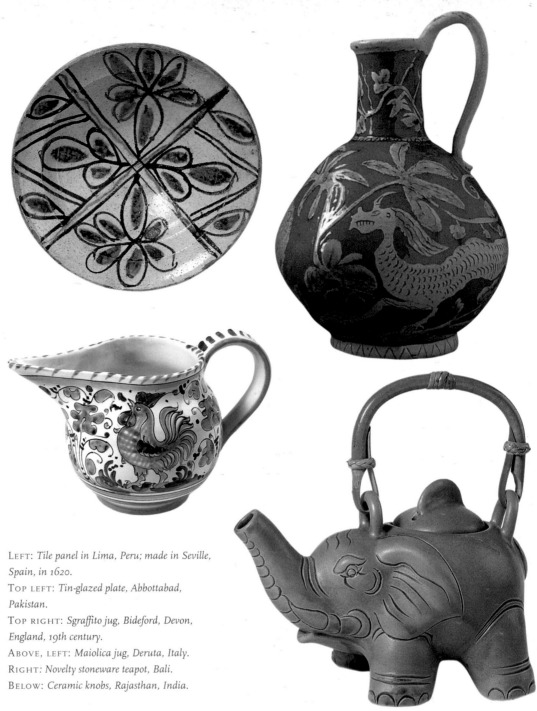

Left: *Tile panel in Lima, Peru; made in Seville, Spain, in 1620.*

Top left: *Tin-glazed plate, Abbottabad, Pakistan.*

Top right: *Sgraffito jug, Bideford, Devon, England, 19th century.*

Above, left: *Maiolica jug, Deruta, Italy.*

Right: *Novelty stoneware teapot, Bali.*

Below: *Ceramic knobs, Rajasthan, India.*

USE AND FUNCTION

USE AND FUNCTION

IN THE first settled communities established in places with a plentiful stock of food – for instance, in Japan where there is a natural abundance of fish and wild plants, or in the Nile and Indus Valleys, time became available for the development of technology and specialized crafts such as pottery. Early functional wares probably copied the forms of containers previously used – baskets or found objects such as gourds and shells – but as they became familiar with their material potters began to build items that exploited the natural properties of the clay.

ABOVE, LEFT: *Elaborate ceramic frontage, Beijing, China.*

LEFT: *Seventeenth-century tiled façade of the Registan in Samarkand, Uzbekistan.*

RIGHT: *The brick and tile Examinations Hall in Honan, China.*

BELOW, RIGHT: *Tiling a roof in Legian, Bali.*

THE QUALITIES OF CLAY

THE MALLEABILITY of clay – it is so easily squeezed and pressed into any shape – provides the inventive and imaginative potter with extensive possibilities, but these are limited by the material's flaccidity when plastic and its brittleness once fired. Thinly walled structures are difficult to build without support and easily broken once fired.

SHAPE AND FORM

CRAFTSMEN HAVE discovered that clay is best used as either solid or hollow forms. Solid forms require slow firing to ensure even drying and heating if they are not to fragment, but if rolled or pressed into slabs or blocks they make strong, hardwearing tiles and bricks. Hollow forms are used for containers and receptacles and may be formed in many ways, but experience has shown that the forms able to withstand the most stress are round or spherical with walls of a consistent thickness which prevents uneven heating and subsequent cracking during firing. The weakest points on any pottery are where two sides join. Objects thrown on the wheel in one piece have particular strength as they have no joints at all.

OPPOSITE, CENTRE, LEFT: *Ben Wittick's photograph taken in the 1880s shows a couple with a Zuni or Acoma water jar. Widely available, they were traded with other tribes and later with tourists.*

OPPOSITE, CENTRE, RIGHT: *Mexican earthenware chiminea, originally used for cooking, they are now popular in the West as patio heaters.*

OPPOSITE, BOTTOM RIGHT: *Old pottery vessels used as plant containers, Ollantaytambo, Peru.*

Thermal shock

C LAY IS vulnerable to the stress of rapid expansion and contraction such as that caused by placing a cooking pot over a fire or exposing a cooking pot to frost. As a precaution, pottery to be subjected to extremes of heat is made from a clay body containing large amounts of temper which opens the body, allowing the free flow of air and moisture. Pottery fired in low-temperature bonfires, such as that built by coiling in West Africa, lacks the structural strength of wares fired at higher temperatures, but, surprisingly, being well tempered, is often much less vulnerable to thermal stress than many stoneware items. Coiled pottery is also more resistant to greater extremes of heat than thrown pottery because the particles of the latter have been made to lie in one direction which creates alignments along which cracks can easily occur.

TOP LEFT: *Keble College at Oxford University, England, was constructed using multi-coloured bricks.*

TOP RIGHT: *Domestic earthenware pottery for sale in Marrakesh, Morocco.*

Porosity

T HE VARYING degrees of porosity possible with fired clay can be exploited for a number of functions. A porous pot allows some evaporation through the walls and can be used to keep its contents cool, while glazed pots or those fired to stoneware temperatures are more impermeable and will prevent the loss of moisture. Glazed surfaces are also resistant to dirt and are easy to clean, making them ideal for use in preparing and serving food.

TILES

Ceramic tiles are long lasting and cut from a slab or shaped in a mould, they are easy to make and offer an excellent surface for decoration. While tiles are drying before firing they should be stacked – spaced with newspaper, biscuit-fired tiles or wooden bats – to stop them warping. To prevent glazed tiles sticking during firing, either to each other or to kiln furniture, it is best to slot them in a rack or crank.

Uses

A ceramic surface is hard wearing, waterproof and easy to keep clean which makes it ideal for rooms such as bathrooms and kitchens where hygiene is important. Tiles were a staple feature of Islamic bath houses long before Europeans considered washing a healthy activity. One of the major uses of blue and white tiles made in Delft, the Netherlands, was the decoration of kitchens. Clay is also resistant to heat and makes an excellent surround for fireplaces and stoves – tiled platforms over a fire once provided a warm place to sit in many Russian homes. Tiles may also be used to keep a room cool and in this capacity have been employed in vast quantities in the palaces and mosques of Islamic lands.

Unglazed tiles

The Romans found terracotta tiles ideal for floors as they absorbed the heat from the hypocaust system beneath which kept rooms warm. Before firing, these tiles were

ABOVE; AND BELOW: *Locally made unglazed tiles on a wall in Maro, Andalucia, Spain; set of four modern Turkish glazed tiles in the Iznik style.*

ABOVE: *Tin-glazed Delft tile made in the Netherlands during the 18th or 19th century.*

BELOW: *Large hand-painted wall tiles from Iran. The middle tile is moulded in relief.*

ABOVE, LEFT: *Large maiolica tile from Italy. The repeat pattern flows on to the adjacent tiles.*

ABOVE, RIGHT: *Selection of floral tiles in the distinctive colours of the blueware produced in Jaipur, Rajasthan, India.*

BELOW, LEFT: *Tile with abstract design, Safi, Morocco.*

BELOW, RIGHT: *Panel of tin-glazed wall tiles at the San Francisco Convent in Lima, Peru; commissioned from Spanish tile manufacturers in Seville in 1620.*

generally dried in the sun and many survive today with the footprints of children and chickens stamped into them. Earthenware tiles, often arranged in a checkerboard of alternating red and black, are known in Britain as quarry tiles – an appellation derived from an old word for a square tile or stone slab. Many European medieval tiles were decorated with heraldic devices by stamping a recessed pattern into a clay slab and filling it with slip of a contrasting colour. This style regained popularity in the 19th century when the designs were dust pressed into encaustic tiles.

Glazed tiles

Easy to clean, glazed tiles have been decorated over the centuries using every known technique – millions are decorated today using transfer printing to copy both old and contemporary designs. Originating in the Middle East, glazed tile techniques were introduced in India by the Mughals, into Spain by the Moors and into Eastern Europe by the Ottomans. The most influential of all tile painting – a style that reached its height in the late 16th century – was carried out at Iznik in western Turkey to supply the needs of the Ottoman Empire. Influenced by Chinese blue and white ceramics, the Iznik style was a fusion of Ming Dynasty designs and

Turkish motifs with twining patterns of foliage, tulips and carnations coloured with underglaze painting in blue, turquoise, green and red.

Arrangements of tiles

Some tiles are plain or decorated with a single motif, allowing them to be arranged indiscriminately, while others are intended to contribute to a larger pattern. This might be a border made by placing them in a row or it might involve a group of tiles that each bear a fraction of a design revealed when laid in a block. The most ambitious tile work panels, such as the religious images of southern Spain, are in effect large fragmented paintings assembled from a number of individually decorated tiles.

MOSAIC

DESIGNS ASSEMBLED from small pieces and used for the decoration of walls, floors and pavements are known as mosaics and the origins of both the name and the technique can be traced back to Ancient Greece. Greek craftsmen introduced mosaics to Italy as early as the 4th century BC and Romans in their turn exported the technique to the farthest borders of their Empire, covering their floors with images of gods, heroes and gladiators.

Tesserae

MOSAICS constructed by the Greeks and Romans were assembled from large numbers of small square pieces called tesserae. They were cut from marble and attractively coloured stone, occasionally pieces of terracotta were used for browns and reds. Some of the most stunning mosaics can be seen in Italy at the Basilica di San Vitale in Ravenna, which was constructed in the 6th century,

and the Basilica di San Marco in Venice, constructed in the 13th century, both of which contain large quantities of glass and gold. Today, mosaics are more often made from ceramic or glass tesserae, making them cheap enough to feature in private bathrooms. The bright colours available have made them a feature of many London underground stations, notably the designs of Eduardo Paolozzi at Tottenham Court Road.

Shaped tiles

A WIDE range of attractive designs can be made by the careful arrangement of regularly shaped tiles – both plain and patterned – including squares, rectangles and triangles. Hexagons were widely used during the 15th century in both Islamic countries, such as Syria, and in Italy. These shapes are cut or stamped out from soft clay before firing, a process that can also be employed to make sets of

TOP RIGHT: *Cistercian patterned floor made from interlocking, differently shaped components, Prior Cruden's Chapel, Ely, England, 1324.*

LEFT: *Roman mosaic assembled from square tesserae of coloured stones and terracotta.*

ABOVE, RIGHT: *'Jigsaw puzzle' style mosaic at Prior Cruden's Chapel, Ely, England, 14th century.*

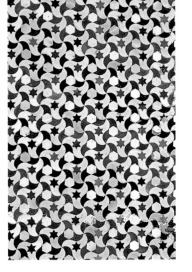

more complex interlocking tiles. The style of mosaic favoured in the religious institutions of the Cistercian order, from the 12th century onwards, was assembled from shaped pieces that fit together like a stained-glass window to form patterns and depict Christian imagery.

The Romans also used the technique of *opus sectile* (cut tile), which can be seen in the Roman Palace at Fishbourne in Sussex, England. This technique of cutting stone into pieces to create complex interlocking patterns was later applied to the cutting of pieces from glazed tiles after firing. The greatest exponents of this art were found in the Islamic world in the cities of Samarkand and Bukhara in Uzbekistan and in Morocco and southern Spain where mosaic is used on walls rather than floors. Islamic cut-tile work is called *zellij* from the Arabic and means glazed or vitrified. The craft thrives in Morocco as the government commissions work for the decoration of public buildings and mosques.

ABOVE, FROM LEFT TO RIGHT: *Mosaic of 19th-century encaustic tiles, Dorchester, England; cut-tile panel, Alhambra Palace, Granada, Spain, 13th–14th century; figures covered with recycled pottery sherds, Rock Garden, Chandigarh, India.*

RIGHT: *Sixteenth-century* zellij *panel, Marrakesh, Morocco.*

Moroccan and Hispano-Mooresque work is replete with repeated motifs and elaborate stars, while in Central Asia panels often include geometric or floral designs as well as stylized calligraphy from the Koran.

Recycled sherds

EXCITING mosaic can be produced using fragments of broken tiles and plates. This is an enjoyable task for the amateur, but has also been employed to dynamic effect by professionals, most notably in Antoni Gaudí's mosaic furniture in the Parque Güell in Barcelona, Spain.

LEFT; AND RIGHT: *Cut-tile patterns on the Shir Dor Madrasah, Samarkand, Uzbekistan, 17th century; bench of reclaimed tile fragments by Antoni Gaudí at the Parque Güell, Barcelona, Spain, early 20th century.*

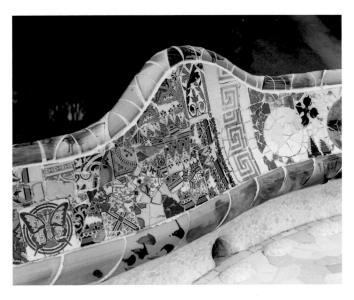

ROOFS

IN THE search for an effective waterproofing layer for buildings many materials have been tried, ranging from grass thatch and palm fronds to wooden shingles, but few are as efficient or widespread as clay tiles. Where rainfall is minimal, the pitch of a roof may be shallow, but in regions where rain falls in torrents a steep pitch is the norm and the water is often carried away down clay guttering and drain pipes. Roofs are primarily functional, but decorative detail is frequently added through the use of texture and, in the case of Chinese glazed tiles, with colour. The silver-grey roofs of many traditional Japanese buildings are made from tiles sprinkled with mica before firing.

Roof tiles

THE simplest tiles are merely rectangular slabs of fired clay lain side by side, sometimes with holes for nails or a lip at the top to attach them to wooden battens. Tiling begins at the bottom of the roof and works up, each row overlapping the one below. By using tiles with a curved bottom edge, an imbricated pattern of scallops can be created. Modern roof tiles often have lips and grooves along the sides which interlock.

Semi-cylindrical tiles may be made from clay slabs rolled out and then curved into shape over a solid former or they may be made from cylinders thrown on a wheel and then cut in half lengthwise. Many of these – like those made in Bihar, India – taper slightly towards the top. Semi-cylindrical tiles are fixed alternately – one concave, one convex – creating a wave-like arrangement of gulleys for water to drain down.

A very efficient system was used by the Romans – it consisted of flat tiles with flanged edges (*tegulae*) linked together by overlapping semi-cylindrical tiles (*imbrices*). The Roman legion ranks included many craftsmen such as potters who could turn out tiles as forts and outposts were established on the outskirts of the Empire.

Decorative details

THE vulnerable opening created at the bottom of a roof covered with curved tiles may be sealed off with a decorative tile. Oriental roofs use circular discs featuring figurative motifs or calligraphy which are often glazed, while end tiles (*antefixes*) made by the Roman army were

generally stamped with the name of the legion to which their maker belonged.

Tiles shaped like an inverted V or more semi cylinders are used to cover the weak point where the slopes of a roof meet at the ridge – this provides an obvious point for decorative detailing. Many roofs are finished off at the gable end with a finial which is generally decorative, but sometimes serves a higher purpose, protecting the house from evil spirits – for instance, the *onigawara* (demon masks) of Ehime in Japan – or advertising the status of its

occupants. Grander Greek buildings continue an ancient tradition where the gable is decorated with an acroterion, a finial shaped like a palmette or moulded into the semblance of one of the gods.

Chimneys

Resistant to heat, fired clay is ideal for the building of chimneys among the most elaborate of which are the spiralling structures of Tudor England. Chimney pots are frequently made from thrown clay, although among the Pueblos of New Mexico, USA, it was once common to see a chimney topped with a beautifully painted coiled jar recycled after its bottom had broken.

BRICKS

SINCE THE first bricks were constructed from river mud in the Middle East 10,000 years ago bricks have been one of the world's most important building materials. The ziggurats of Ur in Mesopotamia were built in 4000 BC from unfired bricks cemented together with bitumen, while 2,000 years later fired bricks were the main building material of the Indus Valley Civilization and the great cities of Harappa and Mohenjodaro. At 1,500 miles in length, the Great Wall of China, a large part of which was constructed from brick, is one of the most ambitious building projects of all time.

for strength. Mud bricks can be employed as soon as they are firm, but those to be fired must dry thoroughly.

A typical method of firing bricks is found in northern India where it is often carried out in a clamp. The bricks are piled in a huge stack interspaced with straw or brushwood and then covered with earth. This type of firing can take place wherever building is to be carried out. Permanent kiln chimneys are visible on the Indian plains and they provide the draught for

Adobe

THE first bricks were built from clay mixed with dung or straw to bind them together and were dried in the sun. Often called by their Spanish name 'adobe', unbaked bricks are still used in many arid regions where rainfall provides little or no threat. Steep roofs and overhanging eaves may protect the vulnerable clay but, when damaged or washed away, adobe buildings are cheap and easy to replace.

Making bricks

BOTH adobe and fired bricks are made in the same way – from prepared clay forced into a wooden mould. The excess is scraped off and the rectangular lump is tipped out to dry. Some moulds have no top or bottom so they can be lifted off, leaving the formed clay to dry where it has been made. Others have a moulded base which can be used to stamp decorative details or to form the recessed 'frog' which will, during building, retain extra mortar

ABOVE, LEFT; ABOVE, RIGHT; AND BELOW: *Adobe bricks, Pachacamac, Peru; the Mezquita in Cordoba, Spain, built from stone, stucco and fired brick; Sky City Pueblo, New Mexico, USA, constructed from stone and mud brick.*

firing in trenches. European industrial brick kilns could once be seen from miles away because of their tall chimneys which created the draught for bottle kilns, but today machine-made bricks are fired on trucks that move steadily through a tunnel kiln capable of holding as many as 80,000 bricks at a time.

Types of brick

OVER the millennia attempts have been made to standardize brick size. The Romans used several formats for different purposes, including the *laterculus* for building hypocausts which measured 8 x 8 x 1½ in. (203 x 203 x 38 mm), while Indian Harappan bricks were made in different sizes, following the proportions of 4:2:1. The standard English brick size is now metric: 65 x 102 x 215 mm.

All bricks need to be fired at a heat above 950°C (1742°F), but the higher the temperature, the harder and more vitrified they will be. A more vitrified surface will

repel water more efficiently and be less subject to wear by the elements. High-fired engineering bricks are particularly hard and impervious which makes them ideal for use in close contact with water, while firebricks, made from clay found in coal measures, will withstand great heat and are used to line kilns and fireplaces.

For decorative purposes bricks can be glazed just like those that can be seen in the monuments and palaces of ancient Persia – for instance, in the palace of Darius at Susa which dates from about 500 BC.

TOP; NEAR RIGHT; AND FAR RIGHT: *'Les Boulangers', a glazed brick panel in Square Scipion, Paris, by Alexandre Charpentier and Emile Muller, 1902; archway with relief brick panel designed by Graham Robeson at the Old Vicarage Gardens, East Ruston, Norfolk, England; English bricks, from top to bottom: Staffordshire blue high-fired engineering brick; weather-resistant facing brick made in Accrington; yellow clay brick with a 'frog' (an indentation to hold extra mortar).*

CONTAINERS

WHILE BRICKS and tiles are formed from comparatively simple blocks or slabs, most pottery employs more complicated techniques to make hollow forms. Whether pinched, thrown or coiled, pots, jars, vases or urns, the majority of ceramics are constructed for use as containers.

ABOVE: PORCELAIN POT FOR CALLIGRAPHY AND PAINTING BRUSHES, YI DYNASTY, 19TH CENTURY, KOREA.

Food and drink

A HUGE variety of ceramics are used to store foodstuffs and the seed from which they are grown, ranging from the little pots used by the indigenous peoples of the American Southwest to store their valuable stock of seed to the massive *pithoi* employed in Crete to store oil and olives. Dry goods may be kept in unglazed containers, while liquids need to be stored in high-fired or glazed vessels which are watertight. The decoration of such utilitarian items is generally minimal, while containers used at the table are likely to be far more elaborate.

Personal use

ITEMS used for self-adornment and beautification such as jewelry, cosmetics, ointments and perfumes have often been stored in fancy containers which may be kept out on display. Just as modern perfumes have elaborate bottles and packaging so the fragrant oils of Egypt and Greece and the cosmetics of ancient China were kept in ornate containers. Some took fanciful forms such as Chinese cosmetic pots or the effigy jars used by the Ancient Puebloans; both are often shaped like turtles.

TOP RIGHT: *Turtle-headed effigy pot for ritual use, discovered at Casas Grandes; made by Mogollon-Anasazi potters (1300–1500), Chihuahua, Mexico.*

ABOVE, RIGHT: *Transfer-printed lid of an English 19th-century pot of 'Gentleman's relish'.*

LEFT: *Hand-thrown earthenware vessels for sale at Port-au-Prince, Haiti.*

RIGHT: *Stoneware ink bottle, England, late 19th or early 20th century.*

Painting and calligraphy

THE paraphernalia of the educated man, able to read, write and paint, has often been given aesthetic consideration. In China coloured pigment was kept in porcelain pots and ink was diluted with water dripped from a special bottle. Islamic calligraphers, too, have stored their ink in fancy vessels. In Morocco, for instance, an inkwell with several interior compartments might be cube shaped and domed like the tomb of a Muslim saint, while the inkwell of a European gentleman might once have been elaborately decorated or gilded, even though the ink itself was transported in very unglamorous stoneware bottles.

Craft and industry

IN times past craftsmen have often kept their tools and materials in ceramic vessels, although the equipment itself might have been of clay. Today, metalworkers, in India for example, often melt the softer metals in a small clay

crucible in their furnaces and the dyers of Kano in northern Nigeria carry out their craft in the traditional way, immersing cloth in huge clay vats sunk into the ground.

Fire

EVEN fire can be contained in a clay pot. The Aztecs in Central America and more recently the inhabitants in Yemen have burnt charcoal or incense in a clay brazier. During the Middle Ages in Europe clay pots containing a live coal were sometimes carried under the clothes to keep the body warm, while nomads crossing the plains of Central Asia may carry their fire with them to make the cooking of the evening meal simpler.

TOP LEFT; TOP RIGHT; AND CENTRE, RIGHT: *Qing Dynasty (1644–1911) water dropper for diluting ink, China; multiple ink pot shaped like a saint's tomb, Safi, Morocco; French faïence inkwell.*

RIGHT: *Basketry cover and indigo dye vats made from large clay vessels sunk into the ground, Kano, Nigeria.*

SEVEN

ABOVE: MODERN
VERSION OF AN
ETRUSCAN MONEY
POT, UMBRIA, ITALY.

DOMESTIC CERAMICS

CLAY HAS been used in the home for the construction of all manner of things from roof, floor and wall tiles to front door knobs and kitchen sinks. Kitchen utensils are very often ceramic and many household chores are facilitated by the use of ceramic objects.

SEVEN

Containers

SOME containers may be adapted for a multitude of uses, but others are designed for a specific function. In many European homes tall cylindrical oriental vases are used for walking sticks and umbrellas, whereas in the Mexican state of Veracruz shelves outside a family home are often filled with pottery hives designed specifically for the native stingless bees.

Children around the world store their saved coins in pottery containers which are often known as piggy banks after one popular form, although they may be shaped in many whimsical forms. Money pots were in use 2,000 years ago in Etruria, Italy, where they are still used, brightly painted with commercial paints. Money is dropped in through a slot at the top and when full the pot is smashed open to retrieve the money.

Stoves and fireplaces

THE focal point of traditional homes in central and Eastern Europe is often a tiled stove. These were first used in the Alps during the Middle Ages and were called *kachelofen* because they were covered with bowls (*cachala* in Old High German) which increased the heated surface area and effectively radiated the heat of the stove. Eventually the bowls were replaced by lead-glazed tiles which were generally decorated in relief. During the 19th and 20th centuries fashionable British homes were equipped with cast iron fireplaces fitted with panels of tiles in the decorative styles of the day.

In the West the fireplace or the mantle above it is one of the choice spots for the placing of decorative objects such as the moulded dogs and cats made in Staffordshire or expensive porcelain figurines from Meissen or Sèvres.

ABOVE, LEFT; TOP RIGHT; AND ABOVE, RIGHT: *Slip-painted earthenware piggy banks made in Oaxaca, Mexico, to sell in Santa Fe, New Mexico, USA; hanging container for feeding garden birds, made in stoneware by Elizabeth Aylmer from Hatherleigh, Devon, England; English transfer-printed tile from a fireplace surround, 1896.*

LEFT: CERAMIC BED LEG, DJENNE, MALI.

BELOW: RUSSIAN HEATED TILED PLATFORM, AFTER AN ILLUSTRATION BY IVAN BILIBIN, 1900.

Furniture

THE principle of the stove was also applied to furniture and in Russia the warmest place to sit is on a tiled platform heated from beneath. A smaller scale version used in China was a drum-shaped ceramic seat which could be warmed by coals placed inside.

Fixtures and fittings

THE grubbiest part of a piece of furniture is probably the handles and by using ceramics these can be kept clean more easily. Thrown and moulded knobs have been produced in many European factories, but are now also available in the West in dynamic colour schemes imported from India and Mexico.

ABOVE: *Chinese ceramic drum-shaped seat.*

RIGHT: *Tin-glazed basin fitted to a wall, Dolores Hidalgo, Guanajuato, Mexico.*

BELOW, LEFT: *The frame of this mirror has been mounted with tin-glazed tiles from Puebla, Mexico.*

BELOW, RIGHT, CLOCKWISE FROM TOP LEFT: *Tin-glazed doorknob decorated with a moon, Dolores Hidalgo, Guanajuato, Mexico; Jaipur blueware light pull, Rajasthan, India; stoneware hot water bottle, England, 1920s; pair of door knobs made from Jaipur blueware, Rajasthan, India.*

OPPOSITE, BOTTOM RIGHT: *A pair of moulded 'fire dogs' placed decoratively on a mantlepiece, 19th century, Staffordshire, England.*

Domestic crafts

TRADITIONALLY many crafts such as weaving have been practised as cottage industries in the home. Clay whorls, used as miniature flywheels when spinning with a drop spindle, have been found in the refuse of most vanished civilizations, including both Roman and Aztec, and can still be seen today in the Andes. In Ancient Greece the legs of women were protected from the chafing of the spindle by a ceramic guard placed on the thigh. Once on the loom, yarn was also often tensioned by clay weights.

HYGIENE

THE ROMAN goddess Hygieia was the daughter of the great healer Asclepius (Aesculapius in Greek) and was responsible for the health of the human race. The word hygiene is derived from her name. The rites of Asclepius included purification by fasting and especially bathing which cleaned both body and soul. Ceramics are ideal for use in the context of washing oneself as they are not only waterproof, but are also easy to keep clean.

LEFT: CHILD USING
A CHAMBER POT,
GREEK VASE
PAINTING, 5TH
CENTURY BC.

SEVEN

Washing

PROVIDING the opportunity to wash the hands and feet has been a part of traditional hospitality since time immemorial and is also an important part of many religious practices. Muslims, for example, must carry out a specific form of ablution every time they pray. Frequently, water is poured from a jug over the hands which are held over a basin. In Mesopotamia 3,000 years ago the jugs connected with ceremonial washing were equipped with extra long spouts so that the water poured out in a jet. In Medieval Europe a jug or ewer used for washing at mealtimes was known as an aquamanile.

Shaving

THE chin or head may be shaved for reasons of religion, hygiene or pure fashion and may be carried out by an individual or a professional barber, men who once were also responsible for drawing teeth and bleeding which was

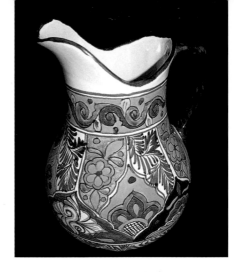

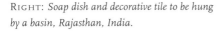

RIGHT: *Soap dish and decorative tile to be hung by a basin, Rajasthan, India.*

CENTRE, RIGHT: *Chamber pot or 'gazunder', early 20th century, England.*

ABOVE, LEFT; AND OPPOSITE, ABOVE, RIGHT: *Mexican ablution jug tin glazed in the 'talavera' style, Dolores Hidalgo, Guanajuato; European jug and bowl set for washing, in common usage before plumbed water was readily available.*

BELOW, LEFT: *Earthenware soap dish by Frannie Leach, Hartland, Devon, England.*

BOTTOM RIGHT: *Industrially produced terracotta drainage pipes.*

considered to be good for the health. From the late 15th century European barbers used special bowls with a notch in one side to fit around the customer's neck and catch the drips. Shaving mugs were still in common usage during the 20th century, fitted with a perforated compartment so that soap could be softened by the hot water beneath.

Baths

BATHS in the Ancient Greek home were much like a smaller version of the modern, Western domestic bathtub. They were made of clay like many throughout the West until the late 19th century. The Islamic bathhouse or *hammam*, the most well known is the Turkish bath, cleans as much by steaming as immersion and to prevent walls and floors deteriorating most are elaborately tiled.

Sanitary engineering

IN the West the chamber pot, also known as a 'gazunder' because it 'goes under' the bed, was used within living memory as an alternative to a night time trip to an outhouse. Toddlers are still toilet trained on potties (which are now usually plastic), just as they were in the times of the Ancient Greeks. The invention of the flush toilet in the mid-19th century saw the first installation of lavatories in the English home. These were mostly moulded and salt glazed and expensive ones were sometimes decorated with transfer-printed floral patterns.

The importance of a clean water supply had been recognized 4,000 years ago in the Minoan cities of Knossos and Malia on Crete which were provided with fresh water from reservoirs distributed through a system of clay pipes. Despite the enlightened attitude of the Arab world to cleanliness, the cities of the Western world were rife with serious diseases such as cholera until well into the 19th century when massive drainage and sewerage systems built with tiles and clay pipes were installed.

OPPOSITE, LEFT; AND OPPOSITE, BELOW, RIGHT: *Berber aquamanile with a large opening for filling and a narrow spout for pouring water over the hands, Morocco; Spanish earthenware aquamanile now being used as a garden ornament.*

LIGHTING

ABOVE: PIERCED LAMP WITH GREEN LEAD GLAZE, IRAN, IITH OR I2TH CENTURY.

AS THEY are fireproof, ceramic materials are an ideal medium for the construction of lighting utensils such as lamps, lanterns and candlesticks. Compared to metal, they are poor conductors of heat and are therefore safer to handle when in use. Even in the modern electric world pottery vases and jars remain a popular base for light fittings.

Light is a symbol of enlightenment and spiritual truth in the religions of the world. Jesus is referred to as 'the Light of the World', while the mosque lamps of the Mamelukes (13th–15th centuries) were inscribed with a text that began, 'God is the Light of the heavens and the earth'. In places of worship lamps are kept burning as a gesture of devotion and as a sign of the presence of the Divine; many festivals such as the Jewish Hanukkah and the Hindu Diwali (festival of light) involve the lighting of lamps or candles.

Lamps

FOR centuries day has been extended into night with simple lamps, increasing the time available for working and socializing. These lamps consist of a reservoir for fuel with, dipped into it, a wick made of twisted fibres which, impregnated with fuel, is ignited at the other end. The simplest consist of no more than a jar and wick and heart-shaped lamps of this type are turned out in their millions for the Hindu festival of Diwali. The other common type resembles a small jug with a wick inserted into its spout. The fuel employed may be animal, vegetable or mineral, ranging from butter, olive oil and paraffin to animal fat. In the 19th century the whaling industry was mainly driven by the demand for pure lamp oil obtained from sperm whale blubber.

The Roman lamp

THE most successful lamp was manufactured in the Roman world, changing little over four hundred years. It was a flattened jug design and exports reached as far as the British Isles, southern Algeria and the Middle East. Some were wheel thrown, but most were press moulded in two-piece moulds, often featuring a design on the flat top which was called the discus. There were two holes, one in the spout for the wick and another in the discus for filling the reservoir. The descendants of this design can be seen in parts of Asia to this day.

Candlesticks

MADE from wax or tallow, candles are rigid and merely need a receptacle with a cup into which one end can be fitted. This means that while many candlesticks are purely functional, modelled or thrown in simple vertical columns, it is quite feasible to create extravagant decorative and sculptural forms. These range from Scandinavian Christmas angels to the folk-inspired confections of Izúcar de Matamoros in Puebla, Mexico, with their tiers of brightly painted mermaids and aquatic creatures.

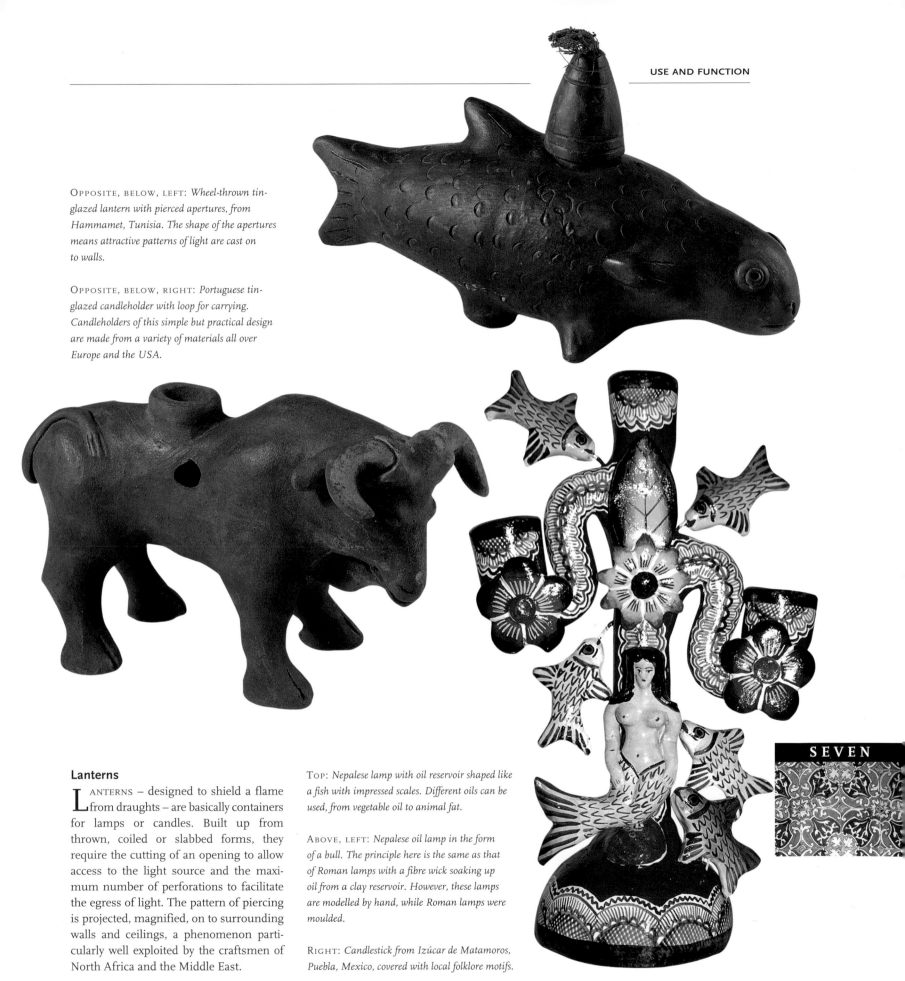

OPPOSITE, BELOW, LEFT: *Wheel-thrown tin-glazed lantern with pierced apertures, from Hammamet, Tunisia. The shape of the apertures means attractive patterns of light are cast on to walls.*

OPPOSITE, BELOW, RIGHT: *Portuguese tin-glazed candleholder with loop for carrying. Candleholders of this simple but practical design are made from a variety of materials all over Europe and the USA.*

Lanterns

LANTERNS – designed to shield a flame from draughts – are basically containers for lamps or candles. Built up from thrown, coiled or slabbed forms, they require the cutting of an opening to allow access to the light source and the maximum number of perforations to facilitate the egress of light. The pattern of piercing is projected, magnified, on to surrounding walls and ceilings, a phenomenon particularly well exploited by the craftsmen of North Africa and the Middle East.

TOP: *Nepalese lamp with oil reservoir shaped like a fish with impressed scales. Different oils can be used, from vegetable oil to animal fat.*

ABOVE, LEFT: *Nepalese oil lamp in the form of a bull. The principle here is the same as that of Roman lamps with a fibre wick soaking up oil from a clay reservoir. However, these lamps are modelled by hand, while Roman lamps were moulded.*

RIGHT: *Candlestick from Izúcar de Matamoros, Puebla, Mexico, covered with local folklore motifs.*

SEVEN

STORING FOODSTUFFS

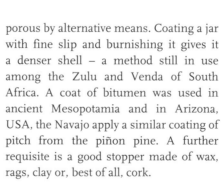

BELOW: EARTHENWARE STORAGE JARS, AFTER PERSIAN MINIATURE, 1554.

S INCE THE most ancient times ceramic vessels have been used for the storage of food and drink as has been proven by the edible contents of jars and pots found during excavations of many of the world's archaeological sites. The discovery of amphorae, for instance, has provided information about trade and the way of life throughout the Roman Empire. Fired clay can be made waterproof and, with a suitable stopper, the contents can be kept safe from rats, insects and air.

Amphorae

A MPHORA is a Greek word which means a two-handled vessel and was used in the Greek and Persian world for storing and transporting oil or wine. During Roman times the classic torpedo-shaped amphora with a capacity of 20 to 80 litres was used across the Empire from North Africa to Britain and from Spain to Cyprus. Wheel thrown, most amphorae had a pointed base which made it easy to store them vertically in sand or stack them, inserted in holes in planks, on a transport ship. Apart from oil and wine, they also held fish sauce, olives, seeds or grain and, once empty, were often recycled.

Waterproofing

I N order to make a container waterproof, a coat of glaze should ideally be applied, but low-fired pottery can be made less

porous by alternative means. Coating a jar with fine slip and burnishing it gives it a denser shell – a method still in use among the Zulu and Venda of South Africa. A coat of bitumen was used in ancient Mesopotamia and in Arizona, USA, the Navajo apply a similar coating of pitch from the piñon pine. A further requisite is a good stopper made of wax, rags, clay or, best of all, cork.

Food

V ESSELS for storing food typically have a wide neck for ease of access and may be covered with a large lid or stoppered with a bung. Beans, grain and vegetable meal are stored dry, while fruits and fresh vegetables, meat or fish may be pickled or

when travelling and discarded at the road side or on railway tracks.

In many parts of the world water is stored in unglazed or partially glazed earthenware jars and is kept cool by the evaporation of moisture through the porous walls. Taste is sometimes incidentally given to the water by the coatings of resin or limewash used for waterproofing, but intentional flavouring is added in Morocco by dabbing the jar with thuya resin, while Yemeni jars are traditionally fragranced by smoking over incense before use.

LEFT: *Chinese porcelain jar of a type commonly used for storing ginger; decorated with overglaze enamelling.*

BELOW, RIGHT: *Coiled and burnished vessel from Lesotho. Large containers like this are used for storing drinking water and brewing beer.*

BELOW, RIGHT, INSET: *Contemporary Cretan terracotta storage jar, its shape and decoration virtually unchanged since the time of the Minoan civilization 3,500 years ago. Identical vessels containing oil and grain were discovered during the excavation of Knossos.*

preserved in syrup or liquor. Some commercial Scottish marmalade is still sold in stoneware jars.

Drink

Today, drink is most often sold in a glass or plastic bottle, but within living memory English ginger beer and Dutch gin were sold in stoneware bottles, while the moonshine illicitly distilled by American bootleggers was traditionally served in a large clay jug. In India clay cups are used

OPPOSITE, ABOVE: *The spout and handle of an amphora retrieved from the sea at Monemvasia in the Peloponnese, Greece.*

OPPOSITE, BELOW, LEFT: *Woman carrying jars to market, Portugal.*

OPPOSITE, BELOW, RIGHT: *Amphora-shaped jar with lead glaze, Sous, Tunisia.*

BELOW, LEFT: *Earthenware pot, from southern Morocco, used for storing butter.*

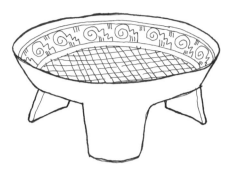

RIGHT: AZTEC *MOLCAJETE* FOR GRATING CHILLIES, MEXICO.

PREPARING FOOD

THE PREPARATION of food is the most important of all domestic tasks. The type of food cooked and eaten is dictated by climate, soil and even religious edicts and so utensils have evolved to satisfy the specific requirements of regional cookery. The popularity of international cuisine in the West has meant that many exotic foods are now exported to distant lands and with them the tools and utensils with which to prepare and cook them.

Dairy products

LIKE water, the milk of cows, sheep or goats is often stored in earthenware jars which may be partially or entirely unglazed to keep their contents cool. The addition of a bacterial culture to a jar placed somewhere warm will eventually thicken the milk into yoghurt, a process first discovered in the Middle East, possibly by nomads carrying milk in skins slung on the backs of their camels. Converting milk into cheese and butter is accomplished by agitating or churning the milk and separating the thick curds from the runny whey by straining it through sieves made from cloth or perforated pottery. In Morocco butter may be made in a ceramic *guerba* which is suspended by ropes and swung backwards and forwards.

RIGHT: MOROCCAN *GUERBA* FOR CHURNING BUTTER.

Seeds and grains

SEEDS, grains and spices need grinding into flour or powder before they can be used. This may involve a stone quern or a stone or ceramic mortar, a heavy receptacle in which substances are ground with a solid pestle. Sometimes the mortar, like the Roman *mortarium*, is made of clay with pieces of grit or grog embedded in it or it may be roughened, like the husking trays of ancient Mesopotamia or the Japanese *suribachi*, by making patterns of grooves inside. The world over, flour is mixed into dough in a large bowl which is often glazed to prevent sticking during the kneading process. Once mixed, dough or paste may be stamped with a mould into attractive shapes before baking into biscuits or cookies.

ABOVE, LEFT: Ceramic lemon reamer. The grooved end is glazed for easy cleaning, while the handle is unglazed to provide a good grip.

ABOVE, RIGHT: English salt 'pig' with slip-trailed decoration. The large opening allows the hand access to grab large quantities of salt during food preparation. Pig is an old term used in Scotland and the north of England to mean an earthenware crock or pot.

RIGHT: Bottle for fermenting yoghurt, made by the Makarunga of Zimbabwe; decorated with ochre and graphite.

SEVEN

ABOVE, LEFT: *Japanese* suribachi *with grooved interior to help with grinding. Other mortars, such as the Roman* mortarium, *may have a gritty surface for the same purpose.*

ABOVE, RIGHT: *Contemporary mould, from the USA, used for shaping cookies.*

BELOW, LEFT: *Lead-glazed colander for draining or staining foodstuffs, Romania, late 19th century. Clean perforations are best cut with a curved or tubular implement.*

BELOW, RIGHT: *Jars, pots and strainers for sale at a Moroccan market.*

Fruit and vegetables

I N Mexico much food is still prepared in the same way as it was in the time of the Aztecs. Chillies, peppers and tomatoes, for instance, are grated and mashed in a special bowl called a *molcajete* which, like the *suribachi*, has a bottom roughened with incised grooves. Before serving, boiled vegetables require straining through a colander, a vessel with holes in it like the Mexican *pichancha* for straining maize. Among the gadgets in European kitchens are wooden, glass or ceramic devices for extracting the juice from lemons or oranges by twisting and squeezing.

Puddings and deserts

T HE same processes are involved in the preparation of deserts – grating, straining and mixing using similar equipment. The most elaborate pieces of equipment were probably the copper or ceramic moulds used for setting jelly and blancmange in the kitchens of the great European houses of the early 20th century. When set and turned out, the contents were revealed as rabbits, lobsters and architectural extravaganzas.

COOKING

A TRADITIONAL COOKERY technique among Romany travellers was to roll a hedgehog in clay and throw it into the fire. The meat cooked as if wrapped in tin foil and the spines came away easily after cooking. Many foodstuffs are placed into a fired clay container before being placed in the fire.

Ovens and ranges

FIRE must be contained in the kitchen and its energy focused. To this end traditional kitchens in India and South America are often fitted with a range made from clay which retains the fire beneath openings over which pots can be placed. Domed bread ovens covered in clay to retain the heat just like a kiln can still be seen in many countries and small versions are now often built in the restaurants of the developed world, catering for the demand for 'exotic' food.

Heat

COOKING pots are constantly exposed to heat and then cool relatively quickly so they must be capable of withstanding thermal shock. Clays fired to stoneware temperatures can survive great heat, but even low-fired pottery can be used provided it has been tempered with materials that allow the easy passage of expanding air and moisture. Turkish casserole dishes tempered with mica-rich clay are brittle and will break easily if dropped, but will stand considerable heat in the oven.

Cooking pots

WHETHER coiled, paddled or thrown, most vessels used in cookery are round or spherical. This is partly ease of manufacture, but is also the best way of making sure that heat is evenly distributed, preventing damage to the pot and ensuring even heating of its contents. Three-legged pots have been used in many parts of Africa, Asia and South America for cooking directly over an open fire. The legs raise the pot to a suitable height above the flames and provide stability. In Cameroon such pots are traditionally used by men

TOP; AND ABOVE: *Tripod pot for cooking directly over a fire, Kirdi tribe, Democratic Republic of Congo (formerly Zaire); lead-glazed earthenware tajine, Morocco.*

BELOW, LEFT: *Earthenware clay ovens, or chimineas, made in Mexico.*

RIGHT: *Traditional lead-glazed earthenware cookwares from Spain.*

cooking over the hearth which is normally considered a female province.

Certain dishes have come to be known by the name of the vessel in which they are cooked – for instance, the casserole (from the French word for an open-mouthed pan), the hot pot (a dish once famously cooked in a salt-glazed pot in Lancashire in the north of England) or the tajine (a Moroccan speciality cooked under a conical lid).

Lead

For thousands of years lead glazes have been used to make pots both water-proof and easy to clean, but in modern times the risk of lead poisoning has raised considerable fears. The greatest danger has always been to the potter working with lead powder and many cases of serious illness were recorded before legislation was introduced. To the user, the greatest risk is from low-fired vessels, particularly when their surface is exposed to the acids present in lemons, tomatoes or coffee. Fully fused lead glazes, fired at higher temperatures, provide little cause for concern.

ABOVE, LEFT: *Salt-glazed vessel used in the north of England for cooking Lancashire hotpot, a dish, like casserole and tajine, that takes its name from the vessel in which it is cooked.*

TOP RIGHT: *Portuguese earthenware casserole dish with trailed slip decoration. Attractive vessels like this are often used to both cook and serve food.*

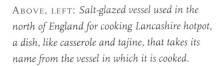

ABOVE, RIGHT: *Cooking pots and ceramic range found on the floating reed islands in Lake Titicaca, Peru. Fire is kept from the reeds by layers of stones and clay.*

LEFT: *Turkish casserole; although fired at a low temperature, the risk of thermal shock is reduced by the quantity of mica in the clay body.*

SEVEN

TABLEWARES

BELOW, LEFT: *Stoneware eggcup, Tintagel, Cornwall, England.*

BELOW, RIGHT: *Faïence soup bowls, Quimper, France.*

BOTTOM: *Tin-glazed platter from Dolores Hidalgo, Guanajuato, Mexico.*

Ceramics used for the serving of food come in a variety of shapes, sizes and styles dictated by their use and the wealth of their owners. The most elaborate and expensive functional ceramics are to be found on the table and some are so valuable or attractive that when not in use they are displayed proudly on a shelf or dresser for the enjoyment of the owner and envy of guests.

History

In Medieval Europe the rich impressed their guests by serving food on gold or silver, banishing pottery to the kitchen, dairy and cellar, while the middle ranks used pewter and the poor relied on wood and clay. The introduction of oriental porcelains, however, led to great change as the gentry vied to impress one another with the latest fashionable imports and their imitations. By the 18th century the tables of the rich were set with porcelain and those of the poor with earthenware.

In the East a far higher value was placed on ceramics as the quality of clay and the sophistication of kiln and glaze technology were much further advanced. Porcelain

ABOVE: ANCIENT PUEBLOAN CERAMIC SPOON, COLORADO, USA, 1300–1500.

SEVEN

172

and celadon glazed bowls had graced the tables of oriental potentates for more than a thousand years and the imperial Chinese porcelain factory at Jingdezhen had been in production since the Five Dynasties period (907–960).

Today, in the West, most households possess factory-made tablewares, although the most expensive items may be painted and gilded by hand. Less sophisticated, but more interesting items, however, can still be acquired at markets supplying communities who retain a pride in their local identity, traditions and regional cuisine or at specialist shops selling culinary equipment.

Uses

THE shape and dimensions of receptacles are affected by both their contents and the way they are eaten. Dishes containing large amounts of juice or liquor, such as soups and stews for example, are best eaten in a high-sided bowl or dish, while drier food can be served on a flat or shallow plate. Individual plates and bowls are not required when the participants cluster around an enormous shared dish from which they eat together, the traditional approach in Islamic countries where dishes such as couscous are enjoyed. In contrast is the system of serving Padang food in Sumatran restaurants where small dishes of every item on the menu are placed before diners who, when they have had their fill, pay for the dishes they have emptied. In Japanese *sushi* restaurants diners make their selection of delicacies from bowls placed on a counter or moving belt. Their bill is calculated by observing the colour with which the empty bowls are glazed.

Cutlery is only occasionally made from clay. Ceramic spoons are traditionally used for eating Chinese soup and were used by the Ancient Puebloans (Anasazi) in the American Southwest for consuming stews made from squashes and beans.

TOP: *Porcelain chopstick rests from China.*

ABOVE, CENTRE: *Chinese porcelain rice bowl with underglaze blue decoration.*

ABOVE, CENTRE, BELOW: *Chinese celadon glaze spoons.*

ABOVE, FAR RIGHT: *Tin-glazed eggcup from Portugal; transfer-printed 'Delft' eggcup, the Netherlands, a souvenir with a practical use.*

RIGHT: *Couscous bowl used for communal eating, Djerba, Tunisia.*

PLATES

Ranging from delicate bone china plates to enormous platters and chargers for whole joints of meat, plates are mostly round or oval and slightly dished. Many plates are never used on the table – their shape makes them an ideal surface for decoration – but are displayed on a dresser or hung on a wall.

Making plates

When a plate is thrown on the wheel, the centred clay is first spread over the surface of the wheel head and then pressed down in the middle to create the central hollow. The fingertips press inwards under the edge to form a flange which is then gently pulled up and out. As the clay is flaccid during this process the flange cannot be made too large at this point, but once leatherhard the plate can be inverted and the flange and foot refined with turning tools. Many industrially produced plates are thrown with the aid of the jigger and jolley. Another method of plate making using a hump or hollow mould requires less practice.

To avoid the risk of plates fusing together during a glaze firing, they may be placed in a special rack or stacked one above the other on three-pointed stilts, although the latter method is likely to leave scars in the glaze.

Decorating plates

Over the centuries a vast range of decorating techniques using slip and glaze have been used on plates, although those with a flat finish are most suited for actual use. The decoration of plates intended only for display has often been decidedly whimsical, a case in point is the work of the French potter Bernard Palissy (1510–90) whose oval dishes were covered with three-dimensional representations of brightly coloured plants and crustaceans that resemble kitsch creations from the 20th century.

Commemorative plates

Many plates are made specifically to celebrate and record a private event, such as a wedding or the birth of a child, or a public occasion such as the coronation of

Above, left; and above, right: *Large tin-glazed charger in the 'talavera' style, Dolores Hidalgo, Guanajuato, Mexico; maiolica plate with floral decoration, Andalucia, Spain.*

Below, left; and below, right: *French lead-glazed plate, from Beot, with trailed slip decoration; earthenware dish with slip and oxide decoration, Romania, 19th century.*

ABOVE, LEFT; AND ABOVE, RIGHT: *Plate with Koranic inscription in underglaze blue; made and decorated by Chinese workmen for the Sumatran market; tin-glazed plate made in Istalif, Afghanistan. Three spots in the centre were caused by the tripod stilts used for stacking plates during firing.*

BELOW, LEFT; AND BELOW, RIGHT: *Greek plate decorated with overglaze enamels, made on Rhodes for the tourist market; a slipware plate made by English ceramist Philip Leach to commemorate the birth of his daughter. Plates like this are intended for display rather than use.*

a monarch. The reigns of Charles II and William III are recorded on English 17th-century tin-glazed delftware, while the victory of the Prussian Duke Ferdinand of Brunswick in 1774 was recorded on German slipware with a long inscription in sgraffito. The coronations of European monarchs and the election of American presidents have been recorded on cheaply made transfer-printed plates and mugs.

ABOVE: ENGLISH TIN-GLAZED 'BLUE DASH' CHARGER, LONDON, 1690.

Inspirational plates

INSCRIPTIONS on plates are often intended to be instructional or inspirational, offering advice on how to have a successful marriage or behave piously. As figurative painting is frowned upon according to the Traditions of the prophet Mohammed many Islamic plates are decorated instead with quotations from the Koran written in beautiful, flowing calligraphy. The work is very skilful and on plates made by the Straits Chinese for Muslims in Sumatra the text is not always as accurate as might be desired!

SEVEN

Bottles and jugs

ABOVE, LEFT: *Eighteenth-century English 'harvest' jug with transfer-printed decoration.*

BELOW, LEFT: *Jug for ghee (clarified butter) with spout made by squeezing a thrown cone, Swat Valley, Pakistan.*

BELOW, RIGHT: *'Toby' jug by Dartmouth Pottery, Devon, England. An effective pouring lip is formed by the front angle of the drinker's tricorn hat. Since the first toby jugs were moulded in the 1760s they have remained popular in England and have been made to represent many historical and topical characters.*

ABOVE: GREEK *OINOCHOE* FOR POURING WINE, RHODES, 650–600 BC.

WATER IS vital for our survival and in places without the benefit of piped water households have always been well stocked with vessels for carrying and storing it. In Ancient Greece, as well as containers for water, there was a whole hierarchy of vessels for wine. It was transported in an *amphora*, mixed in a *krater*, poured from an *oinochoe* and drunk from a *kylix*.

Carrying water

FETCHING and carrying water is traditionally women's work, sometimes involving long walks and often taking up several hours each day. The commonest method is to carry the water jar on the head and this necessitates the use of a bulbous container with a low centre of gravity. Once home, the precious water is poured into a larger vessel, generally made of earthenware and possibly unglazed to keep the contents cool. The Incas and other pre-Columbian people of South America preferred to use an *arybola*, a large vessel with a narrow neck, which was slung on the back for carrying and had a conical base to make pouring easier.

The pilgrim flask

ON journeys water for personal use is carried in a smaller vessel generally slung from a strap. All over the world, in both ancient and modern times, examples of a virtually identical design can be found. The pilgrim flask, the forerunner of the canteen, consists of a flattened round vessel with a narrow neck and two handles at the top for hanging about the person. Variations have been used in South-East Asia, the American Southwest, Medieval Europe and the ancient Middle East. In the past going on a pilgrimage was one of the few reasons for most people to travel any distance and so these vessels were frequently decorated with verses from the Koran or the symbols of Christian saints such as the scallop shell sported by pilgrims on their way to visit the shrine of St James at Santiago de Compostela in northern Spain.

RIGHT: SITKYATKI 'CANTEEN', ARIZONA, USA, 16TH CENTURY.

Bottles and jugs

SMALLER quantities of liquids such as wines, beers, spirits or medicines are stored in bottles with a narrow neck. Before the mass production of glass most bottles were made of clay, but by the 20th century containers for English West Country cider, Dutch gin and Japanese sake were among the few survivors. A jug can be employed for the consumption of volumes of liquids small enough to be lifted and poured easily. Many jugs have been used for the consumption of copious quantities of alcohol during special occasions such as harvest festivities.

Spouts and lips

THE simplest form of jug is a pot or jar which has had its lip pulled out of shape to channel its contents. Teapots, Javanese wine jars and ghee pots from the Swat Valley in Pakistan are all fitted with spouts made from added pieces of clay shaped by throwing, moulding or coiling. Getting a spout to pour well, directing the flow of liquid accurately, is a matter of skill and experience. Once a great source of fun in English alehouses, puzzle jugs were fitted with hidden tubes so the beer inside would not come out where expected and would soak the unsuspecting victim.

ABOVE, LEFT; AND ABOVE, CENTRE: *Navajo resin-coated water jar, Arizona, USA; Nazca arybola, Peru, made between AD 300 and 600.*

RIGHT; AND INSET: *Pilgrim flask with Koranic calligraphy in underglaze blue, made by Straits Chinese potters for the Sumatran market; Acoma woman from Sky City, New Mexico, USA, carrying a water jar on her head.*

177

CUPS AND MUGS

ABOVE: MYCENEAN CUP, 1300–1200 BC, GREECE.

WATER HAS many life-giving qualities and so in many religious philosophies a receptacle for drinking, such as the Holy Grail of Celtic Christian mythology, has become a symbol for life itself and has been one of the items commonly placed by a body in a grave.

ABOVE, LEFT; ABOVE, RIGHT; AND BELOW: Beer pot with impressed decoration, Lesotho; beer pot made from a pinched form, Swaziland; Swazi women drinking sorghum beer from clay pots.

Beakers

THE beaker is a tall, wide-mouthed vessel. The presence of a pair of such vessels in Early Bronze Age graves excavated at Gwithian in Cornwall in the southwest of England inspired archaeologists to name the occupants 'Beaker Folk'. These 4,000-year-old objects were made by coiling with clay tempered with grog (ground-fired clay) and their surfaces were decorated by impressing with a bone comb. Coiled beakers called *keros* were used by the pre-Columbian peoples of what is now Peru for the drinking of chicha, a beer still brewed with maize today.

Pots

ALMOST spherical, pots were once widely used for the drinking of beer, their narrow mouths preventing excess spillage by the inebriated. The collectors of glasses in English pubs are still sometimes referred to as 'pot boys'. In southern Africa round pots are traditionally used for drinking sorghum beer by tribes such as the Zulu and Swazi and are usually black from the reduced atmosphere in the kiln. The size of the pot

is a matter of respect and to offer a small pot may be considered an insult. By contrast, the beer pot of Lesotho, the *sekhona*, has a raised foot and straighter sides. In the Peruvian Amazon the Shipibo-Conibo drink their maize beer from globular pots with linear painted patterns and embossed faces.

Bowls

SHALLOW bowls are used in South-East Asia and China for drinking tea and rice wine. These are served hot and the large area exposed to the air means that the liquid quickly cools, preventing the scalding of the mouth.

Drinking vessels

A CUP is a more or less hemispherical vessel and may or may not have a foot and one or more handles. In the East a tea cup has no handle, but in the West it has one. In Europe traditional large cups for communal drinking sessions might have two, three or even four handles so they could be easily passed around. Wine cups used in Ancient Greece had a pedestal foot and two handles and were frequently beautifully painted, while there was considerable variety across the Roman Empire including beakers, cups with a foot or no foot and with or without handles. Decoration was often in relief and the finest wares were coated with a fine slip such as terra sigillata which was a bright orange-red when fired in an oxygen-rich atmosphere.

OPPOSITE, TOP RIGHT: *Chinese tea bowls decorated with overglaze enamels.*

OPPOSITE, CENTRE: *Moulded German beer stein with pewter fittings. This particular example is fitted with a musical device which plays a drinking song when lifted from the table.*

OPPOSITE, BELOW, LEFT: *Maiolica beakers, Siena, Italy.*

LEFT: *English bone china mug with transfer-printed decoration.*

CENTRE, LEFT: *Coffee cup with underglaze decoration, made by Ben Lucas, Welcombe Pottery, Devon, England.*

ABOVE: *KERO FOR DRINKING MAIZE BEER, TIWANAKU CULTURE (AD 200–700), PERU.*

Mugs are larger than cups, cylindrical and fitted with a handle. Now much used for the informal drinking of coffee, they were once used for drinking beer which was an important part of the diet during the Middle Ages and was known as 'liquid bread'. An example still in use is the German stein which is fitted with a pewter lid.

SEVEN

TEA AND COFFEE

T EA AND coffee have inspired poetry, ritual and a plethora of specialized utensils as diverse as Japanese raku tea bowls and the gaily painted tea and coffee services decorated by Susie Cooper and Clarice Cliff in England during the early 20th century.

Tea

'T HE froth of the liquid jade', legend tells us, was discovered by the Chinese Emperor Shen-nung in 2737 BC when leaves from a tea bush fell into the water he was boiling to drink. The first book on tea, written by Lu Wu (died AD 804), recommended that it could be best appreciated when drunk from a blue bowl. Tea drinking became very popular during the Song Dynasty (960–1279) when it was consumed not only to delight the soul, but also to strengthen the will and repair the eyesight. Taoists claimed it was one of the ingredients of the Elixir of Immortality. Some of the world's finest ceramics were created during this time, many intended

for use in the consumption of tea. Discovering that tea helped to prevent drowsiness, Buddhist monks began to consume large quantities during their long hours of meditation. Elements of Taoism and Buddhism were combined in a new philosophy – Ch'an, better known by its Japanese name Zen – in which the drinking of tea became one of the techniques for self-realization, focusing the attention on the 'now'.

The Tea Ceremony

B Y the 16th century there were many disciples of Zen in Japan and under the guidance of Tea Masters, such as Sen no Rikyu (1521–91) and Kobori Enshu (1579–1647), the Tea Ceremony (*Chanoya*) had developed into an aesthetic ritual carried out in an atmosphere of quiet and austere refinement. The utensils used during the ceremony – flower vases, incense boxes, tea containers, water jars and tea bowls – were

ABOVE: *Lady's porcelain teapot decorated with overglaze enamels, China, 1920s.*

LEFT: *Porcelain tea caddy with stencilled decoration; made by Chinese potters in South-East Asia.*

LEFT: EARTHENWARE PAN FOR ROASTING COFFEE BEANS, HADRAMAUT, YEMEN.

LEFT: TAOISTS TAKING TEA, AFTER A 17TH-CENTURY PAINTED PORCELAIN POT, CHINA.

often made by the participants themselves and were endowed with a primitive, earthy dignity, their appreciation being the conclusion of the ritual. Exquisite individual raku pieces were made by enthusiasts such as the multi-talented Honami Koetsu, while the growing demand provided work for many kilns such as those at Bizen and Shigaraki in producing ash-glazed wares.

In Europe and particularly England, where tea arrived in around 1650, a different ritual is performed, accompanied with sandwiches, cakes or scones, employing a matching service of plates, cups, saucers, teapot, milk jug and sugar bowl, all made from delicate bone china or porcelain.

Coffee

COFFEE was discovered in the Kaffa region of Ethiopia, reputedly by a boy who saw his goats become energized after chewing certain berries. The practice was quickly adopted by local Christian monks to avoid sleepiness, just as the Buddhists

ABOVE, LEFT: *Stoneware teapot with stamped 'peacock eye' pattern, Boleslawiec, Poland. Pottery workshops using the rich resources of local clay were established in Silesia during the 14th century. Stoneware decorated predominantly in blue has been produced in Boleslawiec since the 1830s and employs hand-stamped 'eye' motifs associated with folk art and later popular with Jugendstil, the German Art Nouveau movement.*

TOP RIGHT: *English bone china teacup and saucer with hand-painted decoration. Bone china has probably been England's most successful ceramic export – it has the translucence of porcelain, but is cheaper to produce.*

ABOVE, RIGHT: *Coffee pot from Estapona, Spain. Ground coffee is placed in the upper chamber and water filters through it into the main body of the pot.*

OPPOSITE, BELOW, RIGHT: *Coffee heating on a charcoal brazier in a traditional Ethiopian black coffee pot.*

had adopted tea. For hundreds of years it was eaten, not imbibed, but eventually the drinking of coffee became an important part of the ritual of hospitality. Accompanied by the burning of incense, coffee beans are roasted, ground and then pounded in a mortar before being boiled over a charcoal brazier in a traditional black, round-bellied earthenware pot. The brew is served in handleless cups with, perhaps, a sprig of rue. In a very similar form, the serving of coffee to guests has become widespread in the Arab world – it was first used by Sufis, the mystics of the Islamic faith.

SEVEN

ABOVE: DELFT TULIP
VASE, 1700.

CHINESE PAPERCUTS
OF VASES.

SEVEN

ABOVE: *Glazed vase designed for hanging on
a wall, Sumatra.*

BELOW, LEFT: *Nepalese terracotta planter in the
form of an elephant.*

BELOW, RIGHT: *Ornate moulded terracotta
garden urn, reproduction of an early 19th-century
design, England.*

OPPOSITE, ABOVE, LEFT: *Inspired by Eastern
pottery, vases like this were originally made in the
1890s at Brannams Pottery, Barnstaple, Devon,
but are now made in stoneware in Vietnam.*

OPPOSITE, BELOW, LEFT: *Terracotta planters
based on traditional water jars, Oaxaca, Mexico.*

PLANTS AND FLOWERS

MANY POTS cater specifically for the needs of the gardener and in the West many
items originally intended for other purposes, such as ceramic kitchen sinks,
have also often been used, while some containers, such as the vases of the Ming
period, have been put on display for their own aesthetic merits completely devoid
of flowers.

Flower pots

COOKING pots and flower pots are
opposite sides of the same ceramic
coin. Just as a cooking pot must withstand
the thermal shock of a fire, so plant pots
must be able to withstand frosts and
extremes of weather – the best material
for both is well-tempered clay. Usually
thrown on the wheel, earthenware, and in
particular terracotta, is the most common
choice, although it may be fired at the
higher end of its range for strength.

To prevent plants rotting in soggy soil
most flower pots are porous and have one
or more holes in the bottom for drainage.
In the late 20th century a range of
attractive pottery became available in
Western garden centres which included
bright blue glazed wares from Vietnam
and Chinese lead-glazed vessels with relief
patterns. In Asia the tradition of growing
plants in glazed pots dates back thousands
of years and in former times during the
summer the entrances of households
from Tibet to Thailand and from Kabul to
Kyoto were ablaze with potted blooms.

Planters

LARGE containers for planting are not
necessarily round, but are available
cast or slab built with flat sides. In Europe
rectangular terracotta planters moulded
in imitation of the reliefs on Greek
and Roman stonework are popular. In
Japan bonsai enthusiasts employ shallow
dishes and bowls, mainly with a rustic or
natural feel, carefully selected so that their
clay, glaze and shape will complement
their artificially miniature trees. Chinese

planters intended for use indoors have often been painted in blue and white designs as sophisticated as any tea service.

Forcing

APART from the propagation and growing of plants clay pots are used in the garden to protect and force vegetables. This involves inverting a large pot over a plant so that, starved for light, it grows faster, becoming pale and tender.

Flower arranging

WHETHER Welsh daffodils or Thai orchids, the arrangement of flowers can be a way of bringing beauty into the home or an offering to the gods, spirits or ancestors and the choice of vase is a major part of the composition of a display. This is a particularly important aspect in *ikebana*, the Japanese art of flower arranging, which has risen from an art form to the level of meditation. Vases tend to be bulbous or baluster shaped for stability and are narrowed at the neck to help displayed flowers stand tall. Small vases for a single bloom are narrower with constricted necks.

Although we now associate tulips with the Netherlands, they were introduced to Europe from Turkey in the mid-16th century. Collecting these exotic blooms became such a mania among the wealthy that by the 1700s extravagant, towering structures were constructed for their display – they were of a fashionable material, blue and white tin-glazed earthenware.

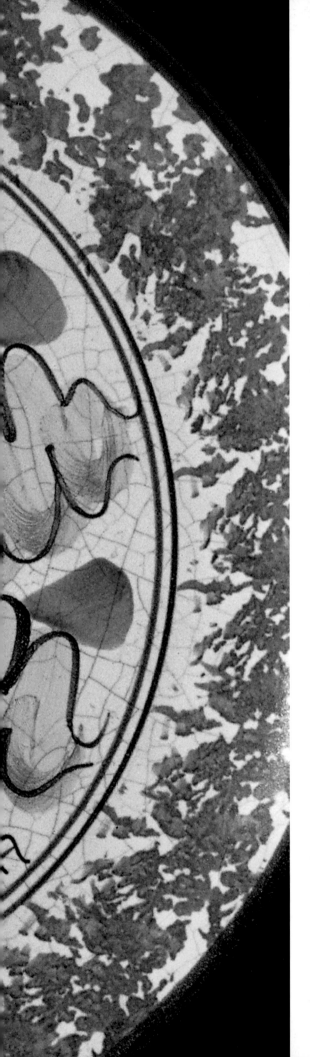

LEFT: *Maiolica plate, Malta.*
ABOVE, LEFT: *Turtle-shaped ocarina, Mexico.*
ABOVE, NEAR RIGHT: *Replica of a terracotta warrior from the tomb of Qin Shi Huang Di (died 210 BC), Xian, China.*
ABOVE, FAR RIGHT: *'Three wise monkeys', souvenir from Nara, Japan.*
CENTRE, RIGHT: *Tin-glazed cross, Dolores Hidalgo, Guanajuato, Mexico.*
BELOW, LEFT: *Tile panel of the Virgin Mary, Antequerra, Spain.*
BELOW, RIGHT: *Church-shaped roof ornament, Ayacucho, Peru.*

EIGHT

THE QUALITY OF LIFE

THE QUALITY OF LIFE

THE TECHNOLOGY and skills of the ceramic craft were first developed when early communities no longer needed to spend all their waking lives finding food. Spare time was also used in the search for pleasure and intellectual and spiritual fulfilment and so new skills were employed to further new pursuits. Some objects were made for use in sport and games – for instance, marbles or the targets employed in clay pigeon shooting, some for sensual gratification such as tobacco pipes and musical instruments, but others were made purely to please the eye.

BELOW, RIGHT: *Slip-cast 'fertility pot', Ute Mountain Pottery, Colorado, USA. The Utes have no pottery tradition of their own, but have drawn inspiration from their neighbours.*

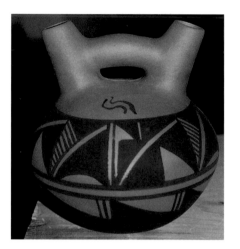

SELF ADORNMENT

THERE IS evidence in prehistoric burials that even the most ancient peoples were wont to decorate themselves for reasons of superstition or pure vanity. Body paint and found objects are still used in many tribal societies, but crafted clay objects have been made in profusion. Beads are one of the oldest forms of decoration and were one of the first trade items. Larger ceramic ornaments such as brooches have also been made despite their weight but, being vulnerable, few have survived. In the Amazon jungle even clothing has been made from pottery – for instance, the ceramic *tangas* worn over their pudenda by girls taking part in the rites associated with puberty. They were worn 1,000 years ago by the Marajoara in the Amazon delta in Brazil and are still in use among the Panoan tribes along the Ucayali River in Peruvian Amazonia.

ABOVE, LEFT: *Good luck figure decorated with beads, Sao people, Chad.*

ABOVE, CENTRE: *Pair of slip-cast bulls placed for luck on the roofs of Andean homes, Pucara, Peru. The bull is a symbol of strength introduced to Peru after the Spanish conquest.*

PLEASURE

THE VERY senses once used to find food and stay safe from danger have diminished in power for those with a sedentary lifestyle, but they still provide a great source of pleasure. The ears are delighted by music, the nose by fragrant smells and the eyes by a pleasing composition of colour and form. Many enjoy the sensory experience of smoking tobacco and other herbs as a form of relaxation, while some like to exercise and amuse the brain with toys and games.

ART

AN INDEFINABLE personal feeling of what is satisfying or pleasing – a sense of
aesthetics – is the basis of art. Although the same criteria may be used to assess
the beauty of functional pottery, in the Western world a higher value is placed on
objects which have no practical function and serve only to be admired for their aesthetic
qualities. Sculptors modelling in clay have a higher status than mere potters making mugs,
bowls and teapots. In traditional societies there is no 'art for art's sake' and beauty and
function are combined, although today making otherwise useless souvenirs to sell to
tourists is a valuable source of income.

TOP: *Brightly coloured figures and animals from
Mexico, South Africa and Japan.*

ABOVE, RIGHT: *Tin-glazed Seder plate used by
Jews to celebrate Passover, Israel.*

LEFT: *Figures of monks holding bird baths or
planters, Mexico.*

RIGHT: *Spanish maiolica plaques on a street wall
in Andalucia.*

HIGHER MATTERS

OUR THOUGHTS are not entirely concentrated on the joys and troubles of this
world. We look for higher meaning in nature, the weather, the stars, in life and
death and we have devised techniques to aid our concentration and objects to
focus our attention on higher matters. Although clay is merely mud or earth, it is, according
to myths and legends, the stuff from which we were originally made, it is the body of our
Mother Earth and with the aid of this dense, mundane substance we look for ways to break
free, to rise up and reach for the celestial.

EIGHT

FRAGRANCE

The inhalation of perfumes and incense has a powerful effect on the human psyche and over the millennia many different aromas have been used to invoke the gods, avert the evil eye, to raise the spirits and to heal the sick.

Clouds of costly frankincense fill the heady atmosphere of Catholic churches just as, in Central America, the rituals of the Aztecs were accompanied by the burning of copal (the resin of a tropical tree) in huge ceramic braziers. The Aztecs believed aromatic fumes could also cure a number of diseases, a belief still held in Yemen.

Aromatic substances

With a few exceptions, such as ambergris and musk (obtained respectively from sperm whales and the scent glands of certain mammals), the most aromatic materials are obtained from plants. Some are distilled from flowers or leaves – rosewater or eucalyptus oil – some are found in wood – like camphor and sandalwood – but the most highly prized are resins such as frankincense and myrrh, both of which were once only found in Yemen from where, according to the Bible, the Queen of Sheba carried them to Jerusalem as a lavish gift for King Solomon.

Incense burners

The simplest method of producing clouds of redolent smoke is to burn incense on a fire. For this purpose many forms of brazier have been used, from the Chinese burners made of metal or clay and shaped like the Celestial Mountain of the Taoists to the spiky braziers of Yemen which are unglazed but brightly decorated with commercial inks. In Yemen the smoke is used to make the home smell sweet and is wafted under the robes of guests as well as scenting clothes draped over a frame, a practice also found among the Tutsis in Rwanda who burn the twigs of the umugwavu tree in their fire pots. During the Renaissance, Italian beauties scented their hair in the same way.

Left: Aztec incense brazier from the Great Pyramid at Tenochtitlan, Mexico.

Left: Oil burner heated with a nightlight; made in Japan.

Below: Chinese incense burner heated with charcoal.

Opposite, above, left: Balinese lamp fuelled with fragrant oils.

Opposite, above, right: Nepalese temple lion made of thrown, moulded and modelled components. The holes in his back are for joss sticks.

Joss sticks

Gaining popularity in the West during the hippy era of the 1960s and 1970s, the joss stick derives its name from deos, the pidgin English corruption of a Chinese word for a religious image. They were originally made by mixing fragrant powders with clay to help them adhere to a stick that was then burned before an image either in a temple or a family shrine. To keep the sticks upright they might be positioned in a pot containing sand or inserted into a perforated stand. Temples in Nepal often contain 'temple lions' which may have holes on their backs for many sticks.

Oil and pastille burners

Pastille burners became popular in the West in the 16th century, using a candle to heat a perfumed tablet placed

Below, left; and below, right: Incense burner, from Mexico, used for burning copal; Portuguese tin-glazed container for pot pourri, a mixture of fragrant dried flowers and spices.

above. The popularity of aromatherapy as an aid to good health and relaxation has seen a proliferation of oil burners which use a nightlight to heat drops of essential oils such as lavender oil which is helpful in curing headaches.

Bottles and alabastron

Ceramic containers have often been used to store fragrant substances, whether pot pourri made of dried petals in a jar perforated to allow the smell to radiate or perfume bottles with a tight stopper to keep it in. Special round-bottomed bottles called aryballos and alabastron were used by the Ancient Greeks to hold the scented oils with which they anointed their bodies.

BEADS

THE ORIGINS of beads are lost in the mists of time, but we know that people living in France 40,000 years ago were making and trading vast numbers of them. Surviving ancient beads are made from many materials including shell, bone and wood as well as clay – both raw and fired. Just how long ago clay was first used is purely conjectural as without firing it is vulnerable to moisture and impact, but clues can be gleaned from the lifestyle of surviving hunter-gatherers. Within living memory the San Bushmen who inhabit the Kalahari Desert in Namibia and Botswana followed a traditional way of life, although it changed rapidly. The Bushmen made beads from pieces of drilled ostrich shell and from pellets of clay, scented with plant extracts, rolled between their fingers. These little balls, simply decorated with patterns imprinted with sticks or fingernails, were hardened off in the baking sun. Similar beads made by the Zulu and Ndebele in South Africa were made from clay mixed with milk.

Function

IN the modern world beads are seen primarily as a medium for self adornment, but closer observation reveals a rich vocabulary of expression. The combination of colours or patterns in a necklace, bangle or embroidery may be a statement of the owner's position in the social hierarchy, their marital status or their ethnic origins. Certain forms, such as those that are triangular or resemble eyes, may be talismanic, intended to ensure fertility or avert misfortune. They may also serve a religious function, forming the counters on a rosary, an aid to prayer common to Christianity, Buddhism and Hinduism.

The great value placed on beads saw the development of an extensive trade network around the world. Probably the most highly prized of all beads were made out of glass in Venice, Italy, from the 16th century onwards and exported to Africa, Asia and the Americas. Some, such as the chevron bead, were so valuable that it became a common practice to substitute cheaper imitations made from local materials such as painted clay.

Making beads

CLAY is an ideal material for the manufacture of beads as a suitable shape is easily achieved by rolling a piece between the hands to make a sphere or on a hard surface to form a cylinder. It is also easy to turn out a set of identically shaped beads by pressing them in a mould, a technique used in Ancient Egypt for the production of scarabs intended for neck collars. Making

OPPOSITE, TOP LEFT: *Dance necklace of ceramic beads painted to look like Venetian glass, Bamileke, Cameroon.*

OPPOSITE, CENTRE, LEFT: *Two large 'blueware' beads from India, five decal beads from Greece and five Japanese imitation turquoise porcelain beads.*

OPPOSITE, BELOW, LEFT: *Necklace of unglazed beads from Ghana; decorated with simple impressed designs.*

OPPOSITE, BELOW, RIGHT: *Glazed beads, from Pisac, Peru, with Inca-inspired designs.*

a hole is best left until the clay becomes leatherhard as at this stage the shape is less likely to be distorted by piercing or drilling. The Egyptians used another method for their faience beads, building up a layer of the paste around a glass rod. During firing the glass melted away leaving a neat hole.

Clay beads may be decorated in a number of ways, by imprinting a pattern, using differently coloured clays or by painting after firing. Decorating with glaze is a tricky process in which it is essential to ensure the glazed surfaces do not touch the kiln or each other during firing, a problem solved by fitting them on to a rack of suitable wire.

TOP LEFT: *Necklace of incised and impressed beads, Djenne, Mali. The designs have been revealed by rubbing white powder into the impressions.*

TOP RIGHT: *Black clay bead necklace, Lesotho.*

ABOVE: *Modern replica of an Ancient Egyptian necklace of faience beads. The necklaces sold in large quantities to tourists are made in the same way as those worn in the times of the Pharaohs.*

EIGHT

SOUND

CLAY CAN be used to generate sound in two ways, either exploiting the resonance of the clay itself or the vibration of air inside a hollow vessel. The resulting noises may be used to entertain children, communicate with the spirit world or to make harmonious music.

Rattles

CLAY rattles are filled with stones or fragments of clay before firing. Some – like human figures made by the Yoruba in Cameroon or Nigeria and the effigy bowls of the Waurá in the Brazilian Amazon, which have small pieces of clay in the hollow base – are shaken as part of rituals either to frighten away malevolent spirits or in a form of sympathetic magic to simulate the sound of thunder and attract rain. Others are intended to entertain children and may be made in amusing shapes. The Ancient Greeks, for instance, made pig-shaped rattles. Rattles used by the Moche and other pre-Columbian peoples in South America often had a bulbous dog's head.

Drums

THE *ghatam* is a large earthenware pot played in villages in India with the fingertips and palms, and tonal variation is achieved by restricting part of the opening with the stomach. The smaller *gharra* is often struck with metal knuckle dusters. A number of Indian drums, such as the *mrdngam*, are made by covering a special pot with a piece of skin. In Morocco hourglass-shaped drums covered with sheepskin are decorated with tin-glazed patterns.

Bells

SMALL bells can be made from thrown or moulded clay, a good ring is achieved with a high-temperature firing. In Japan, where they are called *nendo-suzo*, clay bells are sold as charms at many temples and shrines. Often formed into one of the twelve astrological animals, they were originally hung up near racks of silkworms to attract the aid of the gods in their propagation. Clay bells can also be acquired at many Christian shrines such as the Russian monastery at Valaam.

OPPOSITE, LEFT: *Rattling this female figure deters bad spirits, Yoruba, Nigeria.*

OPPOSITE, BELOW, RIGHT: *Pair of contemporary ocarinas painted with pre-Columbian patterns, Peru.*

ABOVE, LEFT; AND ABOVE, CENTRE: *Slip-painted fish whistle, Japan; Japanese owl-shaped bells.*

NEAR RIGHT; FAR RIGHT; AND TOP RIGHT: *Bird-shaped ocarina, England; replica of Aztec ceramic whistle in 'Tetzcoco redware', 1500, Mexico; bell with sgraffito design, Majorca.*

BELOW, LEFT: *Moroccan clay drum with thrown body, Safi.*

ABOVE: JAPANESE CLAY BELL SHAPED LIKE A RAM.

ABOVE: RATTLING EFFIGY POT, WAURA TRIBE, BRAZILIAN AMAZON.

Whistles

SIMPLE modelled or moulded toys that will produce anything from a peep to a piercing whistle have been made for traditional festivities from China to Mexico. The whistling mechanism, mouthpiece and carefully aligned sound hole must be cut carefully when the clay is leatherhard. Many of these whistling toys are shaped like birds – for instance, those made for the 'Grandma Temple Fair' in the Chinese provinces of Shaanxi and Hunan where tiny birds are bought in the hope of ensuring the birth of grandchildren. In Mexico the shapes reflect local culture and include chickens, horsemen, fish with legs and mermaids playing the guitar.

By carefully cutting a number of extra holes and covering different combinations while blowing it is possible to produce notes of different pitches. Flutes were made by the Aztecs and other South American people from clay cylinders while the ocarina, another traditional instrument still played in the region, acquired its name from its odd globular form which resembles the oca, a variety of locally grown edible tuber related to the sweet potato.

EIGHT

TOYS AND GAMES

RIGHT: ANCIENT GREEK MOUNTED FIGURES, FROM THE GRAVES OF CHILDREN.

PLAY IS an important part of growing up. It is a time when, aided by toys and games designed to improve dexterity or foster the ability to solve problems, a child learns about his or her relationship with the real world and so many toys are miniature versions of the tools and utensils used by adults, such as the water pots carried by their mothers or the herd animals tended by their fathers.

FAR LEFT: *Counters made by Roman soldiers for use in improvised board games. They were constructed from the bottoms of broken pottery. The one on the left is from Wales (1st century AD) and the one on the right is from Leptis Magna, Libya.*

NEAR LEFT: *Painted horseman on whistling horse, Ocumicho, Michoacan, Mexico. Figures like this bear a striking resemblance to those in ancient graves.*

Toys

AT the end of the day potters around the world have squeezed their leftover lumps of clay into crude animal shapes, some taking considerable care. Wheel-thrown toy pigs, for example, were being made in Mesopotamia 4,000 years ago. In China the figures of animals are often brightly painted and fitted with moving parts that wobble on the end of springs. Modelled animals were found in many of the graves of Ancient Greek children. Simple toys are an art form in Mexico where potters use their vivid imaginations to make anything from rabbits to round-abouts, from horsemen to helicopters. The skeletons made for children at the Day of the Dead festival are eagerly played with and ameliorate the children's fear of death.

RIGHT: *Articulated figure made by the author; inspired by Ancient Greek dolls. Modern dolls are generally made with only clay heads and hands.*

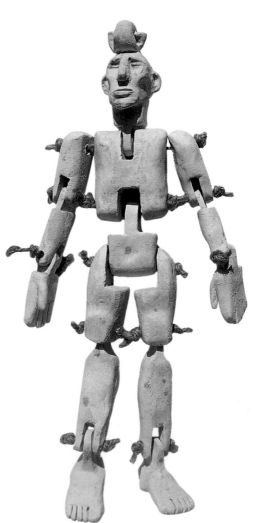

The spinning top, rotated with a cord or whip, has been played with by children since ancient times – those used by Greek children were made from clay.

Wheeled toys

TOYS such as cars or horses that can be moved around on wheels add an extra dimension to play. Wheeled animals were popular with Roman children, but were also surprisingly common in Central Mexico among pre-Columbian societies who did not use the wheel for transport!

Dolls

DOLLS provide a companion with whom children can share darkest secrets or upon whom they can wreak their cathartic wrath. Crude dolls may be shaped in one piece, but more elaborate versions have been fitted with articulated arms and legs such as those made by the Greeks which had their limbs attached with knotted

EIGHT

string. Expensive dolls made in the 19th and 20th centuries for European children frequently had heads, hands and feet made from biscuit-fired clay. Many of these have stood the test of time as adults considered them too precious for children to play with.

Games

CLAY has been used for millennia for counters and playing pieces, such as marbles, either purpose made or recycled. Roman legionaries, for example, improvised using the bottoms of broken wine jugs as counters. At Christmas in Mexico blindfolded children attempt to smash open a clay pot called a piñata suspended in the air. Decorated with coloured paper, the piñata is filled with sweets and small toys that shower down when the pot is eventually broken.

Souvenirs

ON trips to new places both children and adults eagerly acquire mementos of their visit. Such souvenirs were once bought mainly at shrines to assure good luck, but now are more often moulded in the shape of a local attraction, a Dutch windmill, the leaning tower of Pisa or a brightly coloured chameleon from Cape Town.

TOP LEFT: *Painted car and bus with a high level of detail, Ayacucho, Peru.*

ABOVE, CENTRE: *Miniature Acoma water jar, New Mexico, USA. Small versions of adult equipment are widely used in imaginative play.*

ABOVE, RIGHT: *German moulded hard-paste porcelain figure. It once served as the top of a pin cushion.*

BELOW, RIGHT: *Japanese porcelain doll playing the koto.*

ABOVE: PAINTING ON A GREEK CUP OF A WOMAN FLICKING WINE DREGS WHILE PLAYING KOTTABOS.

ABOVE: *Doll in French Breton costume; made in China. Dolls in the traditional costumes of many lands are now made for collectors by factories in China.*

TOBACCO PIPES

THE HABIT of tobacco smoking has spread right round the world after the indigenous population first introduced it to explorers in the New World in the 15th century. Spanish conquistadors observed the Aztecs smoking clay pipes shaped like macaws or indigenous animals and since then many of the pipes of other nations have featured elaborate bowls modelled or moulded with the heads of animals or humans. Clay is ideal for the manufacture of pipes as it is a poor conductor, so the hand is protected from the heat of the burning tobacco leaves. In Britain white, iron-free clays suitable for making pipes are known as pipe clay even though this is not their sole use. Tobacco is the most widely smoked substance, but other contents of a pipe might be hashish, opium or a number of herbal alternatives.

Social and ceremonial smoking

ALTHOUGH the addictive quality of tobacco has ensured there are few social occasions from which it is absent, in many societies it also serves a ceremonial or ritual purpose just as it did in the USA in the 15th century. Today, it is considered polite to give an offering of tobacco when visiting traditional communities in many places from the USA to Indonesia and offerings to the spirits, such as those made each morning in Bali or placed at Voodoo shrines in Haiti, may well feature tobacco. The relationship of tobacco with the spirit world is a result of the heady effect of smoking and the way the smoke ascends up into the air just like incense or burnt offerings.

Taken as snuff or smoked, tobacco is one of the privileges and pleasures of elders in traditional villages around the world where old men meet, like the Makonde in Mozambique, to set the world to rights. In the Congo when the chief smoked his pipe it was a sign that all should be silent while he deliberated. Among the Nguni and Sotho peoples of southern Africa tobacco is associated with power and generosity and is seen as a connection with the ancestors. It is also offered as a gift at weddings and is linked to fertility.

Pipes

THE simplest form of clay pipe, and therefore easiest to make, is probably the *chillum*, used in India for both tobacco and marijuana, which consists of a simple cone open at both ends. Most other pipes have the bowl set at an angle to the stem which is made hollow by forming it around a length of wire or wood. While pipes made for one's own use are modelled, those produced in larger numbers are made by pressing clay into a mould. In Europe, a metal rod was passed through a clay roll which was then placed in a two-

TOP LEFT: *Nineteenth-century moulded pipe bowl; made by Gambier of Paris, France.*

BELOW, LEFT: *Vietnamese porcelain and metal water pipe.*

ABOVE; AND TOP RIGHT:
PAINTED BOWL USED AS A
WATER PIPE, KIRMAN, IRAN,
1700; PIPE OF CLAY, WOOD
AND COCONUT SHELL,
MAKONDE, MOZAMBIQUE.

piece metal mould squeezed together in a gin press. Pulling a lever forced another rod into the clay to form the bowl.

Water pipes

WATER pipes consist of a bowl, two tubes and a container of water to cool the tobacco smoke. The ono-matopoeic title 'hubble bubble' used in the West is actually a corruption of the Arabic *habba bulbul* which compares the bubbling to the singing of the nightingale (*bulbul*). The word *habba*, meaning coconut, refers to the water container which was once made from coconut shell. The water container is now often made of clay, glass or metal, but the bowl is almost always ceramic and may be lavishly decorated.

TOP LEFT: *Modelled terracotta pipe bowl with imprinted patterns, Baganda, Uganda.*

ABOVE, LEFT: *White clay pipe made in a two-piece mould, Scotland. The tip was generally dipped in wax or lacquer to prevent it sticking to the smoker's lips. In Europe the common use of white primary clay with a low iron content in the manufacture of pipes led to its becoming known popularly as 'pipe clay'.*

ABOVE, RIGHT: *Pipe bowl shaped like a ritual mask, Bamileke tribe, Cameroon.*

OPPOSITE, BELOW, RIGHT: *Water pipe with a clay bowl for the tobacco, Aden, Yemen.*

ABOVE: STEATITE CARVING OF A CHIEF SMOKING A CLAY PIPE, MBOMA, DEMOCRATIC REPUBLIC OF CONGO (FORMERLY ZAIRE).

ABOVE: MULTIPLE CLAY PIPE BOWL, CATAWBA, SOUTH CAROLINA, USA, 19TH CENTURY.

RIGHT: *Scottish fisherman smoking a short clay pipe. Many pipes were originally up to a foot long which gave a cooler smoke. Due to the fragility of their stems, they would often snap, but could still be used. With time it was much more prevalent for stems to be made shorter in the first place. In archaeological excavations the discovery of short sections of pipe stems rather than pipe bowls is more common.*

FIGURINES

DURING THE 19th century the mantlepieces of European homes were cluttered with figurines whose purpose was mostly decorative, *objets d'art* in their own right, but the making of figurines and groups has a long history, both contemplative and inspirational. The Victorians would have been shocked to know that the figures made by the Karajá in the Brazilian Amazon were intended to teach children about sex.

ABOVE, LEFT; NEAR RIGHT; AND FAR RIGHT:
*English 19th-century Parian ware statuette of the
Roman goddess Ceres; Hittite votive statuette,
Syria, 2nd millennium BC; Chinese slip-cast
figurine of the Buddhist deity Kwanyin.*

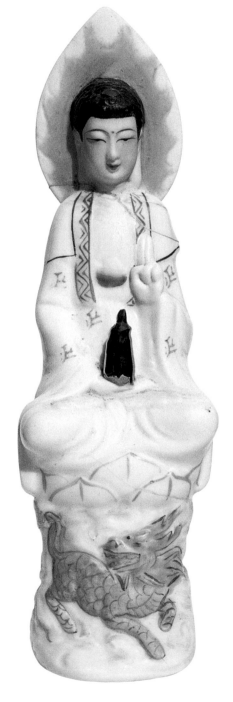

Spiritual statuary

DATING back to the early figures thrown into the fires of Eastern Europe 25,000 years ago, votive plaques and figures have been made to attract the good wishes of a god, spirit or saint and in many traditional homes a special shelf, cupboard or shrine contains images and idols. Statuettes range from the goggle-eyed, bird-headed figures pinched into shape by the Sumerians and Hittites 4,000 years ago to modern Chinese slip castings of the Buddhist deity Kwanyin.

Myths and folklore

CARL Jung said that 'myth is a manifestation of the collective unconscious' – people have always read meaning into the episodes of their mythology, finding inspiration for dealing with the problems of life and warnings of

the results of inappropriate behaviour. One popular subject in Mexican statuary, for example, is the mermaid (*sirena*), the form into which a lazy girl was changed as a punishment for preferring to swim in the river rather than carry out her chores. Another is 'the Weeping Woman' (*La Llorana*) who was condemned to wander forever after murdering her children.

Role models

LIKENESSES of heroes, contemporary, historical and fictional, can be found in places of honour. Moulded figurines made in Staffordshire during the 18th and 19th centuries included Lord Nelson and Rob Roy, a Scottish brigand whose adventures were romanticized by Sir Walter Scott. While other communities produce figures of saints, in Alto Do Moura in north-east Brazil brightly painted miniatures of

heroes, soldiers, bandits and Portuguese footballers are produced.

Genre scenes

Scenes of everyday life have become a popular subject in recent years, bringing potters a good income from tourists, but models of people at work in trade or agriculture have been made since time immemorial, often to be buried in the graves of the dead as they were in Egypt at the time of the pharaohs. Figures of craftsmen such as carpenters and even women in the bathtub were found in Greek tombs. In China models in glazed stoneware may represent fishermen, mah jong players or people practising Tai Chi. In modern Peru a popular subject is women selling chicha, the local beer, or people travelling on the local buses, a subject also common in Colombia and Bolivia. Some figures represent actual living people and may be specially commissioned as gifts for guests and musicians at festivities.

BELOW: *A group of figurines in traditional costume depicting aspects of everyday life in Provence, France.*

EIGHT

RITUALS AND CEREMONIALS

WHERE POTTERY vessels are the norm in everyday life they also feature incidentally in religious and secular celebrations, but clay is itself rich in association and symbolism. It is a symbol of life. Clay is in many mythologies the material from which the first people were made, pots represent the life-giving forces embodied in the water they so often contain and the receptive hollow of a clay vessel is a symbol for a woman's womb and Mother Earth.

ABOVE: INCENSE BURNER SHAPED LIKE A MOUNTAIN, HAN DYNASTY (206 BC– AD 250), CHINA.

ABOVE: *Moulded plaque outside a Catholic house, Mdina, Malta. Maiolica plaques like this one were originally made popular by the Della Robbia family during the 15th century in Florence, Italy.*

BELOW, LEFT: *Terracotta plaque of the Hindu god Ganesh, Molela, Rajasthan, India. Images of Ganesh, the overcomer of obstacles, are placed above doors and are invoked at the beginning of any venture. Molela is home to many potters specializing in iconographic sculpture of this type.*

BELOW, RIGHT: *Nativity scene with painted and varnished clay figures; made by a Mixtec potter in Oaxaca, Mexico.*

Worship

As an aid to focus the attention, the presence of a deity or higher spirit is frequently represented by two- and three-dimensional images in homes and places of worship and also in public locations. Carvings or moulded representations of the elephant-headed Hindu god Ganesh can be seen over gateways and doors the length and breadth of India, while few streets in the Catholic countries of the Mediterranean lack a tiled panel depicting

the Crucifixion or the Virgin Mary. Much of the paraphernalia of religious services may be of clay and often consists of containers for ritual ablution, vessels for sacraments to be drunk or eaten, whether Communion wine or peyote, and lamps and incense burners.

Festivals

The year is punctuated with festivals both temporal and secular. The Christian festival of Christmas is brought

EIGHT

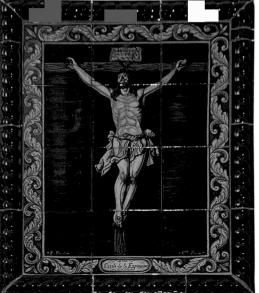

ABOVE, LEFT: *Maiolica tile panel of the Crucifixion, Orgiva, Spain.*

NEAR RIGHT: *Clay lamp decorated with tinsel for the Hindu festival of Diwali, Delhi, India.*

BELOW, RIGHT: *Wedding vase drunk from by the bride and groom at Pueblo weddings, Jemez, New Mexico, USA.*

RIGHT: *Married figures presented for good luck to a bride and groom in Sumba, Indonesia.*

to life all around the world with Nativity scenes of the baby Jesus, his parents, visitors and stable animals, an invention of St Francis of Assisi. In Germany carefully crafted ceramic figures of kings and shepherds are moulded and hand painted, while in Mexico they are crudely modelled and vibrantly coloured. In autumn the return of Rama and Sita is celebrated at the Hindu festival of Diwali when the streets are lit with thousands of tiny lamps made by local potters especially for the occasion. In Judaism Passover is a time for reflection and families eat foods, intended as reminders of the trials of the Jewish people, from a special plate. The climax of the agricultural year in the West is the Harvest Festival which was accompanied in England by a considerable amount of drinking from a Harvest jug which, like the sgraffito versions made in Devon, were replaced each year. In traditional Chinese homes at New Year figures of the twelve animals of the astrological cycle are put out on display.

Rites of passage

THE important episodes of life may also be marked with clay, from the washing of the newborn to the washing of the dead. In North Africa a ritual is performed when a child is seven days old – it involves a vessel with seven spouts, a water pot for a girl and pitcher for a boy. In Ancient Greece a child of three or four was given their first taste of wine at a celebration known, because of the receptacle used, as 'Jugs'. At weddings on the Indonesian island of Sumba the happy couple are presented with a model of a seated man and woman, while in Morocco brides are served with symbolic delicacies piled on a footed dish called a *methred*. The sharing of a drink is a common feature of marriages, a double-spouted vase is used in the Pueblos of New Mexico, USA, a two-handled loving cup in parts of Europe and a gourd-shaped vessel (a symbol of longevity) in parts of China. By way of contrast, modern Greek weddings famously reach their climax with the smashing of plates at the nuptial feast.

ABOVE: CEREMONIAL WINE JAR, ASHANTE, GHANA.

GOOD LUCK

ABOVE: FERTILITY
FIGURE FROM A
GRAIN BIN, ÇATAL
HÖYÜK, TURKEY,
5500 BC.

FOR MANY cultures clay is the actual body of the mother goddess and, imbued with that cosmic power, makes an ideal medium for the manufacture of items intended for communication with the supernatural world. Clay objects set up in the home or place of work, carried on the person or given as offerings at a shrine, are used as a means of averting misfortune and ensuring prosperity, fertility and good health.

Some of the earliest known fired objects, dating from at least 25,000 years ago, were small clay figures thrown into the fire in what is now the Czech Republic. Small female fertility figurines with exaggerated sexual characteristics were being made all over Europe during the Neolithic era and the Ancient Egyptians produced large numbers of miniature faience body parts which most likely represented a plea for healing, a practice that continues to this day at many Catholic pilgrimage sites.

ABOVE, RIGHT: Maneki-neko, *Japanese beckoning cats. Different-coloured cats are placed strategically in a room to attract good fortune.*

BELOW: *Nepalese moulded votive amulets of Manjushri and Tara, beneficent Buddhist deities.*

OPPOSITE, CENTRE: *Reduction-fired votive horse from Bangladesh.*

OPPOSITE, BOTTOM: *The three Chinese Gods of Happiness; slip cast and decorated with overglaze enamels and gilding.*

At home and work

MANY businesses in Japan display the figure of a beckoning cat (*Maneki-neko*). Intended to attract custom, these trace their origins back to 1800 in Ryogoku where a local tea-shop proprietor displayed one and achieved great financial success after the suicide of his wife and her lover. Today, identical cats are found in Chinese establishments and miniature versions in specified colours are placed in designated spots around the home as part of the Feng Shui system which is intended to promote harmony and success.

In the Andean region of southern Peru both physical and spiritual welfare are ensured by placing a pair of bulls and a Christian cross on the roof. In Japan roofs may be protected from malevolent spirits by ridge tiles depicting the faces of demons.

Homes in many regions contain a special niche or shelf for household gods and protective spirits – for instance, the Chinese Gods of Happiness. Often figures or fetishes are placed there as an invocation in times of trouble or need.

Amulets and charms

MANY folk carry a talisman, charm or amulet – sometimes worn as jewelry, but often secured out of sight. These may represent protective spirits such as the little Buddhist deities moulded in Nepal or small animal fetishes are thought to possess qualities which the bearer may desire. In ancient times Egyptians carried charms, including scarabs which were regarded as a symbol of rebirth. A less typical talisman is Tenjin-sama, a Japanese deity made of wood, papier mâché or clay. Representing a scholar of the Heian period (794–1185),

FAR LEFT: *Moulded rabbit, one of the twelve Chinese astrological creatures, Taiwan. Decorated with overglaze enamels.*

FAR LEFT, CENTRE: *One of a pair of bulls placed on roof tops in Peru for good luck; made in Pucara.*

BELOW, RIGHT: Nkisi nkonde, *Congolese spirit emissary with mankind's emotional baggage strapped to his body.*

it is considered an appropriate gift for someone beginning a course of academic study.

Votive offerings

CLAY forms may be given as offerings and these, sometimes unfired, can be immersed in water, thrown in a fire or left to disintegrate at a local shrine or a place of pilgrimage. In India many animal figures are used, but the most common is a terracotta horse intended as a steed for supernatural beings whose identity varies regionally. Modelled, coiled or assembled from thrown segments, they range from hand sized to the massive equine extravaganzas of Tamil Nadu which may be 5 m (16 ft) high! The Sumiyoshi shrine in Japan is peopled by a host of tiny clay women carrying babies, a plea from would-be mothers.

ABOVE: *Coiled earthenware jar used for burials, Yangshao, China, 3500–2500 BC. Many ancient pots discovered in graves have survived intact.*

DEATH

THE MYTHS of many nations tell how the first people were modelled from clay and it remains a widespread practice to lower the departed into the ground to be reunited with the earth from which they came. The care taken by our forefathers over laying their loved ones to rest and providing for their needs in the afterlife has provided us with a wealth of well-preserved ceramic artefacts which enlighten us not only about their owner's deaths, but also about their lives. Pottery has also been used as part of funeral rituals. The Ashante in Ghana, for example, place their shaved hair in a black pot left by the grave, while in parts of the Amazon the ashes of the deceased are traditionally mixed with water and drunk from an earthenware vessel.

Coffins and urns

IN ancient times ceramic coffins of varying shapes were not uncommon for those who could afford them. In Mesopotamia during the Uruk period (4400–3100 BC) green glazed cylindrical caskets were used. They were fitted with a lid which was decorated in relief at one end. During the 2nd millennium BC unglazed, slipper-shaped coffins were made in Lachish, in present-day Israel, with lids moulded like a human head and torso, while in Minoan Crete coffins resembled a bath tub. Large pottery urns, like those from Gansu province in China made

EIGHT

between 3000 and 1500 BC, were once commonly employed to hold the bones or ashes of the deceased. Near the mouth of the Amazon urns used by the Marajoara culture (500–1500) were decorated with stylized faces and those dating from a thousand years ago found by the Maracá river, further west, were anthropomorphic with arms and legs. The Ancient Egyptians, on the other hand, stored body parts separately in 'canopic' jars of alabaster or clay, stoppered with the heads of zoomorphic gods.

Markers and effigies too may be made of clay – graves in the Algerian Sahara are marked with a water pot and in West Africa grave sites are often marked with terracotta effigies. African-American slaves carried their traditions to the New World and marked their burial places with a broken pot, an indicator of stopped time.

Homes for the dead

IN many places care for the spirit continues after death – for example, in Gujarat, India, a bereaved family purchases a lime-washed *dhabu*, a domed dwelling, for the spirit. The Dowayo of Cameroon believe they can speak to a woman's spirit after death when it takes up residence in her water jar.

Grave goods

OBJECTS placed in graves for use in the next life include jars and cups – the Beaker folk of Bronze Age Britain and Europe received their name from the vessels placed, in pairs, in their graves. In Africa and the USA pottery was ritually 'killed' to accompany the dead by smashing or knocking a hole in the bottom.

ABOVE, LEFT: *Canteens like this are placed in graves by Laguna people; decorated with a butterfly symbolizing the soul, New Mexico, USA.*

ABOVE, RIGHT: *Funerary figure of a horseman, T'ang Dynasty (AD 618–906), China. The soldiers buried in the tomb of Qin Shi Huang Di in 210 BC were life-sized, but during the T'ang Dynasty tomb figures were made on a much smaller scale.*

BELOW: *Skeleton candlestick for the Day of the Dead when lost family and friends are remembered all over Mexico.*

Servants and retainers

THE practice of sacrificing wives and servants to accompany the dead was generally superseded long ago by placing figurines in the grave or tomb. Ancient Egyptians were buried with *shabti*, small figures that would carry out essential chores, while in China emperors were buried in style – Qin Shi Huang Di, who died in 210 BC, was buried with clay scribes and bureaucrats and an army of over 7,000 life-sized terracotta warriors. The bodies of these figures were moulded, but their heads were made individually, revealing a great range of character and ethnic origin.

OPPOSITE, BELOW: *Replicas of figures placed in the graves of the Chancay people (1200–1460), Peru. Like the Chinese terracotta army or Ancient Egyptian ushabtis, these little figures were intended to serve the deceased in the afterlife.*

ABOVE: 'KILLED' POT, MIMBRES CULTURE (1080– 1130), NEW MEXICO, USA.

205

ACKNOWLEDGMENTS

As usual my greatest debt is to Polly Gillow who shared this epic task with me and deserves far more credit than she ever gets.

I am also grateful to many potters, collectors and traders for information and permission to take photographs: Abderrahim Adloune and Juliet Guessarian; Ian Arnold at Old Bridge Antiques, Bideford; Terrance M. Chino, Lois Seymour and Lucinda Victorino at Sky City on the Acoma Reservation, New Mexico; Solomon Yigzaw Truzer Ahounem; Amadou and Brothers Niang, Yende Issah, Siko Sherif Muhamed and other traders at the Pan African Market in Cape Town; James and Pauline Austin who are responsible for some excellent photography and very interesting objects; Elizabeth Aylmer; Mark Bahti; Bandigan Arts and Crafts, Sydney; Harry Barclay at Avocet in Aldeburgh; Rosie Bose; John Butler at Burton Art Gallery and Museum, Bideford; Cameron Trading Post, Arizona; Nigel Clark; Robin Clatworthy; Paul, Jan and Sam Cobley; Mike and Jan Craddock; Lucy Davies at Tumi; Durham House Antiques Centre, Stow-on-the-Wold; Kaitlin Fish; John Gillow; Michael and Barbara Hawkins at Port Isaac Pottery, Cornwall; J. R. G. Hinves at MacGregors in Aldeburgh; Alastair, Hazel and Jo at the indispensable Alastair Hull Gallery in Haddenham; Roger Irving Little at Boscastle Pottery; Jackalope, Santa Fe; Harry Juniper at Bideford Pottery; The Kawane family in Tokyo; Judy Kong at Yan, Stow-on-the-Wold; Philip and Frannie Leach at Springfield Pottery, Hartland; Albert Linacre; Ben Lucas at Welcombe Pottery, Devon; Leo Maestas at Naakai's Indian Cultural Trade Centre, Holbrook; Kat Manning and the Mid Sussex Field Archaeology Team at Barcombe Roman Villa; Jeff Montoya at Pojoaque; Moody Dragons in Bideford; Stephen Murfitt, author of the excellent *The Glaze Book*; Sheila Paine; Stephen Parry; Dai Price, archaeologist; Cliff and Mary Prouse; Bob Race; The Gordon Reece Gallery in London; Alfredo Romero; Pablo Seminario Workshop, Urubamba; Milene Sennett at Bonga in Stellenbosch; Alan and Joan Sentance; Paul and Christine Sentance; Robert and Etsuko Sentance; Ute Mountain Pottery, Tawaoc, Colorado; John Walker at Poet's Eye, Dorchester; Helen Williams, Karen Martin, Karen White and Janice Howlett at Waterbeach Primary School; Neil and Lesley Wright, pot hunters.

SOURCES OF ILLUSTRATIONS

The following abbreviations have been used *a*, above; *b*, below; *c*, centre; *i*, inset; *l*, left; *m*, middle; *r*, right; *t*, top

All black and white drawings are by Bryan Sentance; James Austin 1, 6*ar*, 6*br*, 7*bl*, 8, 16*al*, 20*cl*, 22*bl*, 25*l*, 25*cr*, 26*bl*, 26*cr*, 30*bl*, 31*ar*, 31*br*, 32*ar*, 32*br*, 33*bl*, 35*c*, 37*t*, 37*bl*, 42*br*, 43*bl*, 43*cr*, 44*bl*, 46*ar*, 47*bl*, 49*c*, 50*bl*, 51 both, 52*cl*, 54*bl*, 55*bl*, 55*br*, 56*bl*, 57*ar*, 57*bl*, 58*br*, 60, 61*tl*, 61*tr*, 61*br*, 62*cr*, 63*cr*, 63*br*, 65 all, 66*ar*, 66*bl*, 66*br*, 67*r*, 69*ac*, 70*b*, 71*cr*, 72*cr*, 72*bl*, 73*bl*, 73*br*, 74*cr*, 74*bl*, 76*al*, 76*br*, 77*ar*, 77*br*, 78*br*, 79*br*, 81*tr*, 82*br*, 83 both, 84, 85*al*, 85*ar*, 85*bc*, 89*br*, 93*ar*, 94*bc*, 94*br*, 95*c*, 95*r*, 95*bl*, 96*br*, 97*a*, 98*tr*, 99*c*, 99*br*, 101*c*, 101*br*, 103*c*, 104*bl*, 106*br*, 107*ar*, 109*al*, 109*ar*, 109*bl*, 111*bl*, 111*br*, 112*b*, 113*al*, 113*ar*, 113*bl*, 115*b*, 118 all, 121*ar*, 122*br*, 123*ar*, 123*br*, 126*bl*, 126*br*, 127 both, 128*l*, 129*al*, 129*c*, 133*b*, 134*al*, 135*cr*, 136*bl*, 138*al*, 138*bl*, 139*ar*, 139*bl*, 139*br*, 140 both, 141*r*, 143*al*, 144*bl*, 145*tr*, 147*tl*, 147*cl*, 147*cr*, 151*al*, 155*b*, 157*a*, 159*al*, 164 both, 165*ar*, 165*cl*, 166*a*, 167*br*, 169*al*, 169*ar*, 170*br*, 171*ar*, 171*bl*, 172*ar*, 173*cl*, 173*bl*, 174*bl*, 175*al*, 175*ar*, 177*r*, 178*al*, 179*bl*, 179*r*, 180*ar*, 182*bl*, 183*ac*, 185*al*, 185*ac*, 185*ar*, 186*l*, 188*br*, 189*ar*, 189*bl*, 190*cl*, 190*bl*, 190*br*, 191*ar*, 192*l*, 193*al*, 193*cr*, 196*l*, 197*ar*, 199*cr*, 199*b*, 200*br*, 201*ac*, 201*ar*, 202*bl*, 202*br*, 203*tl*, 203*cl*, 203*c*, 203*bl*, 204*b*; Terry Beard 94*ar*; By Permission of the Burton Art Gallery and Museum, Bideford 147*tr*; Ilay Cooper 20*br*, 38*cl*, 42*bl*, 52*bl*, 89*ar*, 134*bl*, 153*ar*; John Gillow 16*bl*, 18*bl*, 72*al*, 153*bl*, 159*b*; Polly Gillow 3, 14*br*, 15*al*, 39*bl*, 39*br*, 44*al*, 55*al*, 61*cr*, 61*bl*, 62*bl*, 67*i*, 82*ar*, 85*bl*, 86*bl*, 93*tl*, 101*tl*, 103*tl*, 105*al*, 105*ar*, 114*ar*, 122*ar*, 135*bl*, 136*al*, 137*bl*, 141*al*, 141*bl*, 149*tr*, 151*br*, 154*cr*, 161*ar*, 163*al*, 168*br*, 170*bl*, 172*b*, 174*al*, 183*bl*, 186*r*, 187*a*, 187*bl*, 203*cr*, 205*bc*; Harry Juniper 91*br*, 135*cl*; By Permission of Ben Lucas, Welcombe Pottery, Devon 77*bl*; Sheila Paine 17*br*; Stephen Parry 12*ar*, 90*br*, 124*al*, 124*bl*; By Permission of Port Isaac Pottery, Cornwall 133*cr*, 143*bl*; Alan Sentance 148*cl*; Bryan Sentance 2, 5, 6*l*, 7*al*, 7*r*, 9*ar*, 9*bl*, 10*bl*, 11 all, 12*cl*, 12*br*, 13*al*, 13*ar*, 14*al*, 15*bl*, 16*cr*, 17*bl*, 18*cr*, 19 both, 20*ar*, 21*al*, 21*bl*, 22*ar*, 22*bc*, 22*br*, 23 both, 24, 25*ar*, 25*br*, 25*bc*, 26*al*, 27 all, 28*al*, 28*bl*, 28*br*, 29 all, 30*ar*, 30*br*, 31*al*, 31*cr*, 32*bl*, 33*ac*, 33*ar*, 34 all, 35*tr*, 35*bl*, 35*br*, 36, 37*cl*, 37*cr*, 37*br*, 38*cr*, 38*bl*, 39*cr*, 40 all, 41 all, 43*al*, 43*tr*, 44*br*, 45*al*, 45*ar*, 45*cr*, 45*br*, 46*ac*, 46*bl*, 46*br*, 47*al*, 47*br*, 48*ar*, 48*bl*, 49*tl*, 49*bl*, 50*tl*, 50*cl*, 50*br*, 52*ar*, 52*br*, 53*al*, 53*cl*, 53*bc*, 53*br*, 54*tl*, 54*cl*, 54*br*, 55*ar*, 56*tr*, 56*cr*, 57*al*, 57*br*, 58*al*, 58*ar*, 58*cl*, 58*bl*, 59*bl*, 59*br*, 62*cl*, 63*al*, 64 all, 66*bc*, 67*al*, 68 all, 69*al*, 69*ar*, 69*bl*, 69*br*, 70*a*, 71*al*, 71*ar*, 71*bl*, 71*br*, 72*ar*, 73*ar*, 73*bc*, 74*tr*, 74*br*, 75 all, 76*ar*, 76*bl*, 77*al*, 78*ar*, 78*bl*, 78*bc*, 79*al*, 79*ar*, 80 all, 81*cl*, 81*bl*, 81*c*, 81*br*, 82*al*, 82*bl*, 85*br*, 86*al*, 86*cr*, 86*r*, 87 all, 88 both, 89*bl*, 89*bl*, 90*tr*, 90*bl*, 91*al*, 91*c*, 91*cr*, 92*al*, 92*ar*, 92*bl*, 93*bc*, 94*cl*, 94*bl*, 95*al*, 96*al*, 96*cl*, 96*bl*, 97*b*, 98*cl*, 98*cr*, 98*bl*, 99*al*, 99*cl*, 99*ar*, 100 all, 101*bl*, 102, 103*tr*, 103*bl*, 103*br*, 104*ar*, 104*al*, 104*cl*, 105*cm*, 105*cr*, 105*bl*, 106*al*, 106*cl*, 106*bl*, 107*al*, 107*bl*, 107*br*, 108 all, 109*br*, 110 all, 111*al*, 111*ar*, 112*ar*, 112*c*, 113*br*, 114*c*, 114*br*, 115*a*, 116 all, 117 all, 119 all, 120 all, 121*al*, 121*bl*, 122*bl*, 123*al*, 123*ac*, 124*br*, 125 all, 126*ar*, 126*bc*, 128*r*, 129*ar*, 130 all, 131*al*, 131*tr*, 131*cr*, 131*br*, 132, 133*ll*, 133*tr*, 134*r*, 135*ar*, 136*br*, 137*al*, 137*ac*, 137*ar*, 137*br*, 138*br*, 139*al*, 142 both, 143*ar*, 143*br*, 144*ar*, 144*br*, 145*cl*, 145*cr*, 145*bl*, 146, 147*b*, 148*br*, 149*tl*, 149*cr*, 149*br*, 150 all, 151*ar*, 151*bl*, 152 all, 153*al*, 153*ac*, 153*cr*, 154*ar*, 154*bl*, 155*al*, 155*ar*, 156 all, 157*bl*, 157*br*, 158*tr*, 158*cr*, 158*br*, 159*ar*, 159*cr*, 160 all, 161*cr*, 161*bl*, 161*br*, 162 all, 163*ar*, 163*cr*, 163*bl*, 163*br*, 165*br*, 166*br*, 167*al*, 167*bl*, 167*bri*, 168*al*, 168*ar*, 169*bl*, 170*tr*, 170*cr*, 171*al*, 171*cr*, 172*al*, 173*t*, 173*cr*, 173*br*, 174*ar*, 174*br*, 175*bl*, 175*br*, 176 all, 177*al*, 177*ac*, 178*ar*, 179*tl*, 179*tr*, 179*cl*, 180*bl*, 180*br*, 181 all, 182*al*, 182*br*, 183*al*, 183*ar*, 183*cr*, 183*br*, 184, 185*bl*, 185*bc*, 185*br*, 186*c*, 187*cr*, 187*br*, 188*al*, 189*al*, 189*br*, 190*al*, 191*al*, 191*br*, 192*r*, 193*ac*, 193*tr*, 193*c*, 193*bl*, 194 all, 195 all, 196*al*, 197*al*, 198 all, 199*al*, 199*ar*, 200*ar*, 200*bl*, 201*al*, 201*br*, 202*ar*, 204*a*, 205*al*, 205*ar*; Paul and Christine Sentance 153*br*.

Glossary

adobe unfired clay bricks

agateware effect resembling agate or marble produced by using clays of more than one colour loosely kneaded together

anvil mushroom-shaped tool of clay or stone used with paddle for shaping clay

azotador Mexican mallet made from baked clay; used for beating clay

barbotine decoration in relief created with trailed slip

biscuit or bisque fired, but unglazed, pottery

blanc-de-chine porcelain with a white glaze

blueware pottery covered predominantly with blue glaze; made in Rajasthan, northwestern India, from a body containing little or no clay

blunger machine for mixing clay and water

body the clay from which a pot is made

bone china English clay body imitating porcelain; contains the ash of animal bones

bordado Spanish word for embroidered; used to describe decoration in clay appliqué in Mexico

burnishing polishing by rubbing with a smooth implement

celadon oriental green glaze produced by iron oxide in a reduction firing

champlevé decoration in which areas of slip are scraped away from the surface

comb toothed tool used when decorating clay

corrugated ware coiled pottery in which the coils are not scraped smooth. Style associated with the Ancestral Puebloans (Anasazi) in the USA

creamware English low-fired earthenware with a body containing Devon white clay and ground flint, developed from 1720 to 1740

cuenca method of containing the flow of glaze in a depression in the surface

cuerda seca Spanish for dry cord; describes a method of containing the flow of glaze with a line of manganese and grease

Delft Dutch tin-glazed wares

delftware English tin-glazed wares produced mainly in the 17th and 18th centuries

earthenware pottery fired between 950 and 1150°C (1742 and 2102°F)

enamels pigments applied over the glaze and fixed with a low-temperature firing

engobe slip containing gum or flux to improve adhesion

faïence French tin-glazed earthenware

faience ceramic body made from ground minerals such as quartz

feathering feathered pattern achieved by combing trailed slip

fettling scraping and smoothing to remove unevenness and evidence of joins

fluting making concave grooves as on a Greek column

flux a mineral which helps the flow of a glaze by lowering the melting point of the mix

frit fused and ground minerals

fritware ceramic body made from frit

glost firing a firing during which glaze is fused

green unfired

greenware an alternate nomenclature for wares with a green celadon glaze

grog fired clay ground into a gritty powder for use as temper

hard paste 'true porcelain', a combination of china clay and china stone; usually refers to porcelain made in the West

harp wire stretched tight with a bow; used for cutting slices of clay

intaglio carving in negative employed when making moulds

jigger mould used to shape an inside profile on the wheel

joggling marbling, creating random swirling shapes from clay of contrasting colours

jolly or **jolley** mould used to shape an outside profile on the wheel

kachelofen German tiled stove

kaolin china clay

kidney kidney-shaped tool for scraping and smoothing

leatherhard clay at a leathery state dry enough to support itself, but still impressionable

levigation separating the particles of clay by soaking. Used for making fine textured slip such as terra sigillata

losetas cut square tiles used in mosaics

luting joining leatherhard clay by roughening the surface and 'gluing' with slurry

maiolica tin-glazed ceramics made in Italy and Spain

majolica ceramics with thick, colourful lead glaze, especially popular in the late 19th century

marbling creating random swirling shapes with clay of contrasting colours

mochaware pottery decorated with tree-like motifs formed by the running of a vegetable infusion over slip

molde baked clay disk used for revolving work in Central America

muffle kiln small kiln in which wares can be protected from direct flames and gases

opus sectile Roman cut tile mosaic

oxidation exposure to an oxygen-rich atmosphere during firing

paddle bat used for beating clay into shape

plastic clay at the stage when it can be squeezed and moulded with the fingers

press moulding shaping a slab of clay with a plaster mould

primary clay clay obtained at the place it was formed

puki concave clay form, often an old pot bottom, used for starting coiled pots by Puebloan potters in the American Southwest

raku pottery fired between 800 and 1100°C (1472 and 2012°F), placed into and withdrawn from a hot kiln

reduction exposure to an oxygen-starved atmosphere during firing

refractory clays clays able to withstand high temperatures

roulette cylindrical stamp for decorating clay with repeated patterns

saggar fireclay box used to protect wares from flames and gases in the kiln

Samian ware Roman pottery made in Gaul; coated in terra sigillata slip

secondary clay clay transported from its place of origin by wind, water, etc. Usually contains more impurities than primary clay

self slip slip used over a body made of the same clay

sgraffito patterns made by scraping through slip to reveal a different colour beneath

slip diluted clay

slow wheel turntable

slurry roughly diluted clay used as 'glue'

soft paste body imitating porcelain, a low-fired mix of white clay and a fusible substance such as quartz

sprig moulded decorative motif attached to a clay surface

stilt clay support for keeping glazed surfaces apart during firing

stonepaste ceramic body rich in ground minerals such as quartz; also fritware or faience

stoneware pottery fired to between 1200 and 1400°C (2192 and 2552°F)

temper non-plastic material added to a clay body to alter its performance

terracotta (corruption of Latin terra cocta meaning fired earth) a low-fired, unglazed earthenware, often red

terra sigillata fine orange-red slip used on Roman tablewares

thumb pot pot shaped by squeezing between the thumb and fingers

tournette turntable

tube lining method of restricting glaze flow with a raised line of trailed slip

turning refining a thrown form on the wheel by shaving at the leatherhard stage

vitrification the fusing together of a body at high temperature

volteador convex baked clay base on which the molde is revolved

wedging slamming clay down on to a solid surface to mix thoroughly and expel air

zellij Arabic for a mosaic made from cut tiles

MUSEUMS AND PLACES OF INTEREST

AUSTRALIA

Adelaide
South Australian Museum
North Terrace, Adelaide, South Australia 5000
T 618 8207 7500
http://www.samuseum.sa.gov.au
Australian, South-East Asian and Pacific crafts

Sydney
Australian Museum
6 College Street, Sydney, NSW 2010
T 612 9320 6000
http://www.austmus.gov.au/about/index.cfm
Artefacts and performances of indigenous peoples

AUSTRIA

Vienna
Museum für Völkerkunde (*Museum of Ethnology*)
Neue Burg, A-1010 Vienna
T 43 1 534 30
http://www.ethno-museum.ac.at/en/museum.html
African and Oceanic collection

BELGIUM

Antwerp
Etnografisch Museum (*Ethnographic Museum*)
Suikerrui 19, B 2000 Antwerp
T 03 220 86 00
http://museum.antwerpen.be/etnografisch_museum/index_eng.html

Tervuren
Musée Royal de l'Afrique Centrale
(*Royal Museum for Central Africa*)
Leuvensesteenweg 13
3080 Tervuren, Brabant
T 02 769 52 04
http://www.africamuseum.be
Central African collection

BOLIVIA

La Paz
Museo Nacional de Etnografía y Folklore
(*Museum of Ethnography and Folklore*)
Calle Ingani 942
La Paz
Bolivian crafts

BRAZIL

Rio de Janeiro
Museo do Indio (*Indian Museum*)
Rua das Palmeiras
55 Botafogo
22270–070 Rio de Janeiro
T 286 8899
http://www.museudoindio.org.br/eng/index.htm

São Paolo
Folklore Museum
Pavilhao Garcez, Parque Ibirapuera,
01000 São Paolo

CANADA

Gatineau
The Canadian Museum of Civilization
100 Laurier Street, Gatineau, Quebec J8x 4H2
T 819 776 7000
http://www.civilization.ca/cmc/cmce.asp

Toronto
George R. Gardiner Museum of Ceramic Art
111 Queen's Park Circle, Toronto M5S 2C7
T 416 586 8080
http://www.gardinermuseum.on.ca/default_flash.aspx

Royal Ontario Museum
100 Queen's Park, Toronto M5S 2C6
T 416 586 8000
http://www.rom.on.ca

CHINA

Beijing
Museum of the Cultural Palace of National Minorities
Chang'an Street, 100 000 Beijing

Hong Kong
Fung Ping Shan Museum
94 Bonham Street, Pokfulam, Hong Kong
T 852 2241 5500
http://www.hku.hk/hkumag/main.html
Chinese ceramics

Hong Kong Museum of Art
10 Salisbury Road, Tsim Sha Tsui, Kowloon
Hong Kong
T 852 2721 0116
Chinese ceramics

Shanghai
The Shanghai Museum
201 Renmin Dadao
Shanghai
Chinese crafts and ceramics

Colombia
Bogotá
Museo Etnográfico de Colombia
(*Colombia Museum of Ethnography*)
Calle 34, No. 6–61 piso 30, Apdo. Aéreo 10511
Bogotá

Czech Republic
Prague
Náprstkovo Muzeum asijskych, africkych
a americkych kultur (*Náprstkovo Museum
of Asian, African and American Culture*)
Betlémské nám estí 1
11000 Prague
T 420 224 497 500
http://www.aconet.cz/npm/eindex.html

Denmark
Copenhagen
National Museum of Denmark
Ny Vestergade 10, Copenhagen
T 45 33 13 44 11
http://www.natmus.dk
Worldwide ethnographic collection

France
Paris
Musée de l'Homme (*Museum of Mankind*)
17 place du Trocadéro
75116 Paris
T 33 1 44 05 72 00
http://www.paris.org/Musees/Homme
Worldwide ethnographic collection

Musée des Arts Décoratifs
(*Museum of Decorative Arts*)
Palais du Louvre, 107 rue de Rivoli
75001 Paris
T 33 1 44 55 57 50
http://www.paris.org/Musees/Decoratifs
French ceramics

Musée National des Arts d'Afrique et d'Océanie
(*National Museum of African and Oceanic Arts*)
293 avenue Daumesnil, 75012 Paris
T 33 1 44 74 84 80
http://www.paris.org/Musees/Art.Afrique.Oceanie/
info.html
African pottery

Germany
Berlin
Museum fur Völkerkunde (*Museum of Ethnology*)
Arnimallee 27, 14195 Berlin-Dahlem
T 030 8301438
http://www.smb.spk-berlin.de/mv/e/s.html
Worldwide ethnographic collection

Dresden
Staatliches Museum für Völkerkunde Dresden
(*Museum of Ethnology*)
Japanisches Palais, Palaisplatz 11, 01097 Dresden
T 0351 8144841
http://www.annegret-schuetze.de/museum
*Ethnographic collection including artefacts from
India and South-East Asia*

Düsseldorf
Hetjens Museum (Deutsches Keramikmuseum)
(*German Ceramics Museum*)
Schulstrasse 4, 40213 Düsseldorf
T 0211 8994210
http://www.duesseldorf.de/hetjens

Frankfurt am Main
Museum der Weltkulturen
(*Ethnography Museum*)
Schaumankai 29, 60594 Frankfurt am Main
T 69 21235913
http://www.mdw.frankfurt.de/home.php
Worldwide ethnographic collection

Frechen
Museum für zeitgenössische Keramische Kunst
(*Ceramics Museum*)
Bonnstrasse 12, 50226 Frechen
T 22 3422891

Stuttgart
Linden-Museum Stuttgart-Staatliches Museum
für Völkerkunde (*Museum of Ethnology*)
Hegelplatz 1, 70174 Stuttgart
T 07 1120223
http://www.lindenmuseum.de
Islamic and Central Asian collection

Greece
Athens
National Archaeological Museum of Greece
Patission 44 St
Athens 10682
T 30 210 8217717
http://www.culture.gr/2/21/214/21405m/e21405m1.html

Crete
Archaeological Museum of Herakleion
1 Xanthoudidou St, Herakleion
Crete
T 30 281 0226092
http://www.culture.gr/2/21/211/21123m/e211wm01.html

Guatemala
Guatemala City
Museo Nacional de Artes e Industrias Populares
(*National Museum of Popular Arts*)
Avenida 10, No. 10–70, Zona 1
Ciudad de Guatemala
T 2380334
Guatemalan folk arts

Hungary
Budapest
Magyar Nemzeti Múzeum
(*Hungarian National Museum*)
Múzeum Körút 14–16
1088 Budapest
T 361 338 2122
http://www.hnm.hu
Hungarian folk arts

Néprajzi Múzeum (*Ethnographic Museum*)
Kossuth Lajos tér 12, 1055 Budapest
T 361 473 2400
http://www.hem.hu/index2.html
Hungarian folk arts

India
Chennai (formerly Madras)
Government Museum
Pantheon Road, Egmore
600008 Chennai
T 91 44 2819 3238
http://www.chennaimuseum.org

New Delhi
Crafts Museum
Pragati Maidan, Bhairon Road
110001 New Delhi
Indian folk arts

ITALY

Faenza

Museo Internazionale delle Ceramiche
(*Museum of International Ceramics*)
Via Campidori 2, 48018 Faenza
T 0546 21240
http://www.micfaenza.org/index.htm

Milan

Museo di Arte Estremo Orientale e di Etnografia
(*Museum of Far Eastern Art and Ethnography*)
Via Mosé Bianchi 94, 20149 Milan
T 024 38201
Asian and Far Eastern collection

Rome

Museo Nazionale Preistorico Etnografico Luigi
Pigorini (*Luigi Pigorini Museum of Prehistory
and Ethnography*)
Viale Lincoln 3, 00144 Rome
http://www.pigorini.arti.beniculturali.it
Worldwide ethnographic collection

Vatican Museum
Città del Vaticano, Rome
T 06 69884466
http://www.vatican.va/museums

JAPAN

Mashiko

Shoji Hamada Museum
3388 Mashiko
T 02 8572 5300
Collection of work by Shoji Hamada

Osaka

Kokuritsu Minzokugaku Hakubutsukan
(*National Museum of Ethnography*)
10–1 Senri Expo Park, Suita, 565–8511 Osaka
T 06 6876 2151
http://www.minpaku.ac.jp/english
Asian and Oceanic collection

Nihon Kogei-kan (*Japanese Folk Art Museum*)
3–7–6 Namba-naka, Naniwa-ku, Osaka
T 06 6641 6309
Japanese folk arts

Tokyo

Nihon Mingeikan (*Japanese Folk Art Museum*)
4–3–33 Komaba, Meguro-ku, Tokyo
T 03 3467 4527
http://www.mingeikan.or.jp/Pages/entrance-e.html

MEXICO

Mexico City

Museo Nacional de Antropología
(*National Museum of Anthropology*)
Avenida Paseo de la Reforma y Calzada, Gandhi
s/n, Bosque de Chapultepec, Mexico City 11560
T 5553 6266
http://www.mna.inah.gob.mx
Pre-Hispanic and folk ceramics

Museo Nacional de Artes e Industrias Populares
del INI (*National Museum of Popular Arts*)
Avenida Juárez 44, Mexico City 06050
T 5510 3404
Mexican folk art

Museo Nacional de Culturas Populares
Avenida Hidalgo 289, Coyoacán, Mexico City
Mexican folk art

Oaxaca

Museo Regional de Oaxaca
Alcalá Street, Oaxaca
T 951 5162991
Folk art of Oaxacan Indians

Tonalá

Museo Nacional de la Cerámica
(*National Museum of Ceramics*)
Constitución 104, Tonalá
Guadalajara
Modern and pre-Columbian Mexican ceramics

MOROCCO

Marrakesh

Dar si Saïd Museum
Rue de la Bahia, Riad Ez-Zaïtoun El Jadid
Marrakesh
T 44 24 64
Moroccan collection

Palais de la Bahia
Signposted from Riad Ez-Zaïtoun El Jadid
Marrakesh
Moroccan collection

Tétouan

Musée Ethnographique de Tétouan
(*Ethnology Museum*)
Zankat Skala, 65 Bab El Okla
Tétouan
T 39 97 05 05
Moroccan collection

THE NETHERLANDS

Leeuwarden

Het Princessehof (*National Museum of Ceramics*)
Grote Kerkstraat 11, 8911 DZ Leeuwarden
Friesland
T 058 2948958
Dutch ceramics

Leiden

Rijksmuseum voor Volkenkunde
(*National Museum of Ethnology*)
Steenstraat 1, 2300 AE Leiden
T 071 5168800
http://www.rmv.nl

Rotterdam

Museum Boijmans Van Beuningen
Museumpark 18–20, 3015 CX Rotterdam
T 10 4419475
www.boijmans.nl
Collection of Dutch ceramics

Wereldmuseum Rotterdam (*Museum of Ethnology*)
Willemskade 25, 3016 DM Rotterdam
T 010 2707172
http://www.wereldmuseum.rotterdam.nl

PERU

Cusco

Archaeological Museum of Cusco
Cuesta del Almirante 103, Cusco
T 084 23 7380
Pre-Columbian ceramics

Museo Inka
Cuesta del Almirante 103, Cusco
T 084 22 2271
Pre-Columbian Andean culture

Lima

Museo de Arqueologia, Antropologia e Historia
(*Museum of Archaeology, Anthropology and History*)
Plaza Bolivar, Pueblo Libre, Lima
T 463 5070
Pre-Columbian artefacts

Museo Arqueologico Rafael Larco Herrera
(*Rafael Larco Herrera Archaeology Museum*)
Avenida Bolívar 1515, Pueblo Libre
Lima 21
T 461 1312
http://museolarco.perucultural.org.pe/english/index1.htm
55,000 pre-Columbian pots

Museo de la Nación (*National Museum*)
Avenida Javier Prado Este 2465, San Borja
Lima
T 476 9875
Crafts and ceramics of pre-Columbian cultures

PORTUGAL
Lisbon
Museu Nacional de Etnologia
(*National Museum of Ethnology*)
Av. Ilna de Madeira
1400–203 Lisbon
T 21 3041160
World ethnographic collection

ROMANIA
Bucharest
Muzeul National de Istorie a României
(*Romanian National History Museum*)
Calea Victoriei nr. 12, 79740 Bucharest
T 40 21 315 82 07
http://www.mnir.ro/index_uk.html
Romanian folk art

RUSSIA
Moscow
Museum of Oriental Art
Nikitsky Bulvar 12a
Moscow 121019
T 095 202 4555

St Petersburg
Peter the Great Museum of Anthropology
and Ethnology
Nab Universitetskaja 3
St Petersburg 199034
T 812 328 1412
http://www.kunstkamera.ru/english
Asian collection

Staatliche Eremitage (*Hermitage Museum*)
Dvortsovaya Naberezhnaya 34–36
St Petersburg 190000
T 812 110 9625
http://www.hermitagemuseum.org
European and Asian collection

SINGAPORE
Singapore History Museum
93 Stamford Road
0617 Singapore
T 6338 0000
Straits Chinese ceramics

SOUTH AFRICA
South African Museum
25 Queen Victoria Street, Cape Town
T 21 481 3800
http://www.museums.org.za/sam
Artefacts relating to the life of indigenous peoples

SPAIN
Barcelona
Museo Etnologic (*Ethnology Museum*)
Parque de Montjuic, 08038 Barcelona
T 934 246402
World ethnographic collection

Madrid
Museu Nacional de Etnológic
(*National Ethnology Museum*)
Alfonso XII, 68, 28014 Madrid
World ethnographic collection

SWEDEN
Gothenburg
Etnografiska Museet (*Ethnographic Museum*)
Norra Hamngatan 12, 41114 Gothenburg
Worldwide ethnographic collection

Stockholm
Etnografiska Museet (*National Museum
of Ethnography*)
Djurgardsbrunnsvägen 34, 10252 Stockholm
T 08 519 550 00
http://www.etnografiska.se/etnoweb/index.htm
Worldwide ethnographic collection

TURKEY
Topkapi Sarayi Müzesi (*Topkapi Palace Museum*)
Sultanahmet, Istanbul
T 90 212 512 04 80
Islamic ceramics and Iznik tiles

UNITED KINGDOM
Barnstaple
Museum of North Devon
The Square, Barnstaple, Devon EX32 8LN
T 01271 346747
North Devon slipware

Bideford
Burton Art Gallery and Museum
Kingsley Road, Bideford, Devon EX39 2QQ
T 01237 471455
http://www.burtonartgallery.co.uk
North Devon slipware

Cambridge
Fitzwilliam Museum
Trumpington Street, Cambridge CB2 1RB
T 01223 332900
http://www.fitzmuseum.cam.ac.uk
European and Far Eastern ceramics

Exeter
The Royal Albert Memorial Museum & Art Gallery
Queen Street, Exeter EX4 3RX
T 01392 665858
English pottery and Devon slipware

Hanley
The Potteries Museum and Art Gallery
Bethesda Street, Hanley, Stoke-on-Trent
Staffordshire ST1 3DW
T 01782 232323
http://www2002.stoke.gov.uk/museums/pmag
Fine collection of Staffordshire pottery

London
British Museum
Great Russell Street, London WC1B 3DG
T 020 7323 8000
http://www.thebritishmuseum.ac.uk
Worldwide ethnographic collection

Horniman Museum
100 London Road, Forest Hill, London SE23 3PQ
T 020 8699 1872
http://www.horniman.ac.uk
Worldwide ethnographic collection

Victoria and Albert Museum
Cromwell Road, London SW7 2RL
T 020 7942 2000
http://www.vam.ac.uk
Worldwide collection of applied arts

Oxford
Ashmolean Museum of Art and Archaeology
Beaumont Street, Oxford OX1 2PH
T 01865 278000
http://www.ashmol.ox.ac.uk
Emphasis on Islam, the Far East and archaeological finds from the Mediterranean

Pitt Rivers Museum
South Parks Road, Oxford OX1 3PP
T 01865 270927
http://www.prm.ox.ac.uk
Worldwide ethnographic collection. Take a torch!

USA

Arizona
Heard Museum
2301 N. Central Ave
Phoenix AZ 85004–1323
http://www.heard.org
T 602 252 8848
*Culture and crafts of Native Americans of
the American Southwest*

Hopi Cultural Center
PO Box 67, Second Mesa
Arizona AZ 86043
T 928 734 2401
http://www.hopiculturalcenter.com
Hopi crafts and pottery

California
Museum of Man
San Diego, Balboa Park
1350 El Prado
San Diego CA 92101
T 619 239 2001
http://www.museumofman.org

The Southwest Museum
234 Museum Drive, Los Angeles CA 90065
T 323 221 2164
http://www.southwestmuseum.org

Colorado
Chapin Mesa Museum
Mesa Verde National Park, Colorado CO 81330
T 970 529 4445

Massachusetts
Peabody Museum of Archaeology and Ethnology
Harvard University, 11 Divinity Ave
Cambridge MA 02138
T 617 496 1027
http://www.peabody.harvard.edu/default.html
Worldwide ethnographic collection

New Mexico
A:shiwi A:wan Museum and Heritage Center
1222 Highway 53, Zuni NM 87327
T 505 782 4403
http://www.ashiwimuseum.org
Zuni culture and pottery

Indian Pueblo Cultural Centre
2401 12th Street NW, Albuquerque NM 87104
T 800 766 4405
Excellent selection of local Native American pottery

Museum of International Folk Art
706 Camino Lejo, Santa Fe NM 87505
T 505 476 1200
http://www.moifa.org
*Dioramas of world cultures compiled from folk art
figures and models*

Pojoaque Pueblo
96 Cities of Gold Road, Santa Fe NM 87506
T 505 455 3460
Pottery of Pojoaque and other Pueblos

New York
National Museum of the American Indian
(Heye Foundation)
The George Gustav Heye Center
1 Bowling Green, New York NY 10004
T 212 514 3700
http://www.nmai.si.edu/http://www.prm.ox.ac.uk

BIBLIOGRAPHY

TECHNIQUES
Cooper, Emmanuel, *The Potter's Book of Glaze Recipes*, London and New
    York, 1980
Fraser, Harry, *Glazes for the Craft Potter*, new edn, London, 1998 and New
    York, 1974
Hamer, Frank and Janet, *The Potter's Dictionary of Materials and Techniques*,
    4th edn, London and Philadelphia, 1997
Leach, Bernard, *A Potter's Book*, 3rd edn, London, 1976
Murfitt, Stephen, *The Glaze Book, a Visual Catalogue of Decorative Ceramic
    Glazes*, London and Iola, Wisconsin, 2002
Pegrum, Brenda, *Painted Ceramics, Colour and Imagery on Clay*,
    Marlborough, 1999
Rhodes, Daniel, *Clay and Glazes for the Potter*, new edn, London, 1988
Warshaw, Josie, *The Potter's Guide to Handbuilding*, London, 2000

AFRICA
Barley, Nigel, *Smashing Pots, Feats of Clay from Africa*, London and
    Washington, D.C., 1994
Hope, Colin A., *Egyptian Pottery*, Princes Risborough, 2001

Jereb, James F., *Arts and Crafts of Morocco*, London, 1995 and San
    Francisco, 1996
Nicholson, Paul T., *Egyptian Faience and Glass*, Princes Risborough, 1993
Phillips, Tom (ed.), *Africa, The Art of a Continent*, exh. cat., Munich and
    New York, 1995
Posey, Sarah, *Yemeni Pottery*, The Littlewood Collection, London, 1994
Sellschop, Susan, Wendy Goldblatt and Doreen Hemp, *Craft South Africa,
    Traditional, Transitional, Contemporary*, South Africa, 2002
Sieber, Roy, *African Furniture and Household Objects*, London, New York
    and Bloomington, Indiana, 1980
Trowell, Margaret, *African Design*, New York, 1971
Visonà, Monica Blackmun, Robin Poynor, Herbert M. Cole, Michael D.
    Harris, Rowland Abiodun and Suzanne Preston Blier, *A History of Art
    in Africa*, London, 2000 and New York, 2001

ASIA
Barnard, Nicholas, *Arts and Crafts of India*, London, 1993
Cooper, Ilay, *Traditional Buildings of India*, London and New York,
    1998

Cooper, Ilay, and John Gillow, *Arts and Crafts of India*, London and New York, 1996

Dato' Haji Sulaiman Othman et al., *The Crafts of Malaysia*, Singapore, 1994

Fahr-Becker, Gabriele (ed.), *The Art of East Asia*, vols 1 and 2, Cologne, 1999

Fehérvári, Géza, *Ceramics of the Islamic World in the Tareq Rajab Museum*, London and New York, 2000

Japanese Crafts, a Guide to Today's Traditional Handmade Objects, The Japan Craft Forum, Tokyo, 2001

Minick, Scott, and Jiao Ping, *Arts and Crafts of China*, London and New York, 1996

Perryman, Jane, *Traditional Pottery of India*, London, 2000

Saint-Gilles, Amaury, *Mingei, Japan's Enduring Folk Arts*, Rutland, Vermont and Tokyo, 1998

Warren, William, and Luca Invernizzi Tettoni, *Arts and Crafts of Thailand*, London and San Francisco, 1994

Watson, William (ed.), *The Great Japan Exhibition, Art of the Edo Period 1600–1868*, exh. cat., Royal Academy of Arts, London, 1981

AUSTRALASIA

Isaacs, Jennifer, *Hermannsburg Potters, Aranda Artists of Central Australia*, Sydney, 2000

Mansfield, Janet, *A Collector's Guide to Modern Australian Ceramics*, Seaforth, N.S.W., 1988

Ryan, Judith, and Anna McLeod, *Tikwani, Contemporary Tiwi Ceramics*, exh. cat., National Gallery of Victoria, Melbourne, 2002

CENTRAL AND SOUTH AMERICA

Bankes, Georges, *Moche Pottery from Peru*, London, 1980

———, *Peruvian Pottery*, Princes Risborough, 1989

Braun, Barbara (ed.), *Arts of the Amazon*, London and New York, 1995

Davies, Lucy, and Mo Fini, *Arts and Crafts of South America*, London, 1994 and San Francisco, 1995

McEwan, Colin, Cristiana Barreto and Eduardo Neves, *Unknown Amazon: Culture in Nature in Ancient Brazil*, London, 2001

Sayer, Chloe, *Arts and Crafts of Mexico*, London and San Francisco, 1990

Villegas, Liliana and Benjamin, *Artefactos, Colombian Crafts from the Andes to the Amazon*, New York, 1992

Wasserspring, Lois, *Oaxacan Ceramics, Traditional Folk Art by Oaxacan Women*, San Francisco, 2000

EUROPE

Black, John, *British Tin-glazed Earthenware*, Princes Risborough, 2001

Bossert, Helmuth Theodor, *Folk Art of Europe*, London and New York, 1954

Copeland, Robert, *Blue and White Transfer-Printed Pottery*, Princes Risborough, 1982 and 2000

de la Bédoyère, Guy, *Pottery in Roman Britain*, Princes Risborough, 2000

Devambez, Pierre, *Greek Painting*, London and New York, 1962

Draper, Jo, *Post-Medieval Pottery, 1650–1800*, Princes Risborough, 2001

Edgeler, Audrey and John, *North Devon Art Pottery*, North Devon Museums Service, n.d.

Gibson, Michael, *Lustreware*, Princes Risborough, 1999

Sekers, David, *The Potteries*, Princes Risborough, 2000

Van Lemmen, Hans, *Delftware Tiles*, Princes Risborough and Woodstock, New York, 1998

———, *Victorian Tiles*, Princes Risborough, 2000

THE UNITED STATES OF AMERICA

Anderson, Duane, *All that Glitters, The Emergence of Native American Micaceous Art Pottery in Northern New Mexico*, Santa Fe, New Mexico, 1999

Bahti, Tom and Mark, *Southwestern Indian Arts and Crafts*, rev. edn, Las Vegas, 1997

Blair, Mary Ellen and Laurence, *The Legacy of a Master Potter, Nampeyo and Her Descendants*, Tucson, Arizona, 1999

Brody, J. J. et al., *Mimbres Pottery, Ancient Art of the American Southwest*, New York, 1983

Bunzel, Ruth L., *The Pueblo Potter, A Study of Creative Imagination in Primitive Art*, London and New York, 1972

Coe, Ralph T., *Sacred Circles, Two Thousand Years of North American Indian Art*, exh. cat., Arts Council of Great Britain, London, 1976 and Kansas City, Missouri, 1977

Dillingham, Rick, *Fourteen Families in Pueblo Pottery*, Albuquerque, New Mexico, 1994

Dillingham, Rick with Melinda Elliot, *Acoma and Laguna Pottery*, Santa Fe, New Mexico, 1992

Feest, Christian F., *Native Arts of North America*, London and New York, 1992

Hayes, Allan, and John Blom, *Southwestern Pottery, Anasazi to Zuni*, Flagstaff, Arizona, 1996

Hucko, Bruce, *Southwestern Indian Pottery*, Las Vegas, Nevada, 1999

Peterson, Susan, *The Living Tradition of María Martínez*, Tokyo and New York, 1989

Whiteford, Andrew Hunter, *North American Indian Arts*, New York, 1970

WORLD

Charleston, Robert J. (ed.), *World Ceramics, An Illustrated History*, London, New York, Sydney and Toronto, 1968

Cooper, Emmanuel, *Ten Thousand Years of Pottery*, 4th edn, London and Philadelphia, 2000

Freestone, Ian, and David Gaimster (eds), *Pottery in the Making, World Ceramic Traditions*, London and Washington, D.C., 1997

MISCELLANEOUS

Coles, Janet, and Robert Budwig, *The Complete Book of Beads*, London, 1990

Hammond, Michael, *Bricks and Brickmaking*, Princes Risborough, 2001

Hilliard, Elizabeth, *The Tile Book, Decorating with Fired Earth*, London and San Francisco, 1999

Hopper, Robin, *Functional Pottery, Form and Aesthetic in Pots of Purpose*, London and Iola, Wisconsin, 2000

Riley, Noël, *Tile Art, A History of Decorative Tiles*, London, 1987

Tomalin, Stefany, *The Bead Jewelry Book*, Newton Abbot and Chicago, 1997

Index